Just War and International Order

At the opening of the twenty-first century, while obviously the world is still
struggling with violence and conflict, many commentators argue that there
are many reasons for supposing that restrictions on the use of force are
growing. The establishment of the International Criminal Court, the growing sophistication of international humanitarian law and the 'rebirth' of
the just war tradition over the last fifty years are all taken as signs of this
trend. This book argues that, on the contrary, the just war tradition, allied
to a historically powerful and increasingly dominant conception of politics
in general, is complicit with an expansion of the grounds of supposedly
legitimate force, rather than a restriction of it. In offering a critique of this
trajectory, *Just War and International Order* also seeks to illuminate a
worrying trend for international order more generally and consider what,
if any, alternative there might be to it.

NICHOLAS RENGGER is Professor of Political Theory and International
Relations at the University of St Andrews. His scholarly interests range
across political theory and international relations and include philosophy,
intellectual history and contemporary philosophical and political theology.
He has published in all of these areas and his recent publications include
Critical International Relations Theory after 25 Years (edited with Tristram
Benedict Thirkell-White, Cambridge, 2007) and *Evaluating Global Orders*
(Cambridge, 2011).

Just War and International Order

The Uncivil Condition in World Politics

NICHOLAS RENGGER
St Andrews University

CAMBRIDGE
UNIVERSITY PRESS

CAMBRIDGE UNIVERSITY PRESS
Cambridge, New York, Melbourne, Madrid, Cape Town,
Singapore, São Paulo, Delhi, Mexico City

Cambridge University Press
The Edinburgh Building, Cambridge CB2 8RU, UK

Published in the United States of America
by Cambridge University Press, New York

www.cambridge.org
Information on this title: www.cambridge.org/9781107644748

© Nicholas Rengger 2013

First published 2013

Printed and bound in the United Kingdom by the MPG Books Group

A catalogue record for this publication is available from the British Library

Library of Congress Cataloging in Publication data

Rengger, N. J. (Nicholas J.), author.
  Just war and international order : the uncivil condition in world politics / Nicholas
Rengger.
    pages   cm
  ISBN 978-1-107-03164-7 (Hardback) – ISBN 978-1-107-64474-8 (Paperback)
1. Just war doctrine.   2. World politics–21st century.   I. Title.
  U21.2.R45 2013
  172′.42–dc23

                                                            2012039600

ISBN 978-1-107-03164-7 Hardback
ISBN 978-1-107-64474-8 Paperback

For Paddy

'Bare is brotherless back'

Contents

Preface

The twenty-first century already offers us many opportunities for observing that human beings in general, like the Bourbons, have learned nothing and forgotten nothing. Far from the new century being a century that would turn its back on the violence and conflict that had disfigured its predecessor, the twenty-first century has indulged itself in major violence even more quickly and, in ironic counterpoint to the reality of a globalizing world, in a geographically far more varied way, than the previous century did.

This, many will doubtless say, is only to be expected, at least in international politics. For is not international relations the world of 'recurrence and repetition', where Hobbes's famous twins 'force and fraud' hold ultimate sway? And there is, indeed, something to that, as we shall see, though not quite what most people think there is. But the persistence of conflict in international relations is not the subject of this book per se; rather I am concerned to trace what I take to be a foolish – and harmful – trajectory in world politics that, I suggest, makes the relative persistence of conflict worse than it need be, and might otherwise be.

Although I think that this trajectory has many aspects and could be explored in many different contexts in contemporary world politics, I have chosen in this book to focus primarily on one: ideas about the justification of the use of force. I do so both because it helps to focus the argument on one particularly pertinent theme that has had very obvious prominence in recent years (and is sadly all too likely to retain it) and also because I think this particular theme brings home the character of that worrying trajectory with special force (no pun intended). But I emphasize that one might take almost any other issue area in contemporary politics and international relations and trace similar problems: it is a *general* trajectory with which I am concerned, however concentrated my discussion of it here will be.

Of course, the constant possibility of the use of force has long been seen as the thing above all else that divides 'international' politics from the domestic variety, which can (at least in some contexts) be seen as 'pacified'. Many of the longest-lasting debates in scholarly studies of international relations dwell on whether this is an inevitable or a necessary condition or a possibly meliorable one. I will come back to this question in the Epilogue but for now let me simply note that 'traditionally' (and the reason for the quotation marks will become apparent later on) the *systematibus civitatum* (the words are Pufendorf's) that was the ancestor of our contemporary international order has mostly been portrayed as an environment of near-permanent instability, when it has not been portrayed as a simple 'war of all against all', usually prefaced by the word 'Hobbesian'.[1] Some, it is true, have sought to correct this picture – the system was famously described by the late Hedley Bull as an 'anarchical society',[2] with the emphasis as much on the second word as on the first – but even here there was a recognition of the instability inherent in a system without an overall locus of authority. The international system has very generally, then, been itself seen as in a permanent 'state of war'.[3] But that, as we shall see, is not quite right, so in what follows I shall refer to this assumption – the assumption of the general unsociability of the states system – as 'the uncivil condition', deliberately distancing it not only from the hallmarks of civility that might be held to obtain in at least some forms of established political community but also from the (mistaken) image of an allegedly 'Hobbesian' state of war, 'a war of all against all'.

---

[1] In fact that is not at all how Hobbes himself understood international relations. For a brilliant demolition of the usual distortions and simplifications of Hobbes in this context – he is actually a remarkably subtle and nuanced interpreter of the international order of his day – see Noel Malcolm's unanswerable argument in 'Hobbes' Theory of International Relations', in his *Aspects of Hobbes* (Oxford: Clarendon Press, 2004).

[2] In, *The Anarchical Society* (London: Macmillan, 1977).

[3] Rousseau used this phrase for his essay on the condition of international relations in the mid 1750s, as we shall see. Somewhat later one of his most acute readers in the literature of international politics, Stanley Hoffmann, used it as the title of a collection of some of his essays. See Jean Jacques Rousseau, 'The State of War', in Stanley Hoffmann and David Fidler (eds.) *Rousseau on International Relations* (Oxford: Clarendon Press, 1991) and Stanley Hoffmann, *The State of War: Essays in the Theory and Practice of International Relations* (New York: Prager, 1965).

In the European tradition, the *ethical* justification of the use of force has, in general, been done in and through one particular tradition of thought: the 'just war' tradition.[4] This is, of course, a tradition of remarkable longevity and great complexity. Some aspects of that complexity will concern me in Chapter 3 but it is worth flagging up now that central to the tradition throughout its history has been its relationship to ideas about authoritative political community. Legitimate force, for the just war tradition, is (whatever else it is) force used by a political community with 'right authority'; that is to say, it is public (not private) violence, and it is exercised by those who have proper authority in the political community. In other words, the justification of force is intimately tied up with questions about what the character of the political community might be said to be. And in the current context, as we will see, that is doubly significant.

The importance of this has, of course, long been recognized in the (many) fields of academic inquiry that touch on it. This is certainly true of International Relations[5] which was conceived as a distinct academic inquiry as a result of one especially appalling war and which has had war – its causes, consequences, matter and form – very much as a central preoccupation from its inception as a field of study. But it is true also of Political Philosophy. For someone who teaches in both these fields, therefore, as I have done now for over twenty years, aspects of the relationship are likely to figure fairly heavily in the teaching schedules and so, indeed, it has proved. And since I have always found that my writing and my teaching have had a strongly symbiotic relationship, not only have I taught on this topic but I have also over the years written on it, in various different contexts.

I had often thought of trying to put my thoughts on the subject together, *more geometrico* as it were, but for a variety of reasons never managed actually to do so. Eventually, however, partly as a result of some not too unwelcome prodding from a variety of sources, but

---

[4] This is not meant to deny that other justifications of the use of force, from straightforward realpolitik to much more idealistic forms, of course exist. They most certainly do, and we shall meet some of them in Chapter 2. But the just war tradition is the most influential language of *ethical* justification of the use of force – and centrally, as we shall also see, on the restriction of such justifications – in the European tradition.

[5] As is now customary I use upper-case letters to indicate the academic study and lower-case letters to refer to what is studied.

partly also (I confess) because of the tenor of the times I decided to put pen to paper (finger to keyboard?) and try and arrange my thoughts more coherently.

In brief, I shall argue that for most of the modern period – and especially for much of the past hundred or so years – the 'scope' of justifications of the use of force has in fact – and contrary to a widely believed narrative – been expanding, not contracting, and that the most influential tradition that is supposed to be about the *restraint* of war (the just war tradition) has in fact been complicit in this. There are reasons to suppose, further, that the contemporary situation displays, and certainly promises, an *even greater* expansion of the scope of the use of force, and not merely in the context of *military* force used in international conflict, but also including the character of force and coercion *within* allegedly 'settled' political communities, even those that would self-identify as – to use a word I dislike – 'liberal'. I submit that for those of us committed to the idea of *civil* politics – a politics composed of limits and self-enacted restraints – this should be seen as deeply problematic, for reasons I will rehearse in the Epilogue. But, as I shall argue too, it is also very problematic for the just war tradition generically and so advocates and supporters of that tradition would do well to think very hard both about how it has developed in the relatively recent past as well as about how they might like it to develop in the future.

The central chapters of the book are thus given over to tracing the manner in which this trajectory has emerged and evolved and the – very deleterious – impact I argue it has had and will, in all probability, continue to have. As I say, I give reasons both in the Introduction and the Epilogue for why I think we should consider this a problematic development, but it is fair to say at the outset – to prepare those of a nervous disposition – that I hold out no great hope that it can be easily reversed. It is deeply embedded in the history and character of contemporary Western polities, of the international order they have largely created and, for both these and other reasons, in many other states as well.

It may be, indeed, that we will have to go through a thoroughly 'uncivil condition' both internationally and perhaps also domestically, before we begin to see the pass to which our own illusions have brought us. And this will take longer than it should, I suspect, because many of the illusions that blind us are hopeful ones, predicated on our desire to do good in the world coupled with our (sadly equally illusory) belief that we are, and can be, complete masters of our fate. I do not doubt, by the way, that many are *sincere* about this desire and I am far from belittling it *in abstracta*. But I close the book by emphasizing that we have come to see such desires in a wholly inappropriate manner; that what should be a matter of limits and restraints, of small-scale and piecemeal actions contextually situated, in the context of a very diverse and plural world, has become the dream of a network of grandiose and hugely complex institutional and political experiments in creating global common purposes that in fact can never succeed. And in failing, they will help to make the world more uncivil still.

Acknowledgements

I owe many debts to a large number of people and institutions for their help with, and support of, the ideas in this book, as well as the book itself, and it is one of the pleasures of bringing any work of scholarship to fruition that such debts can be publicly acknowledged. As John Plamenatz once remarked, 'The artist ploughs his own furrow, the scholar ... cultivates a common field.' And it is a pleasure to recognize and thank fellow labourers in said field (in my case, probably a vineyard!).

St Andrews is a very special place for anyone interested in the kinds of things I am interested in. Across disciplinary boundaries there is a wide community with many shared interests that I have not hesitated to shamelessly plunder, and for that, all involved have my heartfelt thanks. For conversations about, comments on drafts of, or general help with, the present book especially, I should like to thank John Anderson, Ali Ansari, Liz Ashford, Michael Bentley, Mike Boyle, Karin Fierke, John Haldane, Jill Harries, Patrick Hayden, Mark Imber, Tim Mulgan, Oliver Richmond, John Skorupski, Gabi Slomp, Christopher Smith, Jens Timmerman, William Walker, Ali Watson, and the late Paul Wilkinson. Special thanks should go to my colleagues in the School of International Relations, who had good reason to suppose this book would appear much earlier than it has and who have greeted its repeated non-appearance with a tolerance for which I am very grateful. And finally, a very special thank-you should go to Tony Lang. Not only has he discussed the issues herein endlessly with me, and offered comments on many drafts, he has sustained me with the most important thing any scholar can give to another during the process of writing and rewriting: I refer, of course, to coffee.

Then there are my students. I have lectured to both undergraduate and graduate students on topics discussed herein for virtually my whole career to date and have learned an immeasurable amount in the process. I hope they learned something as well, but you'd have to ask them. Perhaps most of all, during the period I was meditating on the book I have had a quite extraordinary group of doctoral students. I think the idea was that I would be advising them on their work, but be that as it may, they gave me more help with mine than I can ever properly thank them for. Particular thanks in this context must go to Amanda Beattie, Jon Boyd, Su Dutta, Sean Elliott, Ian Hall, Renee Jeffery, Torsten Michel, Davood Moradian, Mitchell Rologas, Kate Schick and Marian Tupy.

Much of the book originally took the form of papers given at academic conferences or papers or lectures to academic audiences at universities. In all cases I am grateful for the comments I received, and I would like to thank especially the following for commenting on papers, or discussions on drafts, or about the book in general: Kirsten Ainley, Mathias Albert, the late Hayward Alker, Will Bain, Tarak Barkawi, Ilan Baron, Chuck Beitz, Duncan Bell, Nigel Biggar, Ken Booth, Dai Boucher, Joseph Boyle, Lothar Brock, Barry Buzan, David Campbell, Stephanie Carvin, Ian Clark, Christopher Coker, Ariel Colonomos, Paul Cornish, Alexis Crow, James Der Derian, Tim Dunne, Jean Bethke Elshtain, Toni Erskine, Cecile Fabre, Theo Farrell, Sir Lawrence Freedman, Ian Forbes, Mervyn Frost, Anna Geis, Pierre Hassner, Stanley Hauerwas, Bruce Hoffman, Mark Hoffman, Andrew Hurrell, Kim Hutchings, Viv Jabri, James Turner Johnson, Bob Keohane, Fritz Kratochwil, Ned Lebow, Steven Lee, Andrew Linklater, Richard Little, Jeff McMahan, Larry May, James Mayall, Harald Muller, Terry Nardin, Oliver O'Donovan, Cian O'Driscoll, Onora O'Neill, Noel O'Sullivan, David Owen, Patricia Owens, Dan Phillpot, Thomas Pogge, Gwyn Prins, Esther Reed, David Rodin, Henry Shue, Michael Joseph Smith, Steve Smith, Trevor Taylor, Ann Tickner, the late John Vincent, Ole Waever, Kenneth Waltz, Danny Warner, Jennifer Welsh, Nick Wheeler, Howard Williams, John Williams, Mike Williams and Pete Wright.

There are a few very special debts I would also like to acknowledge here. First, parts of chapters 1 and 2 were, in part, originally papers co-authored with Caroline Kennedy. Not only has she generously allowed me to reuse (and in some cases completely rewrite) material we originally jointly authored, she has been a wonderful conversation partner on strategic, historical and geopolitical questions since we first met. Our fate was sealed, I think, on the day we realized that we both think that *The Searchers* is one of the greatest movies ever made, and if we ever do write that book we have long projected, I think it would be a nice touch if we published it under the composite pen name 'Ethan Edwards'.

A second special thank-you should go to Joel Rosenthal, President of the Carnegie Council for Ethics and International Affairs in New York. Joel has provided the whole community in international political theory, since the mid 1990s, with a truly immense amount of support. In the journal *Ethics and International Affairs*, he has provided a platform for wonderful work across an enormous range of areas, including very prominently the ethics of force, and in the wider work of the Council that he has helped to develop, he has created a hub of ideas and discussion that resonates very widely, in the academy and beyond. To me personally he has been exceptionally generous: hosting me at the Council's Upper East Side headquarters on many occasions in the past ten years, supporting seminars and workshops I organized both financially and through his enthusiasm and seemingly limitless network of contacts and friends and just by discussing the work and commenting on it. Joel, a very big thank-you.

Third, a particular – and slightly peculiar – institutional and personal debt is owed to the Royal Institute for International Affairs, universally known as 'Chatham House'. That august institution and I have a slightly odd relationship. It's not really my kind of place – too close to government and corporations, too policy-oriented and 'relevant'. I'm not really its kind of person – too academic, too philosophical and too much of a Tory anarchist. But somehow, I've been involved, off and on, with both Chatham House in general and its journal *International Affairs* for the past fifteen years, certainly to my great benefit. Distant ancestors of parts of chapters 1, 2 and 4 were originally written for the 2006 and 2008 special issues of *International Affairs* that I guest-edited. So I have a lot to thank Chatham House for, and to Caroline Soper especially, who does such a wonderful job with *International Affairs*, and all her excellent staff over the years, I would like to say a very big thank-you.

Fourth, I would like to announce the winner of the 'above and beyond the call of duty award'. This has to go to Chris Brown. Not only has he heard or seen virtually all of this book at some point or another over the past few years (occasionally even both at the same time), he has always supported me with comments, discussions, an extra glass of the house claret, occasional ribaldry and a well-administered kick when it was required (as it often was). He is unique and has influenced, helped and guided many scholars now plying their trade as international political theorists. Indeed, International Political Theory could not do better than adopt Chris as its patron saint (very chic for an atheist!). He did, after all, finish up in one of my PhD students' thesis – which he examined – as Christ Brown! A misprint, we were told, but then again …

Thanking my family properly would take much longer than I could possibly imagine. My amazing wife Vanessa and our wonderful daughters Corinna and Natalie not only allowed me time on the PC (well, some of the time), put up with my eccentric working habits, and generally tolerated me: they also remind me, on a daily basis, what really matters in life. The book may not be directly improved by that, but its author most certainly is.

I would like to close with one last, but certainly not least, thank-you. My brother Patrick has been my longest-standing conversation partner on the topics discussed here – and, indeed, most others – since we were boys. Despite over twenty years living on different continents, the conversations have never flagged and they are as important (and as entertaining) to me now as they always have been. He has also, as I have not, had experience at the sharp end of the use of force, as an officer in the British army and later as a 'Peacekeeping Poet' in Bosnia. His insights and his example are a permanent inspiration, and, with admiration and love, I dedicate this book to him.

The book draws on a number of papers written at various points in the last few years. Some of the papers have been previously published (a full list appears below), but all those that were have been substantially revised so as to fit with the more general – and very different – argument of this book. Thanks to all editors and publishers for permission to use material which originally appeared in their pages.

The previously published essays that have been incorporated into the present volume are as follows:

'Contextuality, Interdependence and the Ethics of Intervention', in Ian Forbes and Mark Hoffman (eds.) *Political Theory, International Relations and the Ethics of Intervention* (London: Macmillan, 1993)

'On the Just War Tradition in the Twenty First Century', *International Affairs*, 78, 2, 2002, 353–63

'On Democratic War Theory', in Anna Geiss, Harald Muller and Lothar Brock (eds.) *Democratic Wars: The Dark Side of the Democratic Peace* (London: Palgrave Macmillan, 2005)

'The Judgment of War: On the Idea of Legitimate Force in World Politics', *Review of International Studies*, 2005, 143–61

'Apocalypse Now? Continuities and Disjunctions in World Politics After 9/11', in *International Affairs*, 82, 3, 2006

'The Jus in Bello in Historical and Philosophical Perspective', in Larry May (ed.) *War and Philosophy* (Cambridge University Press, 2008)

'The State of War' (with Caroline Kennedy-Pipe) in *International Affairs*, 84, 5, 2008

'The Greatest Treason? On the Subtle Temptations of Preventive War', *International Affairs*, 84, 5, 2008

'Inter arma, silent leges? Political Community, Supreme Emergency and the Rules of War', in Antony J. Lang and Amanda Beattie (eds.) *War, Torture and Terrorism: Rethinking the Rules of International Security* (London: Routledge, 2008)

'A Global Ethic and the Hybrid Character of the Moral World', in *Ethics and International Affairs*, 26, 1, 2012, 27–31.

Introduction

The Fifth. Whence came our thought?
The Sixth. From four great minds that hated Whiggery.
...
                    but what is Whiggery?
A levelling, rancorous, rational sort of mind
That never looked out of the eye of a saint
Or out of drunkard's eye.
The Seventh. All's Whiggery now.

                    Yeats, 'The Seven Sages'

As I remarked in the Preface, this book is principally concerned with tracing the emergence and character of a particular trajectory in European – and now international – thought, by means of a focus on the relationship between justifications offered for the use of force and certain ideas about the character of modern politics. In using the term 'modern' here, I should say that I do not intend to embark on any great discussion of 'modernity' – that most protean, and perhaps overused, term in the modern intellectual lexicon[1] – but rather I am simply gesturing towards the fact that my concern will in general be with the past five hundred years or so, the period in which the modern state – and the states system – came to be formed and the period in which, I shall argue, the just war tradition as a doctrinally articulate tradition also came to be formed. But especially I shall be concerned with how the just war tradition and the particular (teleocratic) trajectory of European thought have been related in the past hundred years or so, the period in which, I shall argue, the relationship between those two increasingly took on a particular, and from my perspective particularly problematic, form, however much it may have been prefigured in earlier thought. The particular trajectory I have in

---

[1] Including by me. See my *Political Theory, Modernity and Postmodernity: Beyond Enlightenment and Critique* (Oxford: Blackwell, 1995).

mind – following Michael Oakeshott, I call it 'teleocratic' – has deep
roots in the modern world, but it has unquestionably become more
embedded and more dominant since the end of the eighteenth century.

The first claim – that the last five hundred years is the period in which
the modern state came to be formed – is relatively uncontroversial,
though there are many controversies associated with how we might
characterize the modern state,[2] but the second – that this is also the
period in which the just war tradition came to be formed – might give
some pause. After all (many might say) the just war tradition goes back
surely to Augustine and Ambrose, perhaps as far back as Cicero, or even
Aristotle.[3] At one level, this is, of course, correct. The just war tradition
tout court indeed pre-dates the modern period but, for reasons I shall
discuss in Chapter 3, I want to argue that just war *doctrine* – that is to
say the tradition as an articulate, self-aware and considered whole –
only emerges as a settled doctrine at the beginning of the modern period
and changes rather dramatically throughout it, most especially in the
period of its so-called 'revival' after the Second World War.

In particular, I will argue that the just war tradition – in the most
recent period especially – has been importantly shaped by the teleocratic understanding of the character of modern politics. I will also
argue that, in their turn, at least aspects of the tradition have provided,
and continue to provide, an important resource *for* that idea, *most
especially* in its contemporary form, and finally that this mutual
shaping has profound implications: for politics in general, for the
tradition itself and for the wider international order in which they both
nest. A chief concern of this book, then, is to trace those relations and
assess those implications.

In discussing the just war tradition one has to say something, of
course, about war more generally, even though war in general is a
much more protean phenomenon. Of the four fabled horsemen whose
provenance Saint John the Divine famously essayed, war is perhaps the

[2] I am aware of course that whole libraries would be needed to house the
controversies about the character of the modern state. I touch on some of this
(a mere fraction) in the next two chapters. But for now it is only the timeline that
I am concerned with and this, as I say, is relatively uncontroversial.

[3] Ironically, as I shall discuss in more detail in Chapter 3, while there are some very
good histories of the tradition, most do not trace the history of the tradition back
as far as Aristotle. For one that, in effect, does, see Robert W. Dyson, *Natural
Law and Political Realism in the History of Political Thought*, vol. I: *From the
Sophists to Machiavelli* (New York: Peter Lang, 2005).

most depressing. Pestilence and famine, after all, are features of the world, avoidable to some degree, but to a large extent outside our control, and Death comes to us all in the end, and cannot be forsworn. But war we bring upon ourselves, have done so since before the beginnings of recorded history and continue to do so today. It is this volitional aspect, as much as its reality in the world, which makes it so protean and so untameable. As the philosopher Stephen Clark suggests,[4] war is perhaps best seen as an Olympian and in that regard we can become caught up in it – in its ecstasies as well as its tragedies[5] – as much as we can get caught up in the delights of that other untameable Olympian, Aphrodite.

Of course, to use the term 'war' at all is also to recognize that there is an ineliminably communal element involved. 'War' is violence waged by, and on behalf of, communities. It is not simply violence as such.[6] Such communities have been, and can be, hugely various: tribes, religious sects, revolutionary movements, empires, city republics, states and so on. But use of the term 'war' implies, in some respect and to some degree, a 'political' connotation. One might (many do) rhetorically speak of the 'war against drugs', or the 'war on poverty' but we all know that it is rhetorical excess, however pardonable, when such phrases are used. In the modern context, the main context of war, certainly in Europe, has been the modern state, and the states system in which that curious and rather ramshackle construction is embedded, and however that might now be changing – and I will offer some suggestions in Chapter 1 to the effect that it may not be changing as much as some think – it is the context of the relationship between war and the state that has shaped the vast majority of modern thinking about war. The context of the relationship has been a central reality in

[4] In his wonderful and much-underdiscussed book *Civil Peace and Sacred Order* (Oxford: Clarendon Press, 1989). I shall return to Clark's argument, briefly, in the Epilogue.

[5] It is a worrying tendency in many – though by no means all – modern treatments of war that they deny it has its ecstasies. It was a commonplace of much ancient writing on war that it did and some moderns too have understood that it is perhaps war's ecstasies that account for much of its power. This is also a failure on the part of those who see war principally in instrumental terms. For a powerful analysis that understands the ecstatic power of war as well as its horrors see J. Glenn Gray, *The Warriors* (New York: Harcourt Brace, 1959).

[6] For two fascinating, philosophically rich discussions of violence per se, see Hannah Arendt, *On Violence* (New York: Harcourt Brace Jovanovich, 1970) and John Keane, *Reflections on Violence* (London: Verso, 1996).

the history of politics and international relations. It has shaped – and is shaping – our world, as it shaped the worlds of our most distant ancestors. Whatever we think about it, however volitional it might indeed be, it seems a permanent presence, good or bad. Machiavelli, one of its greatest students, quoted his master, Livy, in accounting for this: 'war is just', he tells us, 'to whom it is necessary and arms are pious, when there is no hope but in arms'.[7]

There are, historically and culturally, many different ways to write about war, and almost all cultures of which we have any record have a rich literature dealing with many aspects of the subject. Myths abound in discussions of it; history is often written through it; stories of many kinds rely on it. The hero, as Joseph Campbell has it, may have a thousand faces,[8] but it is unsurprising that many of these are faces of the warrior. With rather less literary grace, a broad swathe of literature in historical (and indeed International Relations) scholarship has tended to focus on what I would call the 'explanatory' aspect of war. Why does it occur at all? How does it happen? Why did *this* war break out not *that* one? Why are *these* strategies effective in *this* context in averting (or winning) a war and not in *that* context? And so on. These kinds of questions have generated some of the most impressive studies in the last century or so and will no doubt continue to do so.[9] No one could deny that these are important questions and that answers to them, if they can be found, are likely to be very significant.[10] However, this book is not concerned with these sets of questions or, inasmuch as it is, it is concerned with them only secondarily and to the extent that reflections upon them also cast light on the character of justifications that are offered – in particular contexts and particular settings – for the use of force.

---

[7] Machiavelli, *The Prince*, trans. and Introduction by Harvey Mansfield (University of Chicago Press, 1985), p. 103.

[8] See Joseph Campbell, *The Hero with a Thousand Faces* (Princeton University Press, 1968 (1949)).

[9] See especially, amongst a huge list: Lewis Fry Richardson, *Arms and Insecurity* (Pittsburgh: Stevens, 1960); Thomas C. Schelling, *The Strategy of Conflict* (Cambridge, Mass.: Harvard University Press, 1960); Quincy Wright: *A Study of War* (University of Chicago Press, 1942); Kenneth Waltz, *Man, the State and War* (New York: Columbia University Press, 1959).

[10] I confess that I am less than certain that we *can* expect very much from such discussions. My own suspicion of causal explanation in the human sciences is at the root of this uncertainty – but that is a matter for another day.

A word about method

Before I outline the structure of the book, I should perhaps say something about *how* I am going to go about it, or what would (no doubt) be called by many my 'method'. A lengthy discussion of this would be merely inappropriate in this context: the proof of the pudding being (as always) in the eating. However, a brief discussion might help the digestion. I conceive of this book as a philosophical essay concerned with explicating the relationship between complex sets of ideas – certain ideas about modern politics, certain ideas about ethically justifiable war – and assessing the implications of this relationship for our understanding of the contemporary political and international context. Inasmuch as this is a philosophical essay, therefore, it is not intended as a contribution to 'history' per se, though I certainly draw on historical work, nor is it intended to have an obvious carry-over to the world of practice, though some of the implications I trace clearly have various kinds of practical implication. My intention, in other words, is to try and understand what the character of this relationship is and what implications it could be said to have, has had and might have had. Aside from some brief remarks in Chapter 5, I offer no thoughts as to what implications it *will* have.[11] All of this is to say that, to borrow a helpful distinction from Stephen White, this essay is intended as a contribution to what he referred to as 'World Disclosing' political theory, as opposed, that is, to 'action co-ordinating' political theory.[12]

I emphasize this because I want additionally to emphasize that the story I tell here is not intended to be read as a *necessary* one. I am not suggesting that the relationship I sketch *must* take the form that it has, or that it always *will* take that form. The implications I trace and discuss should be understood, therefore, as I remarked in the Preface, not as a destiny, but as a choice (or perhaps better a series

---

[11] The influence of Michael Oakeshott's conception of the modal character of human knowledge on this will be obvious to anyone who knows it and, of course, that is hardly uncontroversial. I don't intend to defend this view here, however, merely to advertise it as a background against which this essay can be understood. As I will show later, this book draws on Oakeshott's philosophical thought in both particular and general terms, though not always in ways of which he would, I suspect, have approved.

[12] See Stephen K. White, *Political Theory and Postmodernism* (Cambridge University Press, 1991).

of choices), implied by, but not necessitated by, the relations themselves. It could, in other words, be otherwise.

The shape of the book

To undertake this task, Chapter 1, 'Disordered world?', introduces the notion of seeing international order as the 'uncivil condition'. It begins with a consideration of justifications offered for the use of force in the context of various narratives that have emerged from the attacks on Washington and New York in September 2001. Especially salient here are the claims of those that emphasize that these attacks mark a sea-change in the character of twenty-first-century conflict and that 'we' – liberal, modern states – need to change our responses towards it as a result. I argue that those in the twenty-first century who claim that the course of world politics has descended into a new and distinct sphere of conflict understood as (or in some cases prefaced by) a 'global war on terror' vastly misdescribe the character of the context. By claiming that the attacks on the World Trade Center and the Pentagon represented a 'tectonic shift', a reorientation of world politics, and a genuinely new – and very dark – prognosis for the future of world politics, the stage is set not merely for the claim that force is a more or less permanent feature of the world but for the much more problematic claim that its character is radically changing – for the worse – and that, as a result, 'we' have to change our response to it. In this chapter, I argue that the world of post-9/11 is very much the world of pre-9/11, indeed of pre-1989 (and even pre-1945) in many respects. This is not to say that nothing has changed at all but rather to say that what *has* changed does not warrant the kinds of evaluative claims – and political decisions – that have been, and are being, attributed to it. In this chapter I point to what I take to be the chief effect of this sort of claim: to effectively set the stage for claims about the increasing and necessary permissiveness of force in this context; to act, if I may use a strategic analogy, as a 'force multiplier' for a more permissive conception of the use of force, a conception that is being helped, not hindered, by contemporary conceptions of the just war shaped by engagement with teleocratic conceptions of the state, and, indeed, teleocratic conceptions of politics more generally. To set the scene for this, the chapter concludes with a discussion of Oakeshott's account of nomocratic and teleocratic politics.

Chapter 2, which I have called 'War music' – after Christopher Logue's magnificent reimagining of perhaps the greatest literary masterpiece to have been written about war in European history, Homer's *Iliad*[13] – offers a discussion of how we might understand war as part of the modern 'social imaginary' (to use a phrase I borrow from Charles Taylor), and in particular of how we might understand the just war tradition (which of course pre-dates modernity) as part of that imaginary. It looks at claims that war is permanent and valuable, that it is permanent and horrible, and also at various claims that politics can move beyond war, a process that begins really in the eighteenth century but which is now a central plank of international legal and political rhetoric connected with war.[14] I reflect on various ways these claims might be made and outline a rough typology of responses to the reality of war in the world, which together, I suggest, make up the modern social imaginary of war, including, of course, the just war tradition.

In the context of that 'modern social imaginary of war', however, I also consider a central component of that modern imaginary, to wit the claim that a disposition towards war (or away from it) is linked to regime type. Making such a claim, I argue, elides a crucial distinction that has a central significance for the story I want to tell: the distinction between *type of regime* and *mode of association*. The character and implications of this distinction and its elision concern me at the end of the chapter, which amounts to an extended disquisition on the way in which Michael Oakeshott understood the character of the central division of European political thought since the medieval period, to wit, the distinction between what he terms nomocratic and teleocratic modes of association, which I discussed in some detail at the end of Chapter 1.

Which brings me, of course, to how I characterize and understand the just war tradition itself. As Chapter 2 makes clear, the principal

---

[13] This consists of five poetic 'reimaginings' of Homer. *War Music* (London: Faber & Faber, 1988), *Kings* (London: Faber & Faber, 1991), *The Husbands* (London: Faber & Faber, 1995), *All Day Permanent Red: War Music continued* (London: Faber & Faber, 2003), *Cold Calls – War Music continued* (London: Faber & Faber, 2005). As well as being the title of the first volume, 'War Music' tends to be the generic name for the cycle as a whole.

[14] I hardly need to point, surely, to such obvious manifestations of this view as the opening preamble of the United Nations Charter: 'We, the peoples of the United Nations, determined to save succeeding generations from the scourge of war ...' See www.un.org/en/documents.

moral language in which war has been addressed in the European tradition is indeed the just war tradition. But the fact that it is a tradition (and not, as is sometimes assumed, simply a 'theory') is expressive of the obvious fact that there are many ways of seeing it at various points in its history and, of course, that it *has* a history. Chapter 3 thus examines the character and the tensions within the just war tradition. I do not try and offer a history of the tradition – there are many excellent and important studies which do that – but rather concentrate on one central dynamic that, I argue, has operated in the tradition from the beginning: that between seeing the tradition as *centrally* about the limitation of the destructiveness of war, while recognizing its occasional necessity, and seeing it as, again *centrally*, a vehicle for the punishment of wrongdoing. Both were central to the evolving tradition, and they have always been in tension with one another, but it is a version of the latter, I argue, that became increasingly prominent in the twentieth century, especially so in the context of the so-called 'revival' of the just war from the 1970s onwards. I argue that this is intimately connected with the growing dominance of teleocratic conceptions of politics in general.

I situate this initially by discussing perhaps the most important development in the modern just war, the evolution – in the sixteenth century – of the distinction between *jus ad bellum* and *jus in bello*. I argue that the evolution of this distinction, while quite logical in its own terms and at least implied in some earlier versions of the tradition, also introduced an ambiguity that both *enabled* the tradition to function in the increasingly state-dominated world of the seventeenth and eighteenth centuries and also *disabled* at least part of its critical function with respect to emerging conceptions of political authority, and which, in particular, limited its claims about the destructiveness of war. This process became more deeply embedded still by the codification of international law and especially by the development of the laws of war, a phenomenon which went into ever-increasing overdrive in the aftermath of the disastrous wars of the twentieth (and now twenty-first) century. This had the largely unintended effect of making the tradition accommodate itself to a certain jurisprudential reading of law, grounded on state power. In other words to a particular kind of legal positivism which increasingly reflected a teleocratic conception of the state, inasmuch as the state itself was increasingly conceptualized in this way.

In the second part of Chapter 3, in considering the hugely influential rebirth of writing on the just war after the Second World War, in both religious and secular contexts, I argue that the teleocratic conception of politics becomes the central locus of the tradition even when advocates of the tradition are arguing against 'statist' conceptions of politics in general. The chapter thus concludes by looking at the current 'state of the art' in the tradition. In brief, I argue that what is visible, not only in the various different ways of reading the just war tradition but also in a good deal of contemporary international law and, indeed, other approaches to the ethics of force, is a conception of the ethics of force as predominantly about the pursuit of justice, or perhaps better, the elimination of injustice, *rather* than about the restraint of force and that, as a result, it is becoming progressively *less* restrictive, that it is cleaving, in other words, to seeing the tradition as essentially about the punishment of wrongdoing *rather than* (as opposed to alongside) the limitation of destructiveness.

The next two chapters of the book show how the relationship between the just war tradition and modern teleocratic politics has shaped debates over two central questions that have been asked about the justification of force in the world of international politics over the last couple of decades, though in some respects both draw on much earlier ideas. Chapter 4, entitled 'Force for good?', concentrates on the two issues which perhaps more than any other have crystallized the tendencies I have highlighted in the just war tradition in the contemporary period – the linked questions of humanitarian intervention and, following on from that, the possibility of preventive war. Intervention as such, of course, has long been a central question for thinking about the use of force in international relations and, for the European system of states in particular, a hugely important issue given the centrality in the legal and political discourse of that system of the formal norm of non-intervention.

In the 1980s and 1990s an allegedly new debate became inextricably involved with those older ones. In the context of the end of the Cold War and the events that followed it, both in Europe (the collapse of Yugoslavia) and elsewhere (the genocide in Rwanda), debates about so-called 'humanitarian' intervention in the early to mid 1990s, in the context of the evolution of so-called 'new wars', mushroomed.[15]

---

[15] The phrase 'new wars' is most associated with Mary Kaldor. See her *New and Old Wars* (Cambridge: Polity Press, 2007). I will offer a proper discussion in Chapter 3.

In fact, as the pioneering work of Brendan Simms, D.J.B. Trim and their colleagues decisively shows,[16] ideas about 'humanitarian' justifications for the use of force go back to the beginning of the modern states system in the early modern world. And, as we shall see, that is hardly surprising. The growing strength of teleocratic conceptions of politics would create just such a logic.

And the logic of humanitarian intervention is perfectly clear. By caparisoning the use of force with the high moral ground of the protection of rights – most obviously in recent doctrines such as the 'responsibility to protect' – the scope of the possible use of force is extended, not restricted, while the conceptual restrictions on its use – both licit and illicit – are weakened. By seeking to institutionalize such claims, however well intentioned, I argue that contemporary international society is running the risk that undid Dr Frankenstein: making a creature that will exceed anybody's ability to control or direct it.

Perhaps nowhere have the effects of these claims been felt more than in the sudden burgeoning – in academic and political literature, and indeed in fiction and film[17] – of discussions of the necessity, the moral requirement for and the possibilities of 'preventive' force. Of course, as with intervention, discussions about preventive force go back to the beginning of the modern states system (and indeed, arguably, in a rather different manner before that as well),[18] but what is significant is its exclusion from the just war tradition. Including it in the language of ethically justifiable force is what is new. And perhaps most disturbing of all, amongst the contemporary advocates of preventive war one finds strong supporters of the just war tradition (which has always excoriated preventive war) and strong supporters of the international rule of law (which has always outlawed it). It is the arguments of these scholars and thinkers that I chiefly engage in Chapter 4; for, as I say, there have always been advocates of preventive war, but usually these were outside the ranks of those who would civilize war; now they are on the inside and that, I think, is profoundly significant. Given the

---

[16] See Brendan Simms and D.J.B. Trim (eds.) *Humanitarian Intervention: A History* (Cambridge University Press, 2011).

[17] The list is very long indeed, and I will mention some in the chapter itself, so there is no need to do so here.

[18] See for example the discussions in Benedict Kingsbury and Benjamin Straumann (eds.) *The Roman Foundations of the Law of Nations: Alberico Gentili and the Justice of Empire* (Oxford University Press, 2010).

character of contemporary international politics, I argue, such a step is not only unwarranted but foolhardy in the extreme.

If Chapter 4 looks at the justifications of the use of force externally, Chapter 5 takes up what I take to be the most disturbing idea of all to be found in the combination of the teleocratic model of politics generally and the modern just war tradition – the idea of 'Supreme Emergency'. In the context of the just war this idea has been most famously elaborated by Michael Walzer in the 1970s, but in the aftermath of 9/11 this idea, if not always by that name, has been behind a whole range of themes, even policies, now only too well known: abridgement of civil liberties, suspension of habeas corpus, equivocations about 'enhanced interrogation techniques' (for which read torture), and many more.

But again, as with humanitarian intervention and preventive war, these modern conceptions echo a long history of support for 'temporary' abandonment of the 'normal' restraints on violence and power – valorized most obviously in recent decades by Carl Schmitt not only in his now very well known (and perhaps generally not very well interpreted) discussion of the 'state of exception',[19] but perhaps even more so in his much less well known discussion in *Die Diktatur*.[20] In Chapter 5 I go some way beyond Walzer's deployment of the idea (I entirely accept that he seeks to hedge it around with restrictions and qualifications and to restrict it in important ways) but argue that fundamentally, in accepting it at all, he – and indeed the modern just war tradition as a whole – comes close to accommodating itself to a conception of the role of force in politics that is profoundly damaging both to the just war tradition and to (at least civil) conceptions of politics itself. That such arguments are even being considered in polities that claim to be committed to constitutionalism and the rule of law marks the extent, I think, of the growing domination of teleocratic ideas about politics.

In the Epilogue to the book, I move from the specific focus on the use of force to consider more general questions of international order in the light of that argument. I begin by considering two ways of reading

[19] See Carl Schmitt, *Der Begriff des Politischen: Text von 1932 mit einem Vorwort und drei Corollarien* (Berlin: Duncker und Humblot, 2002). The most fashionable contemporary deployment of these ideas can be found in Giorgio Agamben, *State of Exception* (University of Chicago Press, 2005).
[20] See Carl Schmitt, *Die Diktatur* (Berlin: Duncker und Humblot, 1921).

my argument that I do not accept. The first suggests that, on my own terms, I ought to accept world politics as 'the uncivil condition' I mentioned right at the start and not be concerned about the specifics of the changes to relatively minor ideational additions such as the just war tradition. Here I argue that the dynamics I have traced in the specific context of the modern state and the just war tradition are likely to become even more pronounced if one thinks of the context of the states system as a whole, and in particular in the context of both globalization and the evolving geopolitics of the twenty-first century. I argue that the likely consequences of this, for the tradition and at least for 'civil' versions of politics, are parlous indeed.

Second, I consider what I take to be the most influential critique of my position in the West generally which suggests that, in the globalizing circumstances of the twenty-first century a teleocratic conception of politics is inevitable and, despite some possibility of excess, should be welcomed not spurned. Here, I try and suggest why I think this is not so and then expand my response into an argument that suggests why teleocratic conceptions of politics should concern us necessarily and not just contingently: what, in other words is *specifically* problematic about teleocratic conceptions of politics, what we lose if they remain as dominant as they have become.

Plato once remarked that it is the task of the poet to give voices to those who disagree with the common sense of their society.[21] I am far from claiming a poetic mantle, but I do think that the kind of philosophical essay I take this book to be might also, at least in some respects, perform such a task. The book seeks to tell a story that is fraught with difficulties for those who believe in broadly civil politics (as I do), and I do not, in all honesty, offer much by way of hope in the short term at least. But at the end of that journey it is, I think, also important to emphasize that I do not think we are without resources or that we should despair. 'Despair', it is said at one crucial point in J.R.R. Tolkien's great narrative of war, loss and redemption, 'is only for those who see the end beyond all doubt'. We certainly do not, indeed cannot, see the end beyond all doubt. And so for that reason, if for no other, alternative possibilities are always worth investigating; and so that is what I gesture towards at the end of the argument, in the Epilogue to the book as a whole.

---

[21] *Laws*, 719c.

1 | *Disordered world?*

an axe-age, a sword-age,
shields will be cloven,
a wind-age, a wolf-age,
before the world's ruin.
                    Völuspá

The international order at the beginning of the twenty-first century is, many argue, at a crucial turning point. For many, perhaps the majority, the future is likely to be a very positive one, whatever our current difficulties. The growth of humankind's technical and scientific knowledge beckons great improvements across a range of spheres; health, well-being, longevity, food production, energy, and many more. And on top of that there is the possibility of the progressive curtailing or even elimination of age-old scourges such as disease, famine, and even war. But for many others, certainly a sizeable minority, the outlook is much gloomier. A global economy where the rich get richer and the poor much poorer; growing crises over resources (energy, minerals and, perhaps most important of all, water); growing instability in the global order as new powers rise to challenge the existing order; growing ecological breakdown, perhaps verging on catastrophe – a 'coming anarchy', as one writer called it a few years ago.[1]

One book is unlikely to be able to settle these arguments and I do not intend to try. But I do want to examine one aspect, at least, of the negative argument – the claim that the world is becoming a more unstable and violent place than it has been – and assess its significance. For while I shall want to dissent from most of the reasons that are commonly given for assuming this, I shall also want to argue that there is something to the claim after all. This opening chapter will thus seek to show why I reject the usual arguments about a worsening of the contemporary order while at the same time framing the alternative

---

[1] See Robert A. Kaplan, *The Coming Anarchy* (New York: Atlantic Books, 2000).

13

response I want to make in the course of the book as a whole. And I want to begin where many, if not most, of the arguments about the increasingly violent character of world politics also begin: with 9/11.

Apocalypse now?

Today it is a commonplace, of course, to say that 9/11 changed world politics profoundly. World politics had suddenly taken on a much darker, more apocalyptic hue than at any time in recent history. On the evening of 9/11 itself, President Bush declared that 'night fell on a different world'; and in an essay published the following year, the man who had famously – a short twelve years before – announced the end of history remarked that 'world politics, it would seem, shifted gears abruptly after September 11th'. Ken Booth and Tim Dunne, in the preface to their discussion of the 9/11 attacks published the following year, said plainly that 'For years to come, if not decades, the "war on terrorism" will be the defining paradigm in the struggle for global order.'[2]

And the contemporary historian John Lewis Gaddis invoked an even more powerful image to emphasize the 'newness' and radically transformative character of 9/11, in his meditation on the US experience in its wake:

through the days, weeks and months that followed ... most of us managed to return to an approximation of normality. And yet our understanding of what is 'normal' is not what it once was. Just as New Yorkers go about their familiar activities in the shadow of an unfamiliar skyline, so something within each of us has also changed. It's as if we were all irradiated, on that morning of September 11 2001, in such a way as to shift our psychological makeup – the DNA in our minds – with consequences that will not become clear for years to come.[3]

Even after more than ten years, the sense of something profound, new and unsettling in world politics is still very real. The deluge of events and memorials to mark the tenth anniversary of the 9/11 attacks show that, even if little else is agreed about the origins or legacy of that day.

---

[2] See Ken Booth and Tim Dunne (eds.) *Worlds in Collision* (New York: Palgrave, 2002).

[3] John Lewis Gaddis, *Surprise, Security and the American Experience* (New Haven: Yale University Press, 2004), pp. 4–5.

In general terms, one might break up the claims that 9/11 did mark something new and distinct in world politics into three broad groups. These are, first, conceptions about the geopolitical assumptions that govern world politics; second, arguments about the character of the specifics of the use of military force in contemporary world politics; and, third, general ideological alignments that it seemed the events of 9/11 were showing up. Let me take each in turn.

Geopolitical frameworks

One of the areas deemed to be most obviously changed was the relationships between the major players in world politics. From a period of relative stability in these relations – one that is largely traceable to the manner in which the Cold War ended in the early 1990s[4] – it has been argued that we have moved to one of marked geopolitical fluctuation. Very quickly after 9/11, both out of genuine shock and horror and perhaps also out of a recognition of the likely ferocity of the US response, states that had been rivals or even – in the case of Russia – adversaries for much of the previous century stood, and announced that they stood, shoulder to shoulder with the United States. It was a French newspaper that bore the famous headline 'We are all Americans now', but the sentiment was shared in many parts of the globe, notwithstanding the celebrations that broke out in parts of the developing world to gloat over the 'humbling' of the United States. Yet within three years that alliance, that coalition of the willing that had supported and cooperated with the United States in the invasion of Afghanistan – in many cases in very radical ways indeed: think, for example, of the support extended to the US by certain Central Asian states, or by some Middle Eastern states such as Syria[5] – had fractured over the American decision to invade Iraq.

---

[4] Good discussions of this – which emphasize the extent to which the end of the Cold War was effectively a 'peace treaty', with all the concomitant assumptions – can be found in Ian Clark, *The Post Cold War Order: The Spoils of Peace* (Oxford University Press, 2001), and G. John Ikenberry, *After Victory* (Princeton University Press, 2000).

[5] For discussions of relations after 9/11, see e.g. Sally Cummings, 'Negotiating the US Presence: The Central Asian States', and Raymond Hinnebusch, 'Support with Qualifications: Syria', in Rick Fawn and Mary Buckley (eds.) *Global Responses to Terrorism* (London: Routledge, 2003). On the US challenges in Central Asian policy, see Charles William Maynes, 'America Discovers Central Asia', *Foreign*

It is unquestionably true that the events that spun out from 9/11 have created a high level of instability in contemporary international politics; yet it does not seem to me that there is anything especially surprising in such instability. 'It is hardly a surprise', his biographer Porphyry has the ancient sage Plotinus say, 'that sticks and stones should fall, and that men, who must die, should die.' Equally, I suggest, it is hardly radically new or very surprising that states combine balancing and bandwagoning (and sometimes try to finesse a bit of both) in the context of a fluid and changing global political scene; we should see this as entirely normal in the context of the general history of international relations.

Kenneth Waltz has suggested that three basic facts about world politics seem remarkably unchanged by 9/11. The first is what he terms the 'gross imbalance of power' in the world since the demise of the Soviet Union, namely unchallenged US primacy. The second is the gradual proliferation of nuclear weapons in particular and to some extent weapons of mass destruction in general, a trend certainly made worse by events since 9/11 but firmly in place long before it and, indeed, in many respects a central feature of international politics almost from the beginning of the nuclear era. The third is the permanence and prevalence of crises in the world, crises in which, given its position, the US is almost certain to be involved to some extent, but which are, again, a well-known feature of international politics in almost any era.[6]

Without agreeing with all the steps in Waltz's reasoning – and notwithstanding what I shall want to add in a moment – this seems about right. The events of 9/11 and all they have brought in their train provide the context in which international politics, in many aspects at least, is currently played out, but the *manner* in which it is played out seems very familiar. Of course, it was more apparent by the end of the first decade of the twenty-first century – and especially after the

---

Affairs, 82, 2, March–April 2003; Antoine Blau, 'Report Calls on US to Rethink Its Regional Approach', *Radio Free Europe/Radio Liberty*, 10 February 2004, at www.rferl.org/featuresarticle/2004/02.

[6] For Waltz's elaboration of these three claims, see his 'The Continuity of International Politics', in K. Booth and T. Dunne (eds.) *Worlds in Collision* (London: Palgrave, 2002). I should also like to thank Waltz for a long discussion of his argument in the interstices of a conference in his honour held at Aberystwyth in September 2008.

financial crisis that rocked the global economy in 2007–8 – that the position of the United States is rather more precarious than Waltz suggested and that world politics is facing a much more confident and assertive major power in China and several more confident and assertive lesser powers (such as Brazil and India) and thus the international system at the time of writing looks far closer to an emergent multipolar order than, perhaps, did the one observable just after 9/11. Yet this too is hardly new. The 'rise' of other powers has been a continual feature of much International Relations scholarship for half a century (even if the particular 'other power' was infinitely variable) and so it cannot surely be seen as a 'new' or unexpected phenomenon.[7]

In other words, while it is, of course, the case that the character of the international system is shifting this does not appear to have very much, if anything, to do with 9/11, or the response to it, but rather it is a perfectly 'normal' (in historical terms) part of world politics. World politics has always been conflictual – though not necessarily violent – and riven by major differences of interest and power and it still is. Nothing very new here.

Clash of civilizations?

However, a rather different claim has also been made, one which still claims a good deal of support, despite having been enunciated long before 9/11. This is that 9/11 made manifest something very important and different about the real nature of the geopolitical conflicts that face us and which marks a distinct difference from traditional understandings of such clashes: namely, that they are fundamentally civilizational or cultural (and religious) in character, rather than state-based. Among the most widely cited (semi-)academic books that sought to emphasize this was Samuel Huntington's now-celebrated *The Clash of Civilizations and the Remaking of World Order*.[8] Huntington's thesis is now so well known as hardly to need repeating, but it is perhaps worth

---

[7] Contemporary discussions of this are a drug on the market. See, for some relatively restrained and thoughtful examples, Gideon Rachman, *Zero Sum World: Politics, Power and Prosperity after the Crash* (London: Atlantic Books, 2010), Bill Emmott, *Rivals: How the Struggle between China, India and Japan Will Shape Our Next Decade* (London: Penguin, 2009), and Fareed Zakaria, *The Post-American World and the Rise of the Rest* (London: Penguin, 2009).

[8] Samuel Huntington, *The Clash of Civilizations and the Remaking of World Order* (New York: Simon & Schuster, 1996).

pointing out just how widely his ideas have been taken up. For many, and across many 'cultures', it is now a commonplace to speak of the inevitable 'clash' of civilizations as a motor of conflict in twenty-first-century world politics, and there were echoes of this language in academic, journalistic and political commentary alike on, for example, the collapse and bloody wars of the former Yugoslavia, the possible emergence of a Chinese 'threat' to American primacy and, of course, events all over the globe after 9/11.

There are, however, two problems with this claim. First, as has just been made clear, it did not emerge after 9/11. Rather, it has been assumed by those sympathetic to it that 9/11 demonstrates the validity of a hypothesis that had been advanced some time before. Yet if this is so, it is the underlying reality of world politics in its current phase – that it rests on a civilizational or cultural form which both underpins and overlays its more familiar and visible statist form – that is the point, and 9/11 and all that, far from *causing* this, is merely epiphenomenal in this context. The second and much greater problem, however, is that the variety and power of the arguments *against* seeing world politics in fundamentally civilizational terms that were made after Huntington had first outlined his thesis are utterly unaffected by 9/11. They may or may not be convincing, but what makes them so has nothing to do with 9/11; so in that context again, 9/11 adds nothing that was not present in the debates before that point.[9]

The return of 'hard power'

Perhaps the most significant area in which 9/11 is claimed to have exerted a gravitational pull on world politics – away from its previous trajectory, into new and perhaps more dangerous terrain and also one very relevant to the main thesis of this book – concerns claims about the character of the use of force. As we will see in Chapter 2, the rise of what I will call the 'compassionate mode' of responses to the problem of war has increasingly meant that, from the founding of the United Nations onwards, the official rhetoric and (at least arguably) much of

---

[9] For a brief but interesting discussion of the Cold War contest as a contest between civilization defined as democracy and communism as barbarianism, see John Lewis Gaddis, *The Cold War* (London: Allen Lane, 2005), pp. 263–4.

the formal practice of international relations was devoted to the idea of the restraint, limitation and even abolition of war. This was, explicitly, the idea that underpinned the foundation of the European Coal and Steel Community in 1952, and also the Nuclear Non-Proliferation Treaty in 1968.[10] It was also, according to many on both sides, one central theme in the Cold War, the existence of nuclear weapons meaning that a direct confrontation was too horrific and too irrational to contemplate.[11]

Of course, none of this meant that wars did not happen, or that states gave up their right to use force in defence of their own interest, however understood. It was a question of the manner in which such instances of the use of force were justified and legitimated, and of the overall tendency in that use. Perhaps the general assumptions governing this trend were best laid out in the late 1970s by two of the most influential scholars of that generation – one of whom we have already met – Robert Keohane and Joseph Nye. In their now classic study *Power and Interdependence*, they asserted, as one of the three central characteristics of the now-dawning age of interdependence, the 'declining utility of military force', a contention repeated most recently in the third edition of this book in 2000.[12] Nye, indeed, has continued this analysis with his exploration of the idea of 'soft power' – including cultural and economic power – and its uses in an age of interdependence or (increasingly) globalism.[13] A related argument has been pursued by John Mueller, whose *Retreat from Doomsday*,[14] first published in 1989, argued that war between the major powers had gone the way of slavery and duelling: it was a social practice that had simply become 'subrationally unthinkable', and despite the obviously violent history of the past twenty years, Mueller has

[10] On European integration, see Wilfried Loth, *The Division of the World 1941–1955* (London: Routledge, 1988), pp. 219–33.
[11] See John Lewis Gaddis, *The Long Peace: Inquiries into the History of the Cold War* (Oxford University Press, 1987), Chapter 5, 'The Origins of Self-deterrence', pp. 104–47.
[12] See Robert Keohane and Joseph Nye, *Power and Interdependence: World Politics in Transition* (Boston: Little, Brown, 1977; 3rd rev. and expanded edn, 2000).
[13] See Joseph Nye, *Soft Power: The Means to Success in World Politics* (New York: Public Affairs Press, 2004).
[14] See John Mueller, *Retreat from Doomsday: The Obsolescence of Major War* (New York: Basic Books, 1989).

repeated his argument very recently.[15] I will come back to these arguments in more detail in Chapter 2.

For many, however, what 9/11 demonstrated was not the *declining* utility of force but its *growing* utility in an age of globalization. The United States followed up 9/11 not only with the invasion of Afghanistan but also with a new National Security Strategy, which made it perfectly clear that the US now saw preventive war as a legitimate form of force, and also expanded and redefined the general assumptions on which defences of preventive war had rested in the past, a topic to which I will return in Chapter 4.

These shifts, moreover, are by no means limited to the United States or the 'war on terror'. The Iraqi insurgency, the continuing Afghanistan conflict, Russian wars in Chechnya, the conflict in the Great Lakes region in Africa, the possibility of a strike against Iranian nuclear facilities, even the recent NATO mission in Libya: all give substance to the claim that world politics at the opening of the twenty-first century may be even more violent or disposed to violence than the latter part of the twentieth century, and raise the spectre that the century could even be as bloody as – or even bloodier than – its predecessor.[16]

The question, of course, is how much of this was *caused* by 9/11 and all it has brought in its wake, and how much 9/11, as well as these other instances of conflict, were merely *symptomatic* of already existing tendencies in world politics? Surely, much that has shaped contemporary world politics has its roots in the tangled politics of the 1990s or earlier decades, rather than in the particular set of events that triggered 9/11. The rise of militant Islam itself can be traced to episodes such as the Iranian Revolution of 1979, and the passions released by that and by subsequent developments (such as the Iran–Iraq War and the growth of groups like Hamas and Hezbollah), along with the reaction to the Soviet invasion of Afghanistan and the passions that subsequently inflamed the Muslim world.[17] The 2003 invasion of Iraq,

---

[15] See his argument developed in John Mueller, *The Remnants of War* (Ithaca, NY: Cornell University Press, 2004).

[16] See, for example the argument of Colin Gray, *Another Bloody Century: Future Warfare* (London: Weidenfeld and Nicolson, 2005).

[17] For an excellent and thorough analysis, see Gilles Keppel, *The Roots of Radical Islam* (Paris: Saqi Books, 2005). See also Ahmed Rashid, *Taliban: Islam, Oil and the New Great Game in Central Asia* (London: I.B. Tauris, 2001).

far from being an event 'triggered' by 9/11, seems to be much more a case of 'unfinished business' from the First Gulf War (of 1990–1), with 9/11 perhaps providing a justifying reason, but certainly not being the 'exiting' reason, as Hume might have put it.[18]

However, it is often said that what *is* clearly new in the post-9/11 situation is the *character* of the use of force. Here, for example, the point is often made – that al-Qaeda represents a 'new kind of threat' that departs from earlier kinds of 'terrorism' in both its methods and its techniques.[19] A number of related claims usually go to make up this argument:

- that al-Qaeda is a non-state-based threat, and that therefore the character of 'war' has changed and the character of 'war fighting' has also had to change;
- that globalization means that this kind of long war must be fought at all levels, not merely in military action but also in financial, legal and ideological terms;
- that the much-hyped 'revolution in military affairs' was – at best – overstated, for the 9/11 bombers did not use high-tech weaponry but turned basic and 'everyday' technology against the West;
- that the 'nuclear taboo' is becoming eroded both by states and by the desire on the part of non-state actors like al-Qaeda to acquire nuclear weapons or at least some form of weapons of mass destruction (WMD);
- that all these factors require states to change strategy, tactics and doctrine to deal with these new threats: hence the 2002 US National Security Strategy and the rise of preventive war.

The problem, of course, is that these claims, while not necessarily false, can all be seen in a wider context as expressing much more traditional aspects of world politics. It is hardly the first time that 'non-state

---

[18] For Hume's distinction between exiting and justifying reasons, see Book 2 of *The Treatise of Human Nature*. On Islam and the Gulf War, see James Piscatori, 'Religion and Realpolitik: Islamic Responses to the Gulf War', in James Piscatori (ed.) *Islamic Fundamentalisms and the Gulf Crisis* (Chicago: American Academy of Arts and Sciences, 1991).

[19] This is the argument, though in different ways, of both Rohan Guneratna in *Inside Al Qaeda* (New York: Columbia University Press, 2002) and Jason Burke in *Al-Qaeda* (Harmondsworth: Penguin, 2007). For a general argument about the 'new terrorism' see Bruce Hoffmann, *Inside Terrorism* (2nd edn; New York: Columbia University Press, 2005).

actors' have been engaged in wars or conflicts with states. Even if we restrict ourselves to the modern world, most colonial wars of the nineteenth century pitted state militaries against various forms of 'non-state' actors, and 'terrorist' attacks on states (or indeed *by* states) are hardly new either. We need only look at the political violence that took place within the Russian Empire from the late nineteenth century up to 1917, a period during which some 17,000 people were killed or wounded by extremists.[20] Even if it is the case – and this can certainly be disputed – that the manner and matter of 'terrorism' have changed with 9/11, the Provisional IRA did after all for much of its own so-called 'long war' use fairly basic modes of attack in rather spectacular venues: think, for example, of the attacks on Canary Wharf and on Downing Street itself.

A number of scholars – perhaps most notably Colin Gray[21] – have also taken issue with the idea that the 'revolution in military affairs' was in fact anything like as radical as some have claimed, and so the fact that 9/11 was in some respects a very 'traditional' sort of attack is hardly the only reason for doubting these arguments. Again, though, we need to note the almost mystical tone in which responses to the attacks of 9/11 have been couched in certain sectors of the American media and public. Such was the shock that an attack had actually been launched on the United States that in some quarters it was perhaps more comforting to believe that 9/11 must have been inspired by some form of internal conspiracy rather than conceived as an external attack on the symbols of American power and hegemony. Yet, as Bernard-Henri Lévy wrote shortly after 9/11, this type of analysis was to ignore the voices throughout the developing world antagonized by a succession of American policies over a considerable period. As he wrote, 'There are other kamikazes ready to say to the nations of the world, *You ignored us while we were alive: now we are dead: you didn't want to know about our deaths as long as they happened in our own countries; now we throw them at your feet, into the same fire that is consuming you.*'[22] Perhaps we might add that there have always been

[20] See Anna Geifman, *Thou Shalt Kill: Revolutionary Terrorism in Russia, 1894–1917* (Princeton University Press, 1993).

[21] See esp. Colin Gray, *Strategy for Chaos: Revolutions in Military Affairs and the Evidence of History* (London: Frank Cass, 2004), and *Another Bloody Century*.

[22] Bernard-Henri Lévy, quoted in Stephan Chan, *Out of Evil: New International Politics and Old Doctrines of War* (London: I.B. Tauris, 2004), p. 50.

the powerless or the disenchanted in local, regional and global politics who have in various guises launched individual actions against the bastions of local or regional power. Thus 9/11 surely can be seen as part and parcel of longer-term patterns of resistance. And even here it is important to be careful not simply to accept the argument that American foreign policy in the Middle East in itself caused the rise of Islamic fundamentalism. There are also competing arguments that Islamic societies may themselves throw up the radical and the angry.[23]

Even if the resistance of the weak is not new in politics, globalization and technological change – including the deployment and actual or possible use of WMD – certainly are changing the context in which force is used; but again, the logical and structural changes associated with WMD have been acknowledged and discussed extensively since at least the late 1940s, and such discussions have formed part of the panoply of strategic discussion that became deterrence theory.[24] The addition to this debate of the so-called nuclear 'terrorist bomb' may indeed change aspects of the tactical questions, but surely changes nothing in the central strategic or political questions.[25]

We might conclude therefore that while of course world politics changes all the time – the times, as Bob Dylan might have said, are always a-changing – there is little evidence that events like 9/11 have really reshaped its essential character. Of course, to understand contemporary world politics the claim that 9/11 has reshaped world politics must itself be understood; but so must the reasons why this claim is false. It is not the *fact* of 9/11 that has reshaped world politics but rather the ways in which many, including many in the elites of the most powerful states, have chosen to interpret and respond to it. In that respect, there is little new in the situation: the international system has always been shaped by how the major powers choose to respond to the context of international society in their own time. Of course, though, as I shall argue in a moment, the character of the states in

---

[23] See Bernard Lewis, *What Went Wrong? Western Impact and Middle Eastern Response* (Oxford University Press, 2002).

[24] For a good discussion, see Lawrence Freedman, *Deterrence* (Cambridge: Polity Press, 2004).

[25] For the most important and far-reaching general assessment of the impact of nuclear weapons on international politics, see William Walker, *A Perpetual Menace: Nuclear Weapons and International Order* (London: Routledge, 2011).

question – the intellectual and practical assumptions underpinning them – naturally shapes the manner of their response.

A clash of mentalities?

The third claim that is often made about the new situation that 9/11 has created – and from various often very divergent perspectives – has to do with the belief systems that might be said to animate actors. For it is hard not to come to the conclusion that many involved think of themselves as waging some type of a cultural or civilizational 'war' – a war for their beliefs, their faith or their 'values' – at least as much as a war of any other kind. As former President George W. Bush himself argued in the autumn of 2001, 'We wage a war to save civilization itself. We did not seek it, but we must fight it and we will prevail.' The complexities here are obvious. Who can speak for any civilization? How might we understand the notion of a civilization that would allow anyone to speak for it, or in its name? Just how are our notions of civilization and our ideas about civilizations actually related? On top of that, despite the assertions of Western politicians, it is clear that bin Laden and his allies entertain notions of representing a specific type of world-view based on a certain reading of Islam.

Some have therefore seen in the undeniable ideological rigidities and certainties that have characterized world politics since 9/11 – the new and newly polarizing conception of faith or of belief – something new and distinct emerging. Perhaps the aspect of this most often remarked upon – for some years now – is the apparent resurgence of religious sentiment in world and in domestic politics. But here again, I suggest, it is not really that religion has suddenly been resurgent, but rather that Western scholars, policy-makers and journalists have begun to take more note of it. Religious debates have been central to many aspects of world politics in the twentieth century, and one can even see the Cold War, for example, as – in part at least – a religious conflict, or at least a conflict informed by a certain kind of religious sensibility. Eric Voegelin argued long ago that many of the ideologies of the twentieth century are perhaps best seen as 'political religions', and the power of his argument would seem to be borne out by the developments of the last decade.[26]

---

[26] Voegelin's original argument can be found in his *Die politische Religionen*, first published in 1938 and now published in English as volume V of his *Collected*

However, Voegelin's argument is actually a lot more subtle than simply to suggest that we see world politics as an arena of clashing ideologies (religious or secular). His point is that political religions have a particular character – he later characterized it as a 'Gnostic' character[27] – that other formulations of the same or similar ideas do not have. Richard Bernstein has recently argued a not dissimilar case when he suggested that what characterizes the world in the post-9/11 era is not a clash of ideologies, still less a clash of civilizations, but rather a 'clash of mentalities'. The mentalities in question are, on the one hand, those that are inclined towards ever-greater certainty and, on the other, those that accept doubt, scepticism and fallibilism. The point, for Bernstein, is that this clash is manifested in all ideologies and civilizations rather than being the unique property of one (say, Islam, or indeed Christianity). He sees the rigidities and starkness of some of the American responses to 9/11 as a mirror image of the rigidity and unwavering self-righteousness of Osama bin Laden, and contrasts that with the sceptics and doubters on both sides.

For Bernstein, it is this clash of mentalities, far more than any specific difference between 'Islam' and 'the West', that characterizes our era, and he argues unambiguously that we need to support the doubters and the sceptics and problematize the simple certainties of the true believers on any side.

In this respect, I would certainly agree with him. But the point surely is to add that this 'clash' is an old and complex one, reaching much further back than 9/11; its roots lie in some of the most difficult and extensive changes that can be said to characterize the modern world, and its implications are very far-reaching – this, indeed, was part of Voegelin's point in his argument about political religions dating from the 1930s. Indeed, I would argue that, penetrating though his analysis is, Bernstein might perhaps be underestimating the extent of the problem: the clash might be not simply between absolutist certainty and

Writings (34 vols., eds. Manfred Henningsen; Columbia, Mo.: University of Missouri Press, 1999). A writer who has drawn on Voegelin recently to illustrate a similar case is Michael Burleigh. See his (effective) trilogy *Earthly Powers: The Clash of Religion and Politics in Europe from the French Revolution to the Great War* (London: Harper Perennial, 2007); *Sacred Causes: The Clash of Religion and Politics in Europe from the Great War to the War on Terror* (London: Harper Perennial, 2008), and *Blood and Rage: A Cultural History of Terrorism* (London: Harper, 2009).

[27] In *The New Science of Politics* (University of Chicago Press, 1951).

sceptical fallibilism, but also between competing conceptions of the character and implications of that fallibilism. Bernstein's version, influenced by philosophical pragmatism and a democratic sensibility, may not be the only one on offer. Others might take a still more sceptical view. In any case, the problem is not one that has been initiated by 9/11, even if its lineaments have perhaps been shown in rather clearer outline because of that event; so, here again, there does not seem to be much reason to suppose 9/11 initiated anything radically new in world politics.

An agonistic world?

If the claims surrounding 9/11 do not sustain the argument that world politics is becoming more violent or unstable, are there other claims that might warrant further attention? One influential body of thought in the contemporary academy, influential indeed across many fields, would also claim that world politics – perhaps all politics – is increasingly marked by conflict, instability and violence but would also argue that this situation is perhaps constitutive of aspects of the late modern condition, and would situate such tendencies in a culture of 'governmentality'[28] or in conceptions of 'biopolitics'[29] or 'grievable life'.[30]

For such scholars, the character of the current system discloses something necessary or elemental (I will not say, to spare their blushes, essential) about modern politics, indeed perhaps about all politics at all times and places: its necessarily conflictual and agonistic character.[31]

---

[28] This term derives, of course, from the work of the late Michel Foucault, especially his annual series of lectures at the Collège de France between 1977 and his death in 1984, most of which are now making their way into English. See, especially, Graham Burchill and Colin Gorder (eds.) *The Foucault Effect* (University of Chicago Press, 1991) and Michel Foucault, *The Government of Self and Others: Lectures at the Collège de France 1982–83*, ed. Arnold I. Davidson, trans. Graham Burchill (New York: Palgrave Macmillan, 2010).

[29] This language, of course, comes principally from Foucault, but it has been added to at length (I nearly wrote *ad nauseam*) by many others, principally writers such as Giorgio Agamben and, more directly in connection with war, scholars such as Mick Dillon, Jenny Edkins, Julian Reid, and Maja Zehfuss. More general conceptions of political international theory in this broad vein can be found in writers such as William E. Connolly and, as I suggest below, Bonnie Honig.

[30] This locution is Judith Butler's. See her *Frames of War: When Is Life Grievable* (London: Verso, 2008).

[31] See, for example, Michael Dillon and Julian Reid, *The Liberal Way of War: Killing to Make Life Live* (London: Routledge, 2009), Vivienne Jabri, *War and*

As a result, hopes for a world beyond this *agon* were always a dream and perhaps a dangerous dream, since it encourages the essentializing of an always hybrid reality. Of course, suggesting that politics is conflictual does not mean that the conflict must necessarily be violent, and many of these scholars would argue that the trick is turning the conflict of interests that is an inevitable part of political life from a violent to a non-violent one. They would argue that instead of essentializing our differences and supposing such differences generate threats, we should accept and welcome them without presuming that doing this will free us from the consequences of *having* such differences and that such a paradoxical process is the mark of a society committed to democratic values.[32]

Though, as I say, there are many varieties of such thinking, some more radically oppositional than others, I am going to comment on one here. Bonnie Honig has an especially thoughtful variant of this position in her book *Emergency Politics: Paradox, Law, Democracy*.[33] Chapter 5 of that book, entitled 'Proximity', is a version of a commentary she originally offered on a set of Tanner lectures given by Seyla Benhabib.[34] In a postscript to the chapter, Honig considers some criticisms that Benhabib levelled at her, accusing her of 'an anti-statist governmentality-centred Foucauldianism', 'hostility towards institutions' and, perhaps most witheringly of all, not being *serious*, an inevitable consequence, it would appear, of espousing 'movement politics' and that hostility to institutions and the state. In repudiating Benhabib's charges, Honig develops a sophisticated and powerful articulation of the essential position I am getting at here which it is useful, I think, to consider.

the Transformation of Global Politics (London: Palgrave, 2007), Richard Devetak and Christopher Hughes (eds.) *The Globalization of Political Violence: Globalization's Shadow* (London: Routledge, 2008). From a very different, though not unrelated, perspective, see John Milbank, *Theology and Social Theory* (Oxford: Basil Blackwell, 1990) and some of the essays in his *The Future of Love* (London: SCM Press, 2007).

[32] It is worth pointing out, of course, that advocates of this approach are by no means all in agreement with one another. There are many differences of emphasis, some very substantial, and I am to some extent smoothing such differences out for the purposes of summarizing them.

[33] Bonnie Honig, *Emergency Politics: Paradox, Law, Democracy* (Princeton University Press, 2009).

[34] Later published as *Another Cosmopolitanism* (ed R. Post) (New York: Oxford University Press, 2008).

Honig's response to Benhabib consists in refusing the sharp dichoto-
mies Benhabib tries to foist upon her. She is not 'anti-statist', she
responds, 'the state and its institutions are always our addressees'; [35]
nor is she especially 'pro social movements' per se. She says, 'some of
them scare me'.[36] Rather, her point is to emphasize that:

the choice between social movements and a more juridical politics focussed
on state and transnational institutions is a false one. To focus on institutions
of governance without a foot in movement politics and critique is perforce to
perform juridical politics differently than would otherwise be the case,
without the balancing perspective of a life lived otherwise. It is to be left
vulnerable to the self-privileging perspective of statism and its formalisms ...
juridical politics is always in need of the support and orientation of life lived
in political movement. In addition to engaging state and transnational institutions directly, democratic actors must also, and not as a secondary matter,
in some ways begin living now as if we had already succeeded in that first
endeavour. This is a lesson of the paradox of politics.[37]

She concludes her book with the following admonition:

The [book] tracked some of the conceptual resources seen by many ... to
offer great promise to political theory and practice (universal human rights,
the agency of law, faith in progress) while identifying the ways in which their
promise also constrains the democratic imagination in regrettable ways,
limiting opportunities for progressive democratic practice, pressing us in
conservative directions. This does not mean we should reject universal rights,
agentic law and faith in progress. It does mean, however, that reliance on
these resources must be located in a (counter) politics of more life and must
be part of a double gesture that is attentive to their remainders.[38]

As we will see, there is a good deal in this with which I would agree,
though I would (and will) use different language. To recognize the
double-edged aspect of many of the values we enshrine in our political
lives does not, by definition, disable them as valuable and empowering.
It merely reminds us, as Honig's argument suggests it does, of their
potential for being double-edged, And she is surely correct as well
when she repudiates the attempted dichotomy of 'state=good', 'social
movements=bad' with which Benhabib tries to festoon her. But we
might consider whether certain modes or forms of politics *incline* such

[35] Honig, *Emergency Politics*, p. 134.   [36] Honig, *Emergency Politics*, p. 136.
[37] Honig, *Emergency Politics*, p. 135.
[38] Honig, *Emergency Politics*, pp. 140–1.

values to a more 'limiting' role than others or, indeed, whether certain kinds of claims only really make sense within (for example) a certain logic of association. I have always, for example, been something of a sceptic about 'universal human rights', not because I am not sympathetic to much of what the language of universal human rights attempts to capture but because I don't think 'rights' as a political term makes much sense outside of a particular political and intellectual context – so the sense of calling them 'universal' must be called into question.[39]

Honig and I would doubtless have many more general philosophical disagreements. She clearly has a far greater sympathy for certain figures in the wider post-structural firmament, including Foucault, Derrida and Agamben, than I could manage. But in terms of the political contexts discussed here the differences might be relatively small and largely manageable, saving that I am not sure that, properly understood, it makes sense to see politics as 'paradoxical' *by definition*. Rather, I think our current politics often takes on a paradoxical character precisely because we are trying to reconcile two conceptions of what politics is about which, in fact, cannot be reconciled.

Two trajectories in modern European thought

Which brings me to the way in which I do want to suggest that contemporary world politics may be inclining, at least, to greater degrees of violence and instability. In brief, I want to argue that the rise to something like predominance of a teleocratic conception of politics, as discussed by Michael Oakeshott, has had profoundly problematic consequences, for conceptions of political life, for the just war tradition in particular, and for conceptions of international order in general.

Oakeshott's account, indeed his philosophy in general, is, of course, a controversial one and I should perhaps say something to begin with about why I am deploying it here. The obvious response is to say that I am adopting it because I think it is true but, while I do think it is largely true, that will not completely suffice, since I also adapt it and therefore clearly do not think that it is *wholly* true. A fuller answer might be to say that I think that in Oakeshott's account, indeed in his philosophy in

---

[39] For a more detailed discussion of my doubts about human rights see my 'The World Turned Upside Down: Human Rights and International Relations After Twenty Five Years', *International Affairs*, 87, 5, September 2011.

general, there are themes that speak to some of the most central concerns in contemporary political philosophy and international political
theory and that are not highlighted – in quite the same way at least – by
any other contemporary philosopher. And it is also true, I think, that
Oakeshott's work has not been as much reflected upon in the international context as it might have been.[40]

Of course, it is also true to say that, while Oakeshott was a much-
noted political thinker during his lifetime – especially towards the end
of his life – the serious scholarly study of Oakeshott's thought has only
really begun to gather pace since his death in 1990.[41] And one of the
things that this body of work has made unambiguously clear is how
narrow and in many ways unsatisfactory the earlier characterization
of Oakeshott as a 'conservative', a 'traditionalist' or even (sometimes)
a 'reactionary' thinker in fact is. This is not to say that he is not a
conservative of sorts, but the character of his conservatism – in my
view sceptical, Augustinian, bohemian – is very unusual and requires a

[40] I am of course not suggesting that no one else at all has drawn on Oakeshott's
work in the context of international relations. Terry Nardin, a considerable
Oakeshott scholar in his own right, draws on the same distinction I draw on in
his important *Law, Morality and the Relations of States* (Princeton University
Press, 1983), and Robert Jackson draws more generally (and to my mind rather
less convincingly) on Oakeshott in his *The Global Covenant: Human Conduct
in a World of States* (Oxford University Press, 2000). Other scholars, such as
William Bain and Renee Jeffery, have discussed Oakeshott with appreciation
and insight as well. But the use to which we each put his thought is rather
different. Nardin, for example, uses the *societas/universitas* distinction to
contrast two different ways of understanding international society, arguing that
international society could not be distributive (for example) as it is best seen on a
societas model and therefore, strictly speaking, has nothing to distribute. My
point is the rather different one that conceptions of politics and international
relations *as a whole* have become increasingly dominated by teleocratic
understandings of politics – understandings of international society included.
I shall return to the significance of this in the Epilogue.

[41] There could be a long list here. Relatively early studies that repay reading in the
contemporary context would include W.H. Greenleaf, *Oakeshott's
Philosophical Politics* (New York: Barnes and Noble, 1966) and Paul Franco,
The Political Philosophy of Michael Oakeshott (University of Chicago Press,
1989). More recent studies that express views similar to those outlined here
would include Elizabeth Corey, *Michael Oakeshott on Religion, Aesthetics and
Politics* (Columbia, Mo.: University of Missouri Press, 2006), Luke O'Sullivan,
Oakeshott on History (Exeter: Imprint Academic, 2003) and Terry Nardin,
The Philosophy of Michael Oakeshott (University Park: Penn State University
Press, 2004). Of course, I do not suggest these writers would necessarily agree
with my views of Oakeshott, or the use to which I have put them.

good deal more elaboration and discussion than it has so far had.[42] Though this book is not the place to embark on that,[43] I shall return to it, in brief compass, in the Epilogue.

Oakeshott developed his account of teleocratic politics – along with its rival conception, nomocratic politics – most especially in *On Human Conduct*,[44] and I shall start my argument here with a brief consideration of it. In the process I shall also somewhat amend it.[45] It consists essentially in the claim that modern European states – now usually termed liberal democratic states though Oakeshott does not call them that – inherit a political vocabulary that is radically polarized between two different, and opposing, understandings of the *character of the political association and the office of its government*.[46] Oakeshott famously describes these two understandings by borrowing two Latin terms from Roman private law: *societas* and *universitas*.[47]

The former term denotes a mode of association which has

agents who by choice or circumstance are related to one another so as to comprise an identifiable association of a certain sort. The tie which joins them ... is not that of an engagement in an enterprise to pursue a common substantive purpose or to promote a common interest, but that of loyalty to one another, the conditions of which may achieve the formality denoted by the kindred word legality.[48]

---

[42] See here the arguments of Maurice Cowling in *Religion and Public Doctrine in England* vol. I (Cambridge University Press, 1984) and vol. III (Cambridge University Press, 2002).

[43] Though I certainly intend to do so in the not too distant future.

[44] It is worth adding that Oakeshott developed his ideas on these two understandings over many years, and earlier versions appear in many places in his unpublished writings and lectures.

[45] See Oakeshott, *On Human Conduct* (Oxford: Clarendon Press, 1975).

[46] Similar in form, though not at all in content, is Quentin Skinner's development of two equally differing accounts of what he calls 'our common life'; one which sees sovereignty as a possession of the people, the other of the state; one emphasizes the citizen, the other the sovereign. This is implied, of course, in his *The Foundations of Modern Political Thought* (Cambridge University Press, 1978) but developed much more explicitly in his three-volume *Visions of Politics* (Cambridge University Press, 2003) and is crucial to his development of 'republican political thought', as noted earlier. Note, for interest, Oakeshott's critique of Skinner in his review of *The Foundations* in the *Historical Journal*, 23, 2, 1980, 449–53.

[47] A rather different deployment of these ideas, in connection with international relations – indeed as modes of understanding international society itself – can be found in Nardin, *Law, Morality and the Relations of States*.

[48] Oakeshott, *On Human Conduct*, p. 202.

For Oakeshott, a state understood in these terms is thus a *civitas*, a civil association,

and its government (*whatever its constitution*) is a nomocracy whose laws are understood as conditions of conduct, not devices instrumental to the satisfaction of preferred wants.[49] (emphasis added)

Universitas, by contrast, is understood as

persons associated in a manner such as to constitute them a natural person; a partnership of persons which is itself a person, or in some important respects like a person ... [and] a state understood in terms of *universitas* is ... an association of intelligent agents who recognize themselves to be engaged upon the joint enterprise of seeking the satisfaction of some common substantive want ... government here may be said to be teleocratic, the management of a purposive concern.[50]

Oakeshott's point in his essay is to emphasize the extent to which the modern European political consciousness is a *polarized* one and that *these* are its poles. Although Oakeshott denies that we should see these two poles as in any sense 'dominant or recessive' and also is consistent in opposing the view that one pole – the enterprise association or 'teleocratic' pole – is somehow *inevitably* destined to be dominant,[51] he also points out that it is the latter understanding that has been – by far – the more popular over the course of the past two hundred or so years. And he suggests some powerful reasons for this. Chief amongst these is the claim – I think indisputable – that it is enterprise association that best fits what he calls 'the demands of modern war'.[52] He remarks:

In war itself the latent or not so latent ingredient of managerial lordship in the office of the government of a modern state comes decisively to the surface and is magnified ... and what is plenary in a condition of actual war is merely somewhat diminished in the intervals between wars ... war and military preparation imposes this character upon a state more or less completely, not in proportion to its destructiveness, but in proportion to the magnitude of the claims it makes upon the attention, the energies and the resources of subjects; and the wars of modern times have been progressively more demanding in this respect ... (in short) although it may be difficult to find

---

[49] Ibid., p. 203.   [50] Ibid.
[51] The best general discussion of this can be found in Franco's excellent *Political Philosophy of Michael Oakeshott*. See esp. pp. 215–22.
[52] Oakeshott, *On Human Conduct*, p. 322.

any modern European state recognizably the counterpart of Sparta in antiquity (that is a state whose reputed purpose is itself war) the condition of almost continuous warfare in modern times has familiarized Europe with the spectacle of states, significantly, if intermittently, transformed into enterprise associations; and this has been the chief nourishment of the belief that the state is properly to be understood in these terms.[53]

In other words, if we may adapt a phrase of Charles Tilly, 'war made the state and the state made war'[54] but the state that war made was a state understood in a certain way, as a 'teleocratic' enterprise association. To this needs to be added, Oakeshott thinks, the increasingly powerful sense of modern states as agents of the distribution of goods that aim at the satisfaction of particular wants, a sense made progressively more powerful by the rise of mass politics and the interests that this itself generated.[55]

Taken together, I want to suggest (and I think Oakeshott wanted to suggest) that all of these things have created in modern states an orientation that is heavily disposed to see itself in terms of an enterprise association, and a central component of this understanding is the ordering of a society for 'war'. Of course, the common enterprise for which force may be used will shift over time; it may be obviously material in one generation – access to the goods and services of the empire, the 'expansion of England'; and so forth – and more ideational in another – 'intervention for humanitarian purposes' perhaps, as we shall see. Nonetheless, central to the understanding of a modern state as an enterprise association is a willingness to see a 'common purpose' for which, under at least some circumstances, force is an entirely appropriate response; as Oakeshott says, the habits learned through endless preparation for war are retained in times of relative peace.

Nevertheless, of course, there is more than one way of conceptualizing the state as an enterprise association. In *On Human Conduct*, Oakeshott suggests that we might see four different idioms of

---

[53] Ibid., pp. 272–4.

[54] See Charles Tilly, *Coercion, Capital and Modern European States: 990–1990* (Oxford: Blackwell, 1993).

[55] This is discussed in many places in Oakeshott's work – see, for example, his essay 'The Masses in Representative Government' in the expanded edition of *Rationalism in Politics* (Minneapolis: Liberty Fund, 1991(1962)). For another interesting, if idiosyncratic, reading of this phenomenon, see Christopher Lasch, *The True and Only Heaven: Progress and Its Critics* (New York: Norton, 1991).

teleocratic belief. The first considers the state as a religious and cultural enterprise (Oakeshott clearly has in mind Calvinist Geneva as the *sine qua non* of this idea, though other countries at different times and to different degrees approximate to it also). The second idiom understands the state as a corporate enterprise for exploiting the resources of the Earth. This idiom derives ultimately, Oakeshott thinks, from a Baconian vision of the state,[56] though it is more fully developed by Bacon's successors such as St Simon, Fourier, Marx and Lenin (and, one might add, though Oakeshott does not, by many extreme free market productivists as well). A third idiom combines, in a curious way, the first two to provide a model of 'enlightened government', in which the productivist and materialist purpose of the second is yoked to a quasi-moral understanding derived from the first to produce what Oakeshott sees as 'the strongest strand of teleocratic belief in modern European thought'.[57] Finally, one might see the state in this light as a 'therapeutic' corporation, the function of which is remedial: treating an association of invalids or victims (perhaps the version for which Oakeshott expresses most contempt in *On Human Conduct*).

Oakeshott suggests, correctly I think, that all versions of teleocratic belief in contemporary political thought combine, to some degree or other, these four idioms and while, as I remarked, he sees the model of enlightened government as the 'strongest strand' in contemporary thought, it is the second – the state seen as a fully fledged *civitas cupiditas* – that he thinks is, over the long term, the greatest threat to civil association. I think that he is right about this (and will return to it in the Epilogue) but I also think that he underestimates the extent to which this idiom has been subsumed in what might be seen as a version of teleocracy that *unites* a model of enlightened government with a model of the state – or perhaps other agencies as proxies for states – as a therapeutic enterprise. It is, I suggest, this version of teleocratic politics that we find coalescing in much of the twentieth century, the implications of which we shall see in later chapters.

There is also an additional point here to which Oakeshott only briefly alludes, but which is central to the argument I want to make in this book. This is simply that while this polarization originated in the context of the European *state*, it has long since passed into a much

---

[56] Best discussed in Bacon's *The New Atlantis*.
[57] Oakeshott, *On Human Conduct*, p. 286.

more generalized conception of politics which is not tied to the European state alone. As Oakeshott remarks in a footnote:

it is perhaps worth notice that notions of 'world peace' and world government' which in the eighteenth century were explored in terms of civil association have in this century become projects of world management concerned with the distribution of substantive goods. The decisive change took place in the interval between the League of Nations and the United Nations.[58]

I think Oakeshott is wrong here. I think this move can be traced back much further; back to the mid nineteenth century, as we will see, but the general point is crucial: this is no longer simply a matter of 'the state and the office of government', but rather a generalized view of the character of politics and rule *tout court*.

It is the growing dominance of teleocratic styles of politics, first in the European state (and thus states system) and then more generally in the world, that, I want to argue in this book, contributes to a potentially more violent international order. And in particular it is the marriage of teleocratic conceptions of politics with a particular understanding of the just war tradition that opens the door to a much more expansive understanding of the scope of 'legitimate' violence.

Of course, one could, as I remarked in the preface, consider this trajectory in the context of many different issue areas in world politics but I have chosen here to focus on the use of force. I have done this for three main reasons. First, because I think the impact of the predominance of teleocratic politics is perhaps most *stark* in this context, second because in the contemporary context it is perhaps most *visible* there, and third, because it is the use of force and its assumed implications that have long held central place in the distinguishing of international relations from domestic politics. This book will be concerned with exploring each of these three reasons in what follows. At the end of the journey, of course, something will have to be said about the values we attach to each of these conceptions of politics – and I will come to that in the Epilogue. But first, we should turn to the subject of war itself and see how it might fit into our contemporary understanding of the political world.

---

[58] Ibid., p. 313, n. 1.

2 | War music: social imaginaries of war in the modern age

> When the Cambrian measures were forming, They promised perpetual Peace.
> They swore, if we gave them our weapons, that the wars of the tribes would cease.
> But when we disarmed They sold us and delivered us bound to our foe,
> And the Gods of the Copybook Headings said:
> 'Stick to the Devil you Know.'
>
> Kipling, 'The Gods of the Copybook Headings'

Over much of the last decade of the twentieth century – as ironically was also the case in the preceding century as well – there was a cautious but growing optimism that the worst aspects of war were at last being brought under some sort of control. The growing reach and appeal of globalization, the growing 'thickness' of international law and institutions, especially in the area of human rights and their protection, the evolution of notions of 'humanitarian intervention': all were credited, severally or collectively, with helping to tame war, helping to make it increasingly – in the words of one of the academic proponents of this thesis that I have already had occasion to refer to – 'sub-rationally unthinkable'.[1]

From 2001 onwards, however, such views – as we have seen – have become increasingly embattled. Leaving aside the arguments directed at the uniqueness of 9/11 – which as I argued in Chapter 1, do not really hold water – there is the stubborn persistence of conflict in world politics generally. Leaving Iraq and Afghanistan aside, one need only look at the huge war in central Africa in the early twenty-first century, which sucked in as many as six regional powers and cost an estimated

---

[1] John Mueller, *Retreat from Doomsday: The Obsolescence of Major War* (New York: Basic Books, 1989). Mueller's argument is, in fact, extremely nuanced and very subtle and I do not mean to impugn it by simplification here. Nonetheless, he does argue that war, as traditionally understood, is increasingly becoming a thing of the past.

5 million lives, the long-running conflict in Darfur, events in Georgia in 2008, or the Libyan intervention in 2011, to see that state deployment of force is in robust good health. And many of the so-called 'rising powers' – most obviously China, but not excluding the others as well – are engaging in substantial enhancement of their already (in many cases) formidable military forces, although always insisting such moves are peaceful, of course.

But perhaps we should not be surprised. Sometime during 1755 or 1756, Jean-Jacques Rousseau wrote a short, impassioned tract bewailing 'the state of war' in his own time,[2] bewailing, indeed, the contrast between the fine works of civil society and the social state, greatly celebrated, and the reality and barbarity, as he saw it, of the incessant oppressions and wars that disfigured human social life. His irony is savage, and is worth quoting at length:

> I open books on law and ethics and listen to the scholars and legal experts. Permeated with their persuasive talk ... I admire the peace and justice established by the civil order, bless the wisdom of public institutions ... well versed in my duties and happiness, I shut my book, leave the classroom and look around me. I see unfortunate nations groaning under yokes of iron, the human race crushed by a handful of oppressors, a starving crowd overwhelmed with pain and hunger ... and everywhere the strong armed against the weak with the power of law ... I raise my eyes and look into the distance. I see fires and flames, the countryside deserted, towns pillaged ... I hear a terrible sound; what an uproar. I draw near; I see a scene of murder, ten thousand butchered men, the dead piled in heaps, the dying trampled under horses' hooves, everywhere the face of death and agony ... so this is the fruit of those peaceful institutions. Barbarous philosopher! Come and read us your book on the field of battle.[3]

Rousseau's concern, of course, was to mutually implicate what looked to be 'civil' institutions in the 'social state' – law, ethics and so on – with the state of war itself and suggest that they feed off each other. Now, over 250 years later, would Rousseau be pleased at the progress we have made in mitigating and corralling the 'state of war' and

---

[2] See Chris Brown, Terry Nardin and Nicholas Rengger (eds.) *International Relations in Political Thought: Texts from the Ancient Greeks to the First World War* (Cambridge University Press, 2002), pp. 416–25. Though written in 1755–6, Rousseau's text remained unpublished until 1896, when Dreyfus-Brisac published it in his edition of the *Social Contract*.

[3] See Brown et al. (eds.) *International Relations*, pp. 422–3.

making real the constraints of those 'civil institutions', or would he write a new tract for the twenty-first century, bewailing the fact that we have made none?

Rousseau's analysis emphasizes, of course, the interpenetration of our thoughts about ourselves and our societies together with how we should or might understand the fact of war in the world. And that, in brief, is how I shall seek to understand it here.

It is a familiar point, of course, that there are essentially three moral positions that can be taken about the organized use of force by political communities: that it is never justified; that justification in moral terms is hardly the point and that, given its inevitability in our world, we should seek justification in other terms; and that it can, under certain circumstances, be justified. By far the commonest positions, of course, are variations on the latter two, a point that holds across cultures and across time.[4] What is perhaps especially interesting is that the closer one looks, the more blurred the boundaries between these two positions become. Generally speaking even the most hardened realpolitiker does not say that there is no 'moral' justification of war at all; rather they tend to see such justifications as being broadly based in some form of instrumental or consequentialist reasoning where the key assumption lies in the already given value of political community and, therefore, the requirement to use lethal force to enhance, glorify or protect it. This, for example, is the defence offered for Athenian imperialism by Pericles in his funeral oration over the bodies of the Athenian war deed,[5] and it is interesting and significant (in the context of Thucydides' overall position especially) that although the versions of this view offered in the Mytelenian debate and, even more famously, the Melian dialogue, differ in certain respects, they are recognizably variations on a theme.[6]

---

[4] For informative discussions of the general position of world philosophies on such questions see David E. Cooper, *World Philosophies: An Historical Introduction* (Oxford: Blackwell, 1996).

[5] See Thucydides, *History of the Peloponnesian War*, edited by David Grene (University of Chicago Press, 1989). See also Brown et al. (eds.) *International Relations*, Chapter 1.

[6] See the discussion in Brown et al. (eds.) *International Relations*, Chapter 1. See also the very illuminating treatments in J. Peter Euben, *The Tragedy of Political Theory: The Path Not Taken* (Princeton University Press, 1996) and Clifford Orwin, *The Humanity of Thucydides* (Princeton University Press, 1994).

Equally, however, more common moral justifications of war often rely on certain – usually unstated – assumptions about the prior moral worth of self-defence or of righting wrongs, or protecting those who cannot protect themselves, and recognize that there may be circumstances where 'one must do evil that good may come'. An example would be Michael Walzer's condition of 'supreme emergency' to which I shall return later in the book.[7] It is also the case that people who fight wars generally speaking have a conception of their calling which imposes certain restraints or at least rules on the activity. What Michael Ignatieff has called the 'warrior's honour' may not wholly be a moral virtue, but it is certainly partly that.[8]

In other words, it is hard to understand 'war' except in relation to the understandings of it that are prevalent in particular times and places and in particular in relation to conceptions of the political community which might 'authorize' the use of lethal force in question. In many respects we might see such justifications as 'responses' to the reality of war, building blocks in what one might call, following Charles Taylor, a 'social imaginary' concerning war.[9] In his book on the modern social imaginary, Taylor suggests (in Stephen Crocker's words):

The social imaginary ... is (an) elusive set of self understandings, background practices, and horizons of common expectations that are not always explicitly articulated, but that give a people a sense of a shared group life.[10]

Without suggesting that the list is exhaustive, I want to suggest that five 'responses' constitute just such a set of self-understandings in the modern period (roughly from the sixteenth century onwards) and in the European tradition, and want to offer further an interpretation of their constitutive role in shaping the modern imaginary on war – as a precursor to turning to one particular aspect of the imaginary, the alleged role of 'regime type' in the proclivity of societies for war.

---

[7] In his brilliant and rightly influential *Just and Unjust Wars: A Moral Argument with Historical Illustrations* (3rd edn, New York: Basic Books, 2000 (1977)). I shall return to this in Chapter 5.

[8] Michael Ignatieff, *The Warrior's Honour* (London: Jonathan Cape, 1998).

[9] *Modern Social Imaginaries* (Durham, NC: Duke University Press, 2004).

[10] www.cjsonline.ca/reviews/socialimaginaries.html.

The modern social imaginary and war

Let me then briefly outline these responses.

The heroic response

The 'heroic' response runs something like this. War is ugly, it is true, but it is also a peculiarly human institution. Other animals fight and kill; only human beings make war. As a human institution, it is an inevitably evaluative practice and it is equally inevitably subject, in a certain sense at least, to rules. In this context, it is in war that both the highs and the lows of human behaviour are most famously manifest, most especially the idea of the fusion of the individual and the collective, and the notion of the sacrifice. It is no accident that amongst the most powerful and totemic myths of Western culture from ancient times to our own is the warrior hero. As Joseph Campbell pointed out in his exhaustive study of the hero myth, the hero may have a thousand faces but most of these are variations of the face of the warrior.[11] Moreover, as Barbara Ehrenreich has argued, the fact that war has been sacralized in almost all human cultures speaks to its power and centrality in our self-evaluation.[12]

This response was fashioned, of course, out of very disparate strands. Ancient virtue,[13] medieval chivalry, Renaissance ideas of the courtier, aristocratic honour,[14] and the republican tradition in political thought[15] all played a part in it. Its social face is observable in the ritualistic and long-standing evolution of the duel in Western

---

[11] Joseph Campbell, *The Hero with a Thousand Faces* (Princeton University Press, 1968 (1949)).

[12] Barbara Ehrenreich, *Blood Rites: Origins and History of the Passions of War* (London: Vintage Books, 1997).

[13] For interesting discussions of the role of conceptions of ancient virtue on war in the contemporary period see, for example, Nancy Sherman, *Stoic Warriors: The Ancient Philosophy behind the Military Mind* (Oxford University Press, 2005).

[14] For a wonderful essay putting these things together and assessing their influence see Maurice Keen's chapter 'Chivalry and the Aristocracy', in the *New Cambridge Medieval History*, 8 vols., vol. VI ed. Michael Jones (Cambridge University Press, 2000).

[15] A superb examination of the republican context in European thought is to be found in Quentin Skinner and Martin Van Gelderen (eds.) *Republicanism: A Shared European Heritage*, 2 vols. (Cambridge University Press, 2005).

culture[16] and in the emergence and spread of highly advanced techniques of fencing[17] (for example) during and after the Renaissance which became a central way in which the nobility of Europe expressed the essence of what made them 'noble'. The guiding spirit of this response to war is the idea of honour. Initially, of course, this was personal honour, but very swiftly honour was held to apply collectively and communally as well as individually, hence the centrality of national 'honour' in the international relations of modernity.[18]

The realpolitik response

In the history of European thought about war from the late medieval period, this 'heroic' mode existed, however, alongside a response that saw war as simply the pursuit of a ruler's – and later a state's – interest. This response was fashioned in its turn, of course, from the emergence and evolution of the idea of *raison d'état* in early modern Europe, and out of the assumptions that underlay the emergent states system: that sovereigns have the power to make war for their own purposes.[19] Its key concern was for the maximization of state – and later national – interest, and war was seen largely, and sometimes simply, as a vehicle for achieving this. If its prophet was Machiavelli, its presiding genius in the early modern period was perhaps Cardinal Richelieu, but its greatest philosopher was Clausewitz, who saw more clearly than anyone else what this idea represented.[20]

---

[16] A classic study is V.G. Kiernan's *The Duel in European History: Honour and the Reign of Aristocracy* (Oxford University Press, 1988).

[17] A richly rewarding study is William Gaugler, *A History of Fencing: Foundations of Modern European Swordplay* (Bangor: ME Laureate Press, 1997).

[18] It is interesting, and slightly ironic given its historical significance, that notions of honour have had little discussion in general in either contemporary political theory or contemporary international relations theory. Two recent exceptions are Michael Donelan's short but excellent *Honour in Foreign Policy: A History and Discussion* (London: Palgrave Macmillan, 2007) and Ned Lebow's demanding and impressive *A Cultural Theory of International Relations* (Cambridge University Press, 2008).

[19] The literature here is immense. A classic treatment is Friedrich Meinecke, *Machiavellism: The Doctrine of Reason of State and Its Place in Modern History*, (trans. D. Scott) (Boulder: Westview, 1984). Vol. 1: *The Renaissance* of Quentin Skinner's magisterial *The Foundations of Modern Political Thought*, 2 vols. (Cambridge University Press, 1978), also has much of importance to say on this.

[20] For good treatments of Machiavelli on the relationship of war to *raggioni di stato* see Skinner, *Foundations*, vol. 1, pp. 113–89, and Michael Mellet's

In modern times, especially, this mode has been expressed in a way that gives credence to Christopher Coker's claim that the great alternative to what he calls 'existential' ideas about war is an explicitly 'instrumental' understanding of it. Although Clausewitz may not have been guilty of this *reductio ad absurdam* himself,[21] it is certainly how many of his most famous students and followers have tended to see it,[22] and certainly how some of the more influential contemporary strategic thinkers have seen it.[23] Of course, instrumentality does not mean a denial of the obvious fact that men fight wars and therefore the human element in warfare (courage, cowardice, heroism, tragedy) cannot be ignored; nonetheless it places the emphasis on a particular aspect of the relationship between politics and war: that of war's *utility*.[24]

The 'compassionate' response

Both the above responses, of course, assume that war is a permanent feature – perhaps even a necessary feature – of the political world. Yet there has also been another response to war in the modern period, a response rooted in Christian objections to violence, though it has come

excellent chapter 'The Theory and Practice of Warfare in Machiavelli's Republic', in Gisela Bok, Quentin Skinner and Maurizio Viroli (eds.) *Machiavelli and Republicanism* (Cambridge University Press, 1990). On Richelieu and *raison d'état* (both the theory and the practice) a superb study is J.H. Elliot's *Richelieu and Olivarez* (Cambridge University Press, 1984). The best general treatment of Clausewitz in the contemporary literature, to my mind, is Raymond Aron, *Penser la Guerre, Clausewitz* (Paris: Éditions Gallimard, 1976) but honourable mention should also be made of Peter Paret's superb book *Clausewitz and the State: The Man, His Theories and His Times* (Oxford University Press, 1976), his equally excellent collection *Understanding War: Essays on Clausewitz and the History of Military Power* (Princeton University Press, 1992), and the chapter on Clausewitz in W.B. Gallie's pioneering *Philosophers of Peace and War* (Cambridge University Press, 1978).

[21] For a defence of Clausewitz on this point see Gallie, *Philosophers of Peace and War*, Chapter 2.

[22] See the discussions in Peter Paret (ed.) *Makers of Modern Strategy* (Oxford: Clarendon Press, 1986).

[23] See for example – though they are, of course, rich and nuanced treatments and by no means agree with each other – Colin Gray, *Modern Strategy* (Oxford: Clarendon Press, 1999) and Edward Luttwak, *Strategy* (Cambridge, Mass.: Harvard University Press, 1985).

[24] This view seems to be gaining traction exponentially with the rise of 'robotic' war. More on this later.

to have many other sources as well over time. Certainly a minority view – at least until the early to mid nineteenth century – it has nevertheless been a persistent and powerful counterpoint to the dominant traditions from the eighteenth century onwards. Let us call it the 'compassionate' response.

On this view, war was the greatest imaginable mistake, the war system – though nobody called it that then – a disastrous and hugely wasteful spectacle, the heroism empty, and the skill and ingenuity deployed grotesquely misplaced. Strong elements of this view can be found in many of the Renaissance humanists, perhaps most famously Erasmus, whose *Moriae Encomium* and *Querela Pacis* provide perhaps the most eloquent statement of this view into modern times.[25] Yet it was not simply famous and well-known humanists who believed this. Echoes of this view can be found in much religious writing in the sixteenth and seventeenth centuries, especially in the writings of the peace churches, and Quakers, Mennonites and Anabaptists in the late seventeenth and the eighteenth century.[26] It is retained in some of the eighteenth-century writings on the idea and possibility of perpetual peace (for example, the Abbé de Saint-Pierre's famous *Projet de paix perpétuelle*) and it permeates much of the thinking of the Enlightenment on politics, especially, for example, the writings on international relations of Rousseau and Kant. Central to this idea (though certainly not unique to it) is a strong link, as we shall see in a moment, between the *regime* of a state and its predilection, or lack of it, for war.[27]

This emerging confluence of ideas produced what Michael Barnett recently called 'the humanitarian big bang':[28] that set of ideas that emerged out of the eighteenth-century Enlightenment when 'compassion ... moved from part of the private realm and into the public realm,

---

[25] Again, excellent discussions can be found in Skinner, *Foundations*. On Erasmus, Ronald Bainton's *Erasmus of Christendom* (New York: Scribner, 1969) is also extremely useful.

[26] Good discussions can be found in Martin Caedel, *The Origins of War Prevention: The British Peace Movement and International Relations, 1730–1854* (Oxford: Clarendon Press, 1996).

[27] A superb study of Kant's view of these questions can be found in Chapter two of Gallie, *Philosophers of Peace and War*, and for a superb study of the general Enlightenment context Peter Gay's *The Enlightenment: An Interpretation*, 2 vols. (New York: Wildwood House, 1970) cannot be bettered.

[28] See Barnett's excellent study *Empire of Humanity: A History of Humanitarianism* (Ithaca, NY: Cornell University Press, 2011). See especially Chapter 2.

and the alleviation of suffering became a defining element of modern society'.[29] And he is right I think to see its significance for modern thought as almost impossible to overestimate. Here we will focus only on its significance for justifications of the use of force, where it has played an absolutely central role, but its wider significance should not be overlooked. I will say something more about this towards the end of the chapter.

Pacifism as a response

Much older than this 'compassionate' response though clearly related to it, of course, is a fourth response. That response is usually referred to as pacifism. Of course, there is no single pacifist argument. There have been, and still are, many different versions of pacifism and in the space I have here I could not possibly do justice to them all.[30] Rather, I want to highlight certain themes in pacifist thought that share, I shall argue, certain themes with the just war as traditionally understood but which also both link it to, and distinguish it from, most versions of the compassionate response described briefly above.

Let me start by observing that 'pacifism' as I will understand it here stands for a complete rejection of the use of lethal force for political (and quite possibly for any) ends. I am therefore not going to include within it what Martin Caedel refers to as pacificism, that is, 'non-pacifist peace sentiment',[31] which is very much part of what I was referring to as the 'compassionate' response to war above, and which

[29] Ibid., p. 50.
[30] There is no overall historical treatment of pacifism as a phenomenon. Good, though more limited treatments, would include P. Brock and N. Young, *Pacifism in the Twentieth Century* (Syracuse, NY: Syracuse University Press, 1999), and especially Martin Caedel, *Thinking about Peace and War* (Oxford University Press, 1987), Chapter 7, which identifies five different types (arguably in fact ideal types) of pacifism. Caedel has also written three excellent studies of pacifism in the UK, *Pacifism in Britain, 1914–1945* (Oxford University Press, 1980), *Origins of War Prevention*, and *Semi-Detached Idealists: The British Peace Movement and International Relations 1854–1945* (Oxford University Press, 2000). Excellent philosophical treatments of a pacifist position can be found in Richard Holmes, *On War and Morality* (Princeton University Press, 1989) – which also strongly advocates a certain kind of pacifism – and Jan Narveson, 'Pacifism: A Philosophical Analysis', in *Ethics*, 75, 4, 1965 – which most certainly does not. I will come back to explicitly Christian justifications for pacifism in a moment.
[31] Caedel, *Thinking about Peace and War*, p. 102.

might also include (I accept there are profound interpretative questions here) alleged pacifisms such as Gandhi's celebrated 'non-violence',[32] and philosophical advocacy of pacifism such as Richard Holmes who argues for pacifism on what I will call 'instrumental' grounds. As he puts it, 'I maintain that the conditions that might theoretically justify war are simply not met in the actual world; hence war is impermissible in the world as we know it.'[33] Both these views are really part and parcel of what I am calling the compassionate response.

Pacifism, as I understand it here, is then very much a minority position, and it is so because I think that it offers answers to some very hard questions which, for the most part, most people, and most societies, are not prepared to concede. Perhaps the best presentation of this is offered by Grady Scott Davis.[34] He suggests that the pacifist forgoes three particular goods which most people are not prepared to surrender. The first, and least of these, is my person, which I cannot defend against attack; the second of these are my family and friends, whom, again, I cannot defend; finally, I cannot take up arms against an unjust political order, no matter what the circumstances.

I think Davis is correct that pacifism, properly understood, must accept these three conditions and recognize, in doing so, that it is surrendering all hope of political success in the conventional sense. On a strict pacifist analysis, and contra Michael Walzer's famous phrase[35] (which we will meet again in Chapter 3), World War Two *was not* different and the Nazi regime should not have been met by force; in which case, that regime would, of course, have triumphed. Davis argues (and I agree) that a pacifist as I understand the term here must accept that conclusion and this means, for him, the only coherent pacifism is one that can offer a plausible grounding for accepting such

---

[32] Gandhi's non-violence was, as I read it, very much a strategy – though I do not doubt his sincerity and his general abomination of violence – and in that sense not a principled objection to violence as such. At the very least he was often ambiguous about how far his 'pacifism' went. For discussions, see Caedel, *Thinking about Peace and War*, pp. 158–9, and for a rather contrary view see Bikhu Parekh, *Gandhi's Political Philosophy: A Critical Examination* (Basingstoke: Macmillan, 1989).

[33] Holmes, *On War and Morality*, p. 14.

[34] Grady Scott Davis, *Warcraft and the Fragility of Virtue* (Moscow, ID: Idaho University Press, 1992), Chapter 2. I will come back to the argument of this excellent – and inexplicably rarely cited – book in Chapter 4.

[35] To wit, the title of his celebrated August 1971 article in *Philosophy and Public Affairs*, no. 1, 'World War II: Why This War Was Different'.

a conclusion. He further argues that the only such plausible grounding available is that offered by Christian pacifists like the Mennonite theologian John Howard Yoder or his ally and fellow theologian Stanley Hauerwas.[36]

The substantive point Davis is making here is simple enough but, I think, very profound. He suggests that the pacifist renounces the possibility of secular success – victory over evil, intervening to save lives, stopping genocide by military means, and so on – and that such renunciation can only be justified if something like Yoder's version of Christian witness is true. As he puts it: 'In the absence of a story about human relations to the divine that provides a context for such renunciation, pacifism itself is a source of [moral] pollution altogether on a par with the crimes of Oedipus.'[37] I do not want, in this context, to argue the toss about Davis's claim that only Christian pacifism is 'real pacifism', but I certainly want to suggest that he is right to say that adopting a pacifist stance precludes the possibility of using force to achieve a rightfully desired goal – the protection of the innocent, the defence of the weak, and so on. These are things that our general moral world would sanction as unquestionably good, other things being equal, and unless there is some very powerful overriding reason why such a renunciation should be adopted, to allow the weak to be unprotected or the innocent defiled would, almost universally, be considered a profound moral wrong.

It is this recognition, I think, that underpins both the origins and the longevity of the just war tradition. For in many respects the early theorists of what we now call the 'just war' (say Ambrose and Augustine) did share something very like Yoder's account of Christian witness, with the one crucial difference that they did not agree that this generated a blanket ban on the use of force in *all* circumstances, even though it did generate a very healthy scepticism about the kinds of claims that the powers usually resorted to in justifying the use of force.

Augustine, perhaps more than anyone else, was the sceptic *par excellence* in relation both to the claims political authorities give for

---

[36] Yoder's position is detailed most fully in his *The Politics of Jesus* (Grand Rapids, Mich.: W.B. Eerdmans, 1972), Hauerwas's across a huge range of his books and essays. See, as a representative sample, chapters 6 and 7 of *Despatches from the Front: Theological Engagements with the Secular* (Durham, NC: Duke University Press, 1994).

[37] Davis, *Warcraft*, p. 49.

justifying war and to the claims they also give for limiting it and for defending 'peace'. 'Peace and War had a contest in cruelty', he famously remarks, 'and Peace won.'[38] An unjust peace for Augustine was an affront to God as much as unjust war – and, of course, most peace was unjust, as were most wars.

Pacifism and the just war, in other words, share a good deal, but those who developed the idea of what we now call the 'just war' did so because they did not believe that there was a story about human relations with the divine that warranted us giving up on the possibility of moral action here on earth, however limited and partial such action might be. This claim has been the source of much Christian theologizing over the centuries, from the just war tradition to Christian realism, and it is of course open to multiple interpretations. It seems to me, however, that there are two assumptions that make up the claim and, as a precursor to discussing the just war tradition itself in detail, I want to flag both, since I shall return to them in Chapter 3. The first assumption is simply that there are circumstances where, morally speaking, we *must* act – to protect the innocent, defend the weak et cetera – and that it would be a corruption of our moral consciousness if we failed to see this and act – justice must be upheld and injustice and wrongdoing opposed. But the second assumption is that such occasions for legitimate action are likely to be very few and far between given, first, the character of the (fallen) world in which we live, second, the likelihood of the enormous destruction that war brings with it and, third, our own character as flawed, limited and prideful beings. As I understand it, the just war tradition rests on some version of *both* these assumptions, though – as we shall see – one does not have to understand them in distinctively theological ways. It is this that gives it, I want to argue, its real power and poses, for the modern just war tradition, a very real dilemma.

Just war responses

So what about the just war response, then? Where does this fit into the above story? As with the other responses, the roots of the tradition pre-date the modern world. Its origins lie in late antiquity and it became fully developed through the late medieval and Renaissance

---

[38] A remark from Book XIX of *The City of God*, of course.

periods.[39] In the modern world it has, at least from the late seventeenth and early eighteenth century onwards, been very much recessed, with due allowances made for its continuing role in Catholic moral and political thought, until perhaps the mid–late twentieth century. There are many reasons for this, which I will discuss in more detail in Chapter 3,[40] but in the context of the story we have just told it is worth emphasizing that the just war tradition, in its classical form at least, has never seen war as heroic (though it accepts that heroic deeds can be performed in war), has never accepted that political communities can legitimately pursue their interests irrespective of what those interests are (though it certainly accepts that most political communities will and do), and has never supposed that war can be abolished or overcome (which is why it is central to think about how we should comport ourselves in the light of that fact). This is perhaps why the tradition in the modern world has had special difficulties in being understood except as an addendum to one or other of the above responses (most obviously, recently, the compassionate response) – when in fact it is an altogether separate response. The problem is that often it has taken on the 'colouring', as it were, of the dominant response of the time – which, as I shall argue, in the contemporary context exposes very sharply a central tension present in the tradition from the beginning.

The dominant synthesis

It is not, perhaps, too fanciful to suggest that by the mid eighteenth century, the dominant response to the interrelationship of war and politics is best seen as a synthesis of the heroic and the realpolitik responses. Many in European society bemoaned war's follies, while heaping praise on those who took part in it. It was an uneasy synthesis, of course, for its roots took it in contrary directions. If one stays within the limits of the interests of one's state, then wars become tameable,

[39] I will discuss this – thematically, not chronologically – in Chapter 3.
[40] The eclipse was in part due to the emergence of a 'states system' that saw the sovereign power legitimately using force in its interests, as defended, for example, by Vattel in *Les Droit des gens* (1758), thus making one of the central questions the tradition asks – under what circumstances can legitimate force be used – effectively redundant. The tradition only really re-emerged as a living and vibrant tradition once that central claim itself began to be challenged; in other words after Nuremberg. The contextual colouring was by then hugely different.

controllable. One doesn't fight for glory, rather for – political, military or economic – interest; and these interests are *common* interests. 'It is by my order and for the good of the state, that the bearer of this has done what she has done', Dumas's Richelieu tells M'lady de Winter,[41] and this becomes the hallmark of the synthesis. Naturally, it was concomitantly popular amongst those charged with (or who charged themselves with) state responsibility. However, the heroic element in the synthesis often threatened to pull it in the opposite direction. The practices of war in the eighteenth century – the 'honours of war', the significance of 'colours', and so on – are all hallmarks of the heroic response, and the extent to which honour and virtue were seen as inextricably interwoven with the fabric of combat made it very difficult simply to see war as a 'profit and loss' occupation.[42]

The dominant synthesis also, of course, represents at one level the uncertain and precarious balance that existed within European states between the teleocratic and nomocratic understandings of association. The synthesis placed a premium on teleocratic modes, for the reasons Oakeshott suggests and that I highlighted in Chapter 1: the centrality of the idea of a common purpose – 'it is by my order *and for the good of the state* that the bearer of this has done what she has done' (emphasis added) – but it was still restrained by the voice of nomocracy that saw the logic of association in strictly non-instrumental terms. Though there were increasing tensions within it, particularly in the nineteenth century, the synthesis nonetheless held, and it held for the strongest of reasons. Simply put, it allowed the political and martial classes in Europe to do what they felt they needed to do and allowed them to justify it, both to themselves and to others. For this reason the heroic/realpolitik synthesis remained the dominant view of the relationship between war and politics in the states system for most of the post-medieval period. Indeed, one might see it as an abstraction from the practices of that settlement: a way of framing and making sense of

---

[41] In Alexandre Dumas's *The Three Musketeers*.

[42] On the continuing significance of 'honour' and virtue in the politics and international relations of the seventh to the nineteenth centuries and even, perhaps, beyond see Ciro Paoletti's sparkling essay in Peter H. Wilson (ed.) *A Companion to Eighteenth Century Europe* (Oxford: Blackwell, 2008). See also Donelan, *Honour in Foreign Policy* and Lebow, *A Cultural Theory*.

the evolving character of European politics after the fraying and ultimate collapse of medieval political structures.[43] Until, that is, 1914.

The synthesis in the twentieth century

The fate of this synthesis in the nineteenth and twentieth centuries is
easily summarized. It is the story of the slow rise to prominence of the
compassionate mode and the collapse of the synthesis for the simple
reason that the heroic mode was increasingly untenable as a partner to
realpolitik. These two phenomena are, of course, related (though not,
I think, causally so). The decline in the acceptability of the heroic mode
has a number of principal sources; unquestionably the most important
was the growth of mass politics through the nineteenth and early–mid
twentieth century. Coupled with this was the manifest incongruence of
the traditional virtues of the 'warrior' and the weapons increasingly
used for fighting wars. The decline of cavalry and the rise of industrial
technology does nothing directly to damage realpolitik, but it clearly
makes the heroic image of the warrior more and more difficult to
maintain. It is, however, also true that the decreasing acceptability of
certain of the mainstays of the 'heroic' scale of values (duelling, for
example) – which was, in part, caused by the rising acceptability of the
compassionate response – contributed to the heroic mode's decline.[44]

If realpolitik had left the nineteenth century still allied with the
heroic response, it quickly became associated with something else.
As Bracher has pointed out, the twentieth century was the 'age of

[43] Useful discussions of the intellectual architecture of the Westphalian settlement
in this regard can be found in Andreas Bialer, *The States System of Europe*
(Oxford University Press, 1992). A spectacularly good analysis of the
international politics of the eighteenth and nineteenth centuries is Paul
Schroeder, *The Transformation of European Politics 1763–1848* (Oxford:
Clarendon Press, 1994). I emphasize that medieval political structures collapsed;
it is far more interesting and questionable as to whether the assumptions that
underpinned them also did. There are good reasons for supposing that they
perhaps did not, that to a certain extent we still exist in a 'medieval' context.
For arguments that support this claim see the discussion I offer in 'On Theology
and International Relations: World Politics Beyond the Empty Sky', in
International Relations (in press).

[44] There is a good deal more that might be said here, but I do not have the time or
the space to say it. A contrary view to the one I am putting forward can be found
in Lebow, *A Cultural Theory*. A broadly sympathetic one is John Keegan,
A History of Warfare (London: Vintage, 1994).

ideologies'[45] and it was ideology, as well as interest, that became the hallmark of realpolitik during the twentieth century. There were, of course, a number of reasons for this. Again to quote Bracher, one of the hallmarks of ideological politics in the modern age is its need to justify itself and what we might call its 'manner of action'. This is as true of 'liberal democracy' as it was (and is) of liberal democracy's opponents. This development had three specific implications on which it is worth dwelling here. First, the inevitable result of the alliance between realpolitik and 'ideology' was to colour the requirements of realpolitik to include ideological (and not just state) interests, and the logical corollary of this, of course, was that the sphere of geopolitical competition became much greater. Second, and flowing directly from the first, this inevitably meant that war in the twentieth century would increase its tendency already witnessed through the nineteenth to become 'total' – at least in the sense of committing all of the resources of the state behind its cause. Mass politics played its part here too, of course. Third, given the technological changes of the twentieth century, it almost inevitably meant that war would be much bloodier than it had been in the past (the warning of the American Civil War was, of course, there for all to see, but few were looking).[46]

Given that, in much of Europe, the rise of the compassionate response had gone hand in hand with a firm belief in progress and the rise of human (or at least European) civilization to the point at which major powers would no longer use war to settle their disputes, it is not surprising that war, when it did come in 1914, provided such an existential as well as a political shock. It is, of course, this shock that, according to Paul Fussell amongst others,[47] helped to make the perceptions of World War One the paradigmatic perceptions of war for most Europeans and Americans in the twentieth century; despite the attempts of more recent historians (like Niall Ferguson)[48] to tell a somewhat different story about the war, it is Fussell's interpretation

---

[45] Karl Dietrich Bracher, *The Age of Ideologies* (London: Methuen, 1984).

[46] For a brilliant discussion of the manner in which the change in the character of warfare was rationalized in modernity see Daniel Pick, *War Machine: The Rationalization of Slaughter in the Modern Age* (New Haven: Yale University Press, 1993).

[47] The classic treatment is Paul Fussell's *The Great War and Modern Memory* (Oxford University Press, 1977).

[48] Ferguson, *The Pity of War* (Harmondsworth: Allen Lane, 1998).

that has stuck. His point, of course, is not about what the war was actually like, only about how it was perceived and remembered and what effect this had on how we in the West saw war for the rest of the century.

The heroic response to war died, it might be said, in Flanders fields and the result of that was simple: a Western world divided between those who saw war as simply one aspect of state policy among many (in fact very few), those who saw it as anathema under any circumstances (equally few), and those who saw it – when they thought of it at all – as a terrible necessity. However, the logic of the latter view, of course, is that war should only be fought when something considered really valuable is at stake and, given the ideological orientation of the century, that would more often than not translate into fighting war for basic 'values' (whether those were the 'defence of the realm' or the defence of the values felt to be indistinguishable from the realm); under those circumstances the maxim that necessity knows no law is likely to be omnipresent. In other words, realpolitik wedded to ideology is likely to produce 'total' war and the apotheosis of instrumental rationality.[49]

It is, I suggest, against this reality that the compassionate response in the latter part of the twentieth century largely oriented itself. For most advocates of the compassionate view, war must sometimes be fought, but it must also be possible to fight it justly and well. That is the only way to avoid the excesses of ideological war and of a wholly instrumental realpolitik. As so often in this context, it is Michael Walzer who is the lodestar of the debate. His defence of World War Two[50] as the paradigm case of a justifiable war in the modern context (written, of course, against the background of his opposition to the Vietnam War being waged as he was writing) sets the context for his hugely influential rewriting of the just war tradition, but it is significant in this context that he starts from a position which largely accepts much of the ground of the realpolitik position, an acceptance which

---

[49] A logic that is also illuminated at some length in Eric Voegelin's compressed but still magisterial *The New Science of Politics* (University of Chicago Press, 1952). Voegelin's understanding of the character of modern 'gnosticism' and its character as a political religion displays, I think, precisely why modern realpolitik wedded to 'ideology' takes the form it does.

[50] 'World War II: Why This War Was Different'.

only becomes fully fleshed out in *Just and Unjust Wars* with his understanding of the requirements of 'supreme emergency'.[51]

It is in this context that many writers, convinced of the intractability of the problem of war, but equally shying away from the bluntness of the realpolitik position, cast around for something that would enable a response to war compatible with the compassionate approach but allowing a meaningful deployment of the idea of legitimate force. This search led, I suggest, to two things. First, as already mentioned, it led to the 'rediscovery' – and substantial rewriting, as I will go on to argue – of perhaps the most generally significant aspect of the Western tradition of moral and political thought regarding war, the just war tradition, But, second, it led to an increasing emphasis on the Enlightenment-derived claim that war is a problem of 'regime type', a phenomenon that some regimes (autocracies, tyrannies et cetera) are prone to but which other regime types (democracies) are not.[52]

As we will see, this claim also masks the extent to which both compassionate and realpolitik responses are marked by the rise of teleocratic modes of politics. The heroic response to war was always hard to accommodate with a teleocratic understanding, but ironically the supposed opposites of the compassionate and realpolitik modes were much more congenial, partly because they were already inclined to think of themselves as supportive of (very different) common purposes. Moreover, the rise of claims about the significance of regime type allowed the parallelism of their arguments to pass largely unnoticed, as we shall see. So before we turn to the manner in which teleocratic politics reshapes the just war tradition, we should pause a while to examine the second phenomenon I mentioned. For it, too, plays its role in potentially expanding, not constricting, the possible use of force.

Regime type and the use of force

Forms of political community of course exist in many varieties and even long-standing forms have complex and plural histories. But for all such forms war was perhaps the one inescapable reality. The question

---

[51] For a critique of Walzer's argument about supreme emergency and how it can (and has) been used by far less interesting and scrupulous writers subsequently, see Chapter 5.

[52] Obviously there are ancient precedents as well.

was how they related to it, understood it, and accommodated themselves to it. But as Michael Howard, amongst others, has pointed out,[53] it is especially in the eighteenth century that some thinkers increasingly came to see war not as a permanent, however regrettable, feature of human experience but rather as a 'problem' that could, in principle at least, be 'solved' (that is, eliminated). Of course, this view was much broader than simply the belief that war need not always be with us – that we might, by God or providence, be delivered from war. Rather it was a belief in the capacity of individuals and societies *to reshape* the character of politics such that established traditions – in this case the tradition that there was nothing that could be done about war as such, though always things you could do about particular wars – weakened their grip on the European mind.

As we saw earlier, such a view was central to the rise of the 'compassionate' response, and I believe many of the innovations in nineteenth-century international relations are traceable to this idea. The foundation of the Red Cross is a good example, as are the disarmament conferences of 1899 and 1907.[54] Indeed, the very notion of 'disarming' and 'disarmament' is surely dependent on the idea that, at least in principle, it is not irrational to wish, and act, for a world without war.[55] Indeed, much of the history of institutional change and 'reform' in international relations in general throughout the nineteenth and twentieth centuries is inexplicable in the absence of this belief, and even much of the negative reaction to such attempts speaks volumes about the extent to which both reformers and their opponents occupied the same essential mental universe; as Michael Oakeshott once remarked apropos Hayek's critique of centralized planning, 'a plan to resist all planning may be preferable to its opposite, but it is still part of the same style of politics'.[56]

And it is here, I think, that we see two crucial assumptions being made. First, we must assume that humanity *can* progress morally

---

[53] See Howard's *The Invention of Peace* (London: Profile Books, 2001).

[54] For the best general treatment of this see Geoffrey Best, *Humanity in Warfare: The Modern History of the International Law of Armed Conflicts* (London: Allen and Unwin, 1978).

[55] For a wonderful illustration of this, as well as a superb discussion of the evolution of this sensibility in modern thought as a whole, see Best, *Humanity in Warfare*, and *Law and War* (Oxford: Clarendon Press, 1996).

[56] The remark is made in Oakeshott's *Rationalism in Politics* (London: Methuen, 1962).

(note, not that we *must* make such progress, or even that we *are* doing so, only that we *can* do so). Second, not only must we believe in the possibility of a world without war, but we must have a plausible vehicle for getting us there.

The chosen vehicle has, of course, been variable — Kant's *foedum pacificum*,[57] the growth of 'civilization' suggested by some in the nineteenth century,[58] economic interdependence as was hinted at by Kant and claimed more generally by Norman Angel,[59] and subsequently by many others – but there has been a growing conviction both that it was possible, and that this possibility could be made law. That is to say, there has been a predilection to see the 'problem' of war, principally at least, as a matter of political forms.

The best-known version of this claim in modern thought is, of course, the so-called 'democratic peace thesis', and however this is understood in detail it is clear that the core argument depends upon the idea that there is a clear and unambiguous relationship between a political regime and its manner of acting in the world.[60] As Montesquieu claimed, monarchies (for example) are war prone (if not always warlike), while republics are peaceable (if not always peaceful). This claim, while of course it has ancient roots, is traceable in its modern form to the Enlightenment.[61] However, it is worth

---

[57] Elaborated most fully in his essay '*Zum ewigen Frieden*' (*On Perpetual Peace*). See Brown et al., *International Relations*, pp. 432–50.

[58] A classic discussion is Geritt W. Gong, *The Standard of Civilization in International Society* (Oxford: Clarendon Press, 1984).

[59] Most famously in *The Great Illusion* (London: Heinemann, 1933(1911)).

[60] There is now an immense literature on the democratic peace thesis, and I could not even begin to scratch the surface if I were to write another book. The modern *locus classicus* is Michael Doyle, 'Kant, Liberal Legacies and Foreign Affairs', *Philosophy and Public Affairs*, 12, 1983: 205–35, 323–53, and 'Liberalism and World Politics', *American Political Science Review*, 80, 4, 1986. A critical response is Christopher Layne, 'Kant or Cant: The Myth of the Democratic Peace', *International Security*, 19, 2, 1994: 5–49.

[61] There is a good deal to be said about the extent to which Enlightenment and post-Enlightenment understandings of the character of a regime (most obviously in Montesquieu and Tocqueville) draw upon ancient ideas about the 'character' of a regime and to what extent they differ from them. The most obvious difference is the emphasis, certainly in both Plato and Aristotle, on the equivalence between the soul and the city – Plato's discussion of the declining character of the souls/cities in books 8 and 9 of the *Republic* is an example – of which there is no real equivalent. However, there are other differences as well. For good discussions of the idea of the regime and its effect in antiquity see, famously, Kurt Von Fritz, *The Theory of the Mixed Constitution in Antiquity*

pointing out – especially given what I want to say at the end of this chapter – that the Enlightenment did not speak with one voice on this matter. The claim is often associated with Montesquieu's *De l'esprit des lois*, and a widely cited passage in the context is his claim that 'the spirit of Monarchy is war and enlargement of dominion; peace and moderation are the spirit of a republic'.[62] From this, of course, it seems to follow that if you changed the social form of Europe from monarchy to republics, you could – in principle – abolish war. However, Montesquieu's point is actually the very different one that war is not a feature of the human condition as such but rather of social (but not merely constitutional) form; the character of the 'spirit of the laws' determines a society's predilection towards or away from the use of force, but it is a mistake to equate the spirit of the laws, as Montesquieu understands this, merely with constitutional form or – as we might say today – with 'regime type'.[63]

The thinker who certainly does make this claim – and as I have already said in contemporary terms he is easily the most influential advocate of the democratic peace *avant la lettre*, as it were – is Immanuel Kant. In a series of essays published in the 1780s and 1790s, Kant outlined a subtle and philosophically rich account of human social development that suggested, first, that properly 'republican' (as he would call them) states would have little to go to

(New York: Columbia University Press, 1954) and the classic Alfred Zimmern, *The Greek Commonwealth* (Oxford: Clarendon Press, 1911). Much contemporary writing from the friends and admirers of the late Leo Strauss has also stressed the importance of the notion of the regime and has also considered its modern imitators. Good examples would be Thomas Pangle's interpretive essay to his (excellent) translation of the *Laws* (University of Chicago Press, 1980). For his take on the Enlightenment version see his *Montesquieu's Philosophy of Liberalism* (University of Chicago Press, 1973). A much more recent discussion, specifically on Aristotle, but very good on the idea of the regime and its significance, is Bernard Yack, *The Problems of a Political Animal* (Berkeley: University of California Press, 1993).

[62] Montesquieu, *The Spirit of the Laws*, ed. A. Cohler, B.C. Miller and H.S. Stone (Cambridge University Press, 1949), 5.

[63] This point is made by Oakeshott in *On Human Conduct* (Oxford: Clarendon Press, 1975); see the discussion on pp. 245–51. Accounts of Montesquieu that would broadly share this view (though from very different perspectives) would include Judith Shklar, *Montesquieu* (Oxford University Press, 1987) and John Plamenatz, *Man and Society*, 2 vols. (Harlow: Longman, 1961), vol. 1, pp. 284–91. Accounts that would be rather different would include Thomas Pangle, *Montesquieu's Philosophy of Liberalism*.

war over and, second, that history (or, as Kant preferred to say, 'providence') was effectively creating a situation where more and more states would indeed become republican. However, for Kant this development was not irreversible (or at least not so in any meaningful timescale), and so republican states had to look to protect themselves from other kinds of states that would, for a long time, be in the majority. To this end, he thought, they should create a *foedus pacificum*, or pacific union of republican states, peaceful towards one another but prepared to defend each other against aggression.

This way of thinking helps to create a very different way of thinking about war (that is entirely characteristic of the dominant tenor of post-Enlightenment thinking about war).[64] It assumes that the problem of war is essentially solvable if we move away from political and social forms that encourage it (monarchy or the 'martial spirit', for example) and towards political and social forms that discourage it (liberal republics/democracies), *and* that there is an historical process that can bring this about. This has given liberal and democratic thinking on war in general an institutional flavour which permeated much of the international relations theory of the twentieth century, from Zimmern's *League of Nations and the Rule of Law* in 1936 to the most recent edition of Keohane and Nye's *Power and Interdependence* in 2000.[65] One might even suggest that much conventional Marxist thought on international relations is a variant on the same theme: it is the contradictions of capitalism that will bring about the abolition of war, not the republican state – indeed states too will be abolished – but the form of the argument is essentially the same.[66]

Kant, of course, additionally believed (as did Marx) that a progressivist philosophy of history was required to turn this argument from a fairly banal one relating regimes to behaviour, prefigured in antiquity, to a much more significant comment on the emerging possibilities for

---

[64] In this context I mean, of course, post-Enlightenment in the sense of following on in the *spirit* of the Enlightenment, not merely chronologically post-Enlightenment.

[65] Alfred Zimmern *The League of Nations and the Rule of Law* (London: Macmillan, 1936). Robert Keohane and Joseph Nye, *Power and Interdependence: World Politics in Transition* (Boston: Little, Brown, 1977; 3rd rev. and expanded edn, 2000).

[66] For an excellent discussion of Marxist accounts of international relations see Vendulka Kublakova and Andrew Cruikshank, *Marxism and International Relations* (Oxford University Press, 1989).

humankind. Without what Kant famously called an 'idea for a universal history with a cosmopolitan purpose',[67] which emphasized the extent to which republics would, over time, become the norm in international politics, his thesis is merely a recognition of the fact that republics would have to wage war – and perhaps wage it with considerable ferocity – if they were to survive in a world where most states were still not republics and were, in all probability, hostile to such republics. The other face of the *foedus pacificum*, in other words, is a democratic *war* theory, an account of how and why republics will fight wars and a recognition that such wars may be very fierce and very frequent until such time as the *foedus pacificum* covers the earth.

Modern versions of the democratic peace thesis have been – to put it mildly – ambiguous about what, in particular, has been the key factor in explaining peace between 'democracies'. Is it perhaps democratic political mechanisms?[68] Or a liberal political culture?[69] Or a combination of these things coupled with an active free market and trade? Or the salience and binding force of international institutions? Or all of the above? I should add, of course, that latterly both in respect of politics in general and in respect of international politics in particular, there is a burgeoning literature that argues for 'republican' forms of government that are democratic but, in important ways at least, very critical of liberalism.[70] But the key points in all these arguments, of

---

[67] The German title is 'Idee zu Allgemeinen Gesichter in Weltburgerlicher Absicht'.

[68] This argument is developed in detail by Bruce Russett in *Grasping the Democratic Peace* (Princeton University Press, 1993).

[69] Implied, at least, in Fareed Zakaria's *The Future of Freedom* (New York: Norton, 2003).

[70] The growth of interest in 'republican' political thought, its history, character and contemporary provenance is, of course, one of the great stories of the past forty years of intellectual history and political theory. Probably the two leading historians of ideas responsible for much of this recapturing are J.G.A. Pocock – especially in *The Machiavellian Moment: Florentine Political Thought and the Atlantic Republican Tradition* (Princeton University Press, 2003(1975)) – and Quentin Skinner, much of whose work deals with republicanism in some form or another but whose pioneering historical work in *Foundations* bore specific fruit in *Liberty Before Liberalism* (Cambridge University Press, 1997). The dominant voice in contemporary republican political thought is probably Philip Pettit whose *Republicanism: A Theory of Freedom and Government* (Oxford University Press, 1997) was the first fully worked out contemporary appropriation of the ideas of classical republicanism and who has recently moved into thinking about the international implications of this, in his 'A Republican Law of Peoples', in the *European Journal of Political Theory*, 9, 1,

course, are that, first, whatever factor is identified should be seen as having, potentially at least, universal scope; and second, that however interpreted, the key assumption has to be that there is a direct and unmediated connection between a liberal democratic (or republican or what have you) political regime and its behaviour in regard to (in this instance) war.

Of course, if it is the case that the royal road to international peace and security runs through the establishment of what we might today term 'liberal democratic' societies, then there is an obvious logic – I don't say unimpeachable logic – in seeking to create as many democracies as possible, even perhaps, in some circumstances, in imposing them. Something like this seems to have been at least part of the rationale for certain actions of the Bush administration after its epiphany on 11 September 2001, but it is worth adding that to a lesser (and less obviously aggressive) extent such policies had been prefigured in the Clinton period and have been followed also by the Obama administration, and are part of the widely shared rhetoric of the contemporary West. Western reactions to the Arab uprisings in the spring of 2011 show a similar imprint, saving that the 'democracy promotion', which Western governments are welcoming, comes from people within the region rather than from outside. Put this way, however, it is clear that there is one crucial claim in any argument about regime type and war: that there is a clear and traceable link between regime type and certain kinds of behaviour in the international sphere.

So can we find such a link? I want to suggest that we cannot, and we cannot because the argument about regime type and war elides a distinction that is central to the story I want to tell in this book. It is an obvious point, to begin with, that liberal democracies are themselves notoriously diverse. Of course they have certain institutional similarities, which is why it is fair enough to call them by a common name, but it is equally certain that there are many differences. For there to be anything properly meaningful in the democratic peace thesis, however, one would have to be able to say that it was the liberal democratic aspect of a political community – that is, the regime

January 2010. Other scholars who have articulated a distinctive republican position in International Relations are Nick Onuf in *The Republican Legacy in International Thought* (Cambridge University Press, 1997) and Daniel Deudney in *Bounding Power: Republican Security Theory from the Polis to the Global Village* (Princeton University Press, 2007).

type – that mattered most, that *this* aspect of country A or B would overcome national or ethnic partiality, religious sensibility (or lack of it), or simply perceptions of profit and loss.

It seems unlikely that this would necessarily be the case; surely it would depend upon the context. In this case one is looking for *the context in which* the existence of a democratic (or liberal democratic) political culture will lead to a certain kind of political behaviour, rather than the mere fact that the state in question is or was (in whatever sense) 'liberal democratic'.

Some defenders of the thesis have sought to link the fact of liberal political cultures or democratic political systems with relevant contexts, but even when they have succeeded, the implications for the liberal democratic peace are not really as rosy as many of its advocates would have us believe. Not only do 'really existing democracies' of course differ among themselves, in many ways and for many reasons; it is surely also reasonable to suppose further that even the specific form of government we might describe as liberal (or representative) democracy will have many fault lines within it.

If we return to Oakeshott's distinction I discussed in Chapter 1, another major problem becomes apparent. One does not have to accept the whole of Oakeshott's case,[71] of course, to accept that what we today call liberal democratic states are a very odd ragbag and that there is little reason to believe that the mere fact of them all possessing, in some form and to some degree, liberal politics and democratic institutions generates any particular commonality of behaviour. But if that is the case, then the democratic peace thesis, at least as a thesis, disappears along with the claim that proclivity towards war goes along with regime type. In order for it to be plausible, we need the direct link between regime type and behaviour that Oakeshott's argument suggests is absent. There is no such direct link because inasmuch as modern states are the inheritors of the consciousness, polarized between nomocracy and teleocracy, the mere fact of them being liberal democratic states will matter much less than the character of the association they chiefly display.

The democratic peace thesis – as a thesis, that is to say as an hypothesis about the political world – represents, it seems to me, in a

---

[71] I would amend Oakeshott's case in various ways and hope, in future work, to do just that. But the broad outlines of it, as I said in the previous chapter, I certainly would endorse.

particularly pure form, an error common in the history of European political thought over the past two hundred years and especially common today and to which Oakeshott also points.[72] This is simply the confusion between describing the character of a regime, that is, a particular set of constitutional arrangements, and disclosing the logic of a certain mode of association. As we saw in Chapter 1, 'belligerence is alien to civil association',[73] but this has nothing specifically to do with the constitutional arrangements (republican, liberal or whatever) of a state (which will in any case be an admixture of civil and enterprise association) and everything to do with how one understands the logic of association itself.[74]

This error has a number of very unfortunate corollaries. It not only conflates regime type with mode of association, it also allows for the identification of certain kinds of *behaviour* with certain kinds of regime rather than, as would be much more appropriate, the logic inherent to a certain mode of association. Moreover, it tends to encourage the belief that one can change or adapt behaviour deemed desirable or undesirable for various reasons by changing the relevant regime. This gives an additional impetus, if one were needed, for 'liberal democratic' states to believe that force can be used to bring about 'regime change' and therefore allegedly secure changes in regime 'behaviour'. As I already remarked, there certainly seems to be something of this logic behind at least some justifications of the United States invasion of Iraq in 2003.[75] As Oakeshott himself remarks at one point in *On Human Conduct*, we ourselves have long ago 'suffered the voice of civil association to be confused with a "liberal" [almost always put in scare quotes in Oakeshott's writing] concern for constitutional devices'.[76] He is clear, and I agree with him, that it should not be.

---

[72] See, especially, his discussion in *On Human Conduct*, pp. 272–4.

[73] Ibid., p. 273.

[74] See, for example, Oakeshott's acerbic footnote (ibid.): 'Kant and others conjectured that a Europe composed of states with republican constitutions would be a Europe at peace. This absurdity is often excused on the ground that it is a plausible (although naïve) identification of war with so-called dynastic war, but it is in fact the muddle from which Montesquieu did his best to rescue us, the confusion of a constitution of government (republican) with a mode of association.' Cf. the discussion of Montesquieu above.

[75] Witness, for example, some of Paul Wolfowitz's comments in an article in *Prospect*, 18 December 2004.

[76] See Oakeshott, *On Human Conduct*, p. 297, n. 2.

In other words, this kind of conflation, especially given the other aspects of the character of contemporary 'liberal democracy' mentioned above, might make democracies *more* war prone rather than the reverse. So a world composed largely of liberal democracies conceptualized as teleocracies might not be any less war prone than the existing international order, and indeed, in some respects – as we shall see – it might be rather more so.

Conclusion

This is to say, of course, that the hopes invested in the democratic peace thesis (and, indeed, other suggestions that war as a phenomenon can be somehow 'solved' or 'eliminated') are likely to prove illusory. The compassionate response to war might well have dominated in the Europe of the late twentieth century but, as Christopher Coker has remarked in an impressive (and disturbing) account of the rise of 'humane warfare', that might simply end up making war more inhumane than ever before.[77] And realpolitik, as we know, has hardly gone away. This, then, is the current version of the 'modern social imaginary of war' – an uneasy and unstable combination of realpolitik, just war, and compassionate modes yoked to (in large part) teleocratic understandings of politics. It is that version that frames our consideration of the 'shape' of war in the twenty-first century. But central to this, I want to argue, is the 'rebirth' of the just war tradition in the twentieth century, after at least three centuries of relative stagnation, a rebirth profoundly affected by the increasingly dominant teleocratic conception of the state and indeed of politics more generally. It is to the just war tradition, then, that we must now turn.

[77] Christopher Coker, *Humane Warfare* (London: Routledge, 2001), p. 151.

3 | *Just war: ambiguous tradition*

Whether the State can loose and bind
   In Heaven as well as on Earth:
If it be wiser to kill mankind
   Before or after the birth –
These are matters of high concern
   Where State-kept schoolmen are;
But Holy State (we have lived to learn)
   Endeth in Holy War.
…

Whatsoever, for any cause,
   Seeketh to take or give
Power above or beyond the Laws,
   Suffer it not to live!
      Kipling, 'MacDonough's Song'

The period since the end of the Second World War, and most especially the period from the 1970s to the present, has seen a revival of normative theorizing about war unparalleled since the seventeenth century. Both religious and, especially, secular theorizing have focused to a very large extent on working broadly within the parameters of the most influential European tradition of thought connected with war: the just war tradition. This is true even where (as in some recent cosmopolitan work) the tradition is also greatly reworked and true also in the worlds of political rhetoric and military law, as witnessed by the constant recitation of central *in bello* principles by senior Allied officers in Afghanistan and Iraq, and by the regular invocation of the tradition by politicians.

Thus, for many, the just war tradition can rightly be seen to have triumphed as the appropriate moral language for the evaluation of the use of force. Indeed, in a recent essay, Tony Lang and Cian O'Driscoll argue that:

The just war tradition is the predominant moral language through which we address questions pertaining to the rights and wrongs of the use of force in international society … it furnishes us with a set of concepts, principles, and analytical devices for making sense of the moral-legal questions that war raises … *the just war tradition manifests, on the one hand, a tragic resignation to the necessity of war in this fallen world, and, on the other hand, a determination to restrict its destructiveness.* (emphasis added)

They stress further that:

the just war tradition is central to the practice of international relations. Its influence is evident in the legal codes that govern how modern militaries perform their duties, and it has featured prominently in the rhetoric surrounding the war on terror and the recent invasions of Iraq and Afghanistan.

They conclude that the tradition

reflects an enduring effort to sustain the idea that, even when he finds himself in the trenches, man occupies a moral world. As such, the tradition should not be misconstrued as a simple *techne* or set of guidelines stipulating what is permissible in war. Rather, it comprises a tradition of political theory that invites us to think about war on a philosophical register. It challenges us to peer beyond the possibility of a narrowly defined 'ethics of war', toward a broader engagement with the practice of rules and responsibilities, and rights and duties, as they relate to the violent edge of world politics. Underpinning this is a sustained inquiry into the relation between power and authority in international life.[1]

There is much in this, of course, with which I would agree. But there are also some reasons for being cautious about these claims, and it is these reasons – my differences rather than my agreements – on which I want to dwell in this chapter. One disagreement, in particular, will occupy me, but let me start by flagging a couple of other areas where I entertain a doubt or two.

In the first place, whereas it is true that in Europe and its cultural analogues elsewhere the just war tradition is probably 'the predominant *moral* language through which we address questions pertaining to the rights and wrongs of the use of force' (emphasis added), that would not be true in all cases in the 'West' (however we might understand that rather slippery term) and would obviously not be true in many other cultural and evaluative contexts. There was (for example) much sneering on the part of some (so-called) neoconservative theorists and

---

[1] Background paper for the United States Institute of Peace conference 'Just War: A State of the Art' (Washington, DC, 25–26 August 2010).

policy-makers, at the time of the Iraq invasion and before, about the just war tradition and its antiquated sense of 'playing by the rules' and many (in my view rather risible) references to the need for a 'pagan ethos' (or what have you) to govern the use of force.[2] In a different context, I doubt that the Chinese political elite have much time for notions of the just war, whatever their public protestations of support for international law. So while in some circles the just war is indeed a 'predominant moral language', it is certainly not without challengers.

In the second place, Lang and O'Driscoll emphasize that 'the just war tradition manifests, on the one hand, a tragic resignation to the necessity of war in this fallen world, and, on the other hand, a determination to restrict its destructiveness'. Again, I think this is fair enough, but would make two qualifications. Many just war thinkers today – including many of the most influential such thinkers – would, of course, have some problems in seeing this world as a 'fallen world' – the theological overtones are rather too overt for comfort for those who do not share a confessional orientation. Second, and much more important however, this way of conceptualizing the tradition – though it is close in some respects to my own – does not give anything like enough weight to the concerns of many who see the tradition as at least as much about the promotion of justice, or at least the elimination of injustice, as it is about the limitations of destructiveness.

In this chapter I want to argue that the tradition historically was about *both* the limitation of destructiveness and the elimination, or punishment, of wrongdoing, but also that these twin pillars of the tradition have always sat rather uneasily together. In writers like Augustine, the tension is noted but explained as the inevitable dissonances of that 'fallen world'. With the emergence of what James Turner Johnson calls 'just war doctrine' in the sixteenth century, however, and especially in the evolution of the distinction between *jus ad bellum* and *jus in bello*, the dichotomy becomes more pronounced and, over time, the tension too becomes more pronounced. This is partly, I shall argue, a reaction to the growing dominance of the *jus in bello*, a dominance strongly reinforced by the obvious fact that the emergent states system in the seventeenth and eighteenth centuries assumed that sovereigns

---

[2] This reference is to Robert Kaplan's short book *Warrior Politics: Why Leadership Demands a Pagan Ethos* (New York: Vintage, 2003), actually one of the better and more literate of such arguments.

had the right to use force to uphold their interests and that therefore discussions of the *jus ad bellum* were (outside explicitly theological contexts) somewhat redundant. It is also noteworthy that it is precisely during this period, I think, that the notion of authority, so central to every thinker from Augustine to Vitoria, becomes increasingly muddy – a point to which I will return briefly in the Epilogue. This process was further deepened, I will argue, by the development in the nineteenth century of the codification of international law and especially by the development of the 'laws of war', in that these were understood in the nineteenth century and later in terms of a certain jurisprudential reading of law, grounded on state power, in other words on a particular form of legal positivism.

It is this setting that has framed the hugely influential rebirth of writing on the just war after the Second World War, in both religious and secular contexts. But as I have already argued, this period also sees the growing dominance of the teleocratic conception of the state – and of politics more generally – and in this chapter I want to argue that this becomes the central frame for the tradition after the Second World War. In this same context, ideas about punishment and wrongdoing became centrally entwined with ideas that suggested that a political community (however understood) should act as the promoter of justice or at least the eliminator of its opposite, a development which, in the academic theorizing of the past forty years, has been strongly enhanced by the burgeoning justice industry which followed the astonishing success of Rawls's *A Theory of Justice* in 1971[3] but was already implicit in the rise of the compassionate response to war that I discussed in Chapter 2.

In brief, then, I want to argue that what is visible, not only in the various different ways of reading the just war tradition that are influential in moral and political theory today, but also in a good deal of contemporary international law and, indeed, other approaches to the ethics of force, is a conception of the ethics of force as predominantly about the elimination of injustice, as a growing priority *over and above* the restraint of force and that, as a natural corollary in a violent and conflictual world, the tradition has become, and is becoming, progressively *less* restrictive of reasons for, and the manner of the exercise of,

---

[3] John Rawls, *A Theory of Justice* (Harvard: Belknap Press, 1971).

lethal force.[4] Where injustice is everywhere, the reasons to use force to oppose it are not hard to find, even if they are not always politically apposite or, indeed, possible. And in the context of modern states that has, I think, extremely pernicious consequences, as we shall see.

The just war tradition: dilemmas of origin and interpretation

The traditional distinction that is often held to define the just war tradition – between *jus ad bellum* (justice of war) and *jus in bello* (justice in war) – is, of course, a very familiar one to us today. It is as well to remember, therefore, that in fact it has a history and that the history it has is by no means devoid of general philosophical interest, and so I want to dwell for a moment on that general philosophical interest that I take the history to have, since I shall want to return to it towards the end of the chapter.

As I discussed a moment ago, among the more important aspects of the recent development of the tradition has been the move to a particular kind of jurisprudential logic for it, one that has partially replaced or overlaid the earlier casuistic form that the tradition took in its medieval and neoscholastic heyday (and which included, of course, a rather different form of jurisprudential reasoning). Among the reasons for this shift, I want to argue, is the dominance of the *jus in bello* in the literature of the just war roughly from the early to mid seventeenth century onwards. This fact has not perhaps been as much discussed as it really warrants: in Geoffrey Best's very apt words, during the modern period 'while the *jus ad bellum* withered on the bough, the *jus in bello* flourished like the Green Bay Tree'.[5] In other words, the particular history of the *jus in bello* in the early modern – and then later modern – period has played a large role in shaping the just war tradition as a whole in the modern world, how it is understood and how it is deployed. I shall return to the significance of this in more general terms later, but I want for the moment merely to comment on the obvious implication that it is the *jus in bello* and not the *jus ad bellum* that has structured the inner logic of the tradition in the modern context.

---

[4] Though as we shall see there are some countervailing tendencies, especially in cosmopolitan just war theorizing.
[5] Geoffery Best, *War and Law since 1945* (Oxford: Clarendon Press, 1994), p. 20.

This has a number of implications for the way we think about the tradition itself. For example, if we ask the obvious question of what the tradition allows us to do, in the first place, the just war tradition cannot tell us – and is not designed to tell us – whether this or that particular instance of the use of force is 'just' (that is, morally legitimate) or not in the generality. To quote Oliver O'Donovan:

> it is very often supposed that just war theory undertakes *to validate or invalidate particular wars*. That would be an impossible undertaking. History knows of no just wars, as it knows of no just peoples … one may justify or criticize acts of statesmen, acts of generals, acts of common soldiers or of civilians, provided one does so from the point of view of those who performed them, i.e. without moralistic hindsight; but wars as such, like most large scale historical phenomena, present only a question mark, a continual invitation to reflect further.[6]

What, then, is the tradition designed to do? We can grasp something of this, I think, if we reflect for a moment on one aspect of the tradition little considered by moderns: right intention. James Turner Johnson, in his account of the tradition, accepts that this aspect of the tradition is 'not explicitly addressed' in the modern just war, being subsumed under questions of just cause and right authority.[7] Yet in classic 'just war' writing, from Augustine to the sixteenth century, right intention was most emphatically not so subsumed. Partly this was because it cut across the 'dividing line' of *jus ad bellum* and *jus in bello*.[8] While part of the 'right intention' discussion is meant to apply to rulers – they must not have the intention of territorial or personal aggrandizement, intimidation or illegitimate coercion – part of it is also meant to apply to those who do the fighting: the enemy is not to be hated, there must be no desire to dominate or lust for vengeance, and soldiers must always be aware of the corruption that can flow from the *animus dominandi*.

---

[6] Oliver O'Donovan, *The Just War Revisited* (Oxford University Press, 2003), p. 15

[7] James Turner Johnson, *Morality and Contemporary Warfare* (New Haven: Yale University Press, 1999), p. 30.

[8] For an extremely powerful account of the views on war of the School of Salamanca in general, and Vitoria in particular, see the introduction to Anthony Pagden and Jeremy Lawrance (eds.) *Francisco de Vitoria: Political Writings* (Cambridge University Press, 1991). An extremely good account of the background can also be found in Pagden, *Lords of All the World: Ideologies of Empire in Spain, Britain and France c. 1500–1800* (New Haven: Yale University Press, 1995).

The point here, of course, is that what the tradition – from Augustine onwards – insisted upon, and what right intention was meant to gesture towards, was the extension into the realm of war of the normal practices of moral judgement. Of course, classic just war thinkers – Augustine above all – also recognized that war was an *extreme* realm and so such an extension represents (in O'Donovan's formulation) 'an *extraordinary extension* of ordinary acts of judgment'[9] but an extension of them all the same. This was why the two poles of the classic just war tradition were always authority on the one hand and judgement on the other, and why, when we come to think about judgement, the two central terms of reference were (as they are now known to us) discrimination and proportion. In the classic treatments of the tradition it is *these* distinctions that give rise to discussions about just cause, right authority, and right intent (for example). O'Donovan refers to the *jus ad bellum/jus in bello* distinction as a 'secondary ... and not a load bearing'[10] distinction, which I think nicely captures how we should view it. It is a useful heuristic, no more. The problem is that it has become elevated to an architectonic, and for very significant reasons, as we shall see.

The just war tradition and the *jus in bello*

At this point we should perhaps introduce a further distinction. As I noted in the Introduction and Chapter 2, normative attitudes on what it is permissible to do in war are features of virtually every culture and time period. In European history, such constraints can certainly be traced back to classical antiquity, if not before. The Greek practice of war, for example, operated under a series of conventions that were, for the most part, adhered to and which, when violated, brought genuine opprobrium, and sometimes worse, on the heads of the violaters. The ransoming of prisoners, the possibility of burying the dead who had fallen on the battlefield, the honouring of certain sacred truces (such as those celebrating the Olympic Games): these were conventions that had the effective force of law. When they were violated, the shock and anger was heartfelt, as Thucydides makes clear in his account of the

---

[9] O'Donovan, *The Just War Revisited*, p. 14, emphasis added.
[10] Ibid., p. 15.

Peloponnesian War.[11] It is perhaps worth adding, though, that many
of these restraints were meant to apply in general only in intra-Greek
wars; they were not held to apply to wars with others (though some
philosophers, perhaps including Plato, may have dissented from this
view).[12] The Romans, by contrast, while they also had complex conventions concerning war – indeed, in Rome the whole process of going
to war was heavily formalized – had few *in bello* constraints at hand
once a war was itself deemed legitimate, which led some medieval
commentators to use the term *bellum Romanum* – to describe a war
without limits or restraints.[13]

The just war tradition itself, however, emerges out of the encounter
of such general practices of war fighting and legitimation with specifically Christian concerns about the legitimacy of fighting at all.[14] And it
is this encounter that gives the tradition its early logic, much of its
power, a good deal of the tensions that still exist within it and, in

---

[11] See Thucydides, *History of the Peloponnesian War*, trans. Thomas Hobbes, ed.
David Grene (University of Chicago Press, 1989).

[12] See, for a good introduction, Josiah Ober, 'Classical Greek Times', in Michael
Howard, George Andreopoulos and Mark R. Schulman (eds.) *The Laws of War:
Constraints on Warfare in the Western World* (New Haven: Yale University
Press, 1994). Plato's ambivalence to the traditional Greek 'particularist' view
of conventions in general, and war in particular, can perhaps be seen in a
number of places in the *Dialogues* and *Letters* (notwithstanding the dubious
authenticity of many of the latter), perhaps most clearly in the passage in the
Republic where Socrates refers to the city built in speech as viable also for
non-Greeks 'beyond the limits of our vision' (though, of course, there is a question
about how one interprets the specific sense of any remark in the *Dialogues*). It is
also perhaps not entirely without significance that a number of the Hellenistic
schools that were avowedly critical of traditional Greek civic morality – for
example the Cynics and the Epicureans – claimed Platonic licence for this view.

[13] A good discussion of how the Romans saw war in general is in F.E. Adcock,
Roman Political Ideas and Practice (Michigan: Ann Arbor, 1964). See also the
discussion in Bruno Coppieters and Nick Fotion (eds.) *Moral Constraints on
War: Principles and Cases* (Lanham: Lexington Books, 2002).

[14] It is well known that early Christian communities were largely pacifist,
influenced by a literal reading of the Sermon on the Mount, and by a particular
view of the character of Christian witness. It is this view that one finds held up as
the legitimate way of thinking about war by many modern Christian pacifists,
perhaps most notably John Howard Yoder and Stanley Hauerwas, as discussed
in the last chapter. For a brilliant historical interpretation of the debates between
early Christians on this topic see Peter Brown, *The Rise of Western
Christendom*, 2nd edn (Oxford: Blackwell, 2003). Yoder's account of the
Christian basis of pacifism can be found in his *The Politics of Jesus* (Grand
Rapids, Mich.: W.B. Eerdmans, 1972).

particular, creates the assumptions out of which the distinction between *jus ad bellum* and *jus in bello* grows. However, it is worth emphasizing that this distinction does not appear at all in the work of those thinkers most associated with the early development of the tradition, Augustine of Hippo and Thomas Aquinas. Indeed, one of the most influential interpreters of the tradition today, James Turner Johnson, goes so far as to say that to all intents and purposes

there is no just war doctrine, in the classic form as we know it today, in either Augustine or the theologians or canonists of the high Middle Ages. This doctrine in its classic form, including both a *jus ad bellum* ... and a *jus in bello* ... does not exist before the end of the middle ages. Conservatively, it is incorrect to speak of classic just war doctrine existing before about 1500.[15]

Johnson's argument here is predicated on the claim that what came together to create what he terms 'classic just war doctrine' was a religious (that is to say theological and canonical) doctrine largely concerned with questions about the right to make war and a secular doctrine whose content was largely confined to discussions of the proper mode of fighting and which was derived from cultural constraints on violence, such as the knightly code and the civil law.

In this chapter I shall largely agree that, understood as an identifiable part of the just war tradition and as a coherent body of thought, the distinction between *jus ad bellum* and *jus in bello* does not pre-date the sixteenth century. While I do think that there is much of interest in earlier writers (most especially, I think, Augustine) that touches thinking about how war should be conducted), this argument has the merit of allowing us to concentrate to begin with on the key periods in the evolution of the *jus in bello* – not accidentally, I think, also the period in which the teleocratic approach to politics also developed and became, as I have stressed, increasingly dominant – roughly the early modern period (between about 1500 and 1758) and what I shall call the period of international juridicalization (roughly 1800–1950).

[15] See James Turner Johnson, *Ideology, Reason and the Limitation of War* (Princeton University Press, 1975), pp. 7–8. Similar points are made by John Finnis in 'The Ethics of War and Peace in the Catholic Natural Law Tradition', in Terry Nardin (ed.) *The Ethics of War and Peace: Religious and Secular Perspectives* (Princeton University Press, 1996) and by Thomas Pangle and Peter Ahrensdorf in *Justice among Nations: On the Moral Basis of Power and Peace* (Lawrence: University Press of Kansas, 1999).

The early modern *jus in bello*

Johnson's basic argument is that the modern *jus in bello* comes about largely through the rejection, initially by the neoscholastics and after them by many others, of the key arguments developed in the late medieval period for a parallelism between the just war doctrine and holy war doctrine. In this respect, it is a critique of the familiar claim – made by amongst others Roland Bainton – that thinking about war in the medieval period and after can basically be divided into three kinds: pacifist, just war and holy war.[16] By contrast, Johnson's view (and mine) is that holy war doctrine in the late medieval and early modern period is a version of just war not something separate from it – that is to say that, for Johnson, the language of holy war in the sixteenth and seventeenth centuries arises out of the same heritage of Christian thinking about war that generates what he refers to as modern just war thinking. The reason for this is straightforward enough. Holy war theorizing comes out of the medieval just war doctrine partly as a reaction to the political events of the late medieval and early modern period, specifically the Reformation and Counter-Reformation and the wars these movements engendered. As Johnson puts it:

Holy war doctrine and modern just war doctrine developed out of their common source during the same period of time – the approximately one hundred years of serious and virtually continuous warfare between Catholics and Protestants, the end of which might be put at the close of the Thirty Years War, but which in truth did not finally conclude until the Puritan revolution was fought in England.[17]

The point, then, is that holy war theorizing is really about how and why God might require us to use force to pursue His ends: it is about war for religion.

This claim can be strengthened still further if we ponder the additional claim, found perhaps most persuasively in Skinner's *Foundations of Modern Political Thought*, that many humanist responses to war – such as Erasmus's celebrated *Querela Pacis* (The Complaint of Peace), to which Bainton alludes in his discussion of pacifism – were also in very large part reactions to – and in some cases adaptations

---

[16] The mature statement of this view is to be found in Roland Bainton, *Christian Attitudes towards War and Peace* (Nashville, Tenn.: Abingdon Press, 1960).

[17] See Johnson, *Ideology, Reason and the Limitation of War*, p. 82.

of – the medieval just war doctrine. As Skinner says, glossing Erasmus, 'Christians often claim, [Erasmus] says, to be fighting a "just and necessary war"', even when they turn their weapons 'against another people holding exactly the same creed and professing the same Christianity'. But it is not necessity and justice that make them go to war; it is 'anger, ambition and folly' that supply 'the compulsory force'. If they were truly Christian, they would instead perceive that 'there is scarcely any peace so unjust that it is not preferable, upon the whole, to the justest war'. For Peace is 'the most excellent of all things' and if we wish to 'prove ourselves to be sincere followers of Christ' we must embrace Peace at all times.[18]

We can agree, then, that rather than there being three separate doctrines justifying war we have at most two, and even pacifism is strongly dependent upon the way that the just war is understood. Which brings us to the real origins of the manner in which we have come to understand the *jus in bello* in the modern period. The wellspring from which all else flows in this context is simple enough in outline: it is the School of Salamanca. To be sure, there are also influential voices in England (especially) and the Netherlands who shaped this particular climate of opinion – Johnson, for example, mentions especially Mathew Sutcliffe, William Fulbecke and William Ames – but the essential logic – which is what is central for us here – was provided by the School of Salamanca, and by two members of the school in particular, Francisco de Vitoria and Francisco Suarez.

Before turning to the specific arguments relevant to our concerns here, let me say something about the School itself. Salamanca was one of the most important and prestigious universities in Catholic Europe, and its most important chair of Theology was held by Vitoria for twenty years until his death in 1546. His lectures, on a wide variety of subjects, became central to the revival of scholastic and Thomistic philosophy both in his own day and for several centuries afterwards. He is generally regarded as the founder of the school, broadly neoscholastic and neo-Thomist in general philosophical and theological orientation, and sharing with Aquinas and with many of his own successors membership in the Dominican order. The school went on to boast a distinguished roster of theologians and philosophers, including Vitoria's

---

[18] Quentin Skinner, *The Foundations of Modern Political Thought*, 2 vols., vol I: *The Renaissance* (Cambridge University Press, 1978), p. 246.

two immediate successors in the pontifical chair of theology, Melchor Cano and Ferdinand de Soto, plus his supporter and representative of the school in their debate with the Spanish crown at the famous Valladolid debates in 1550, Bartoleme de Las Casas, and perhaps his greatest philosophical descendant, Suarez.[19]

Vitoria lectured many times on topics connected with war, including on conquest and the laws of war.[20] But the issues that occasioned his most influential reflections on the topic were all connected with the Spanish conquest of America and its treatment of the native inhabitants it found there, and his two most influential *relectiones*, *On the Indians* and *On the Laws of War*, both delivered in 1539, came about through his reflections on it.

Vitoria showed the direction his recasting of the just war was to take unambiguously in *De Indis* (more properly *De Indis et de Jure Belli Relectiones*).[21] Vitoria is straightforward: 'Difference of religion', he says, 'is not a cause of just war'. The only justification for war is wrong received, and the only way of identifying wrong received and therefore whether a war is just or not is through the application of the natural law, common to all, Christian and non-Christian alike. It was this claim that led him to state, controversially in his own day (to say the least), that the Spanish crown was not justified in using force against the non-Christian inhabitants of its New World colonies in order to deprive them of their property. This basic argument was supported and then developed by Suarez and it is important to see that while the basic

---

[19] A good general account of the philosophical and theological views of the School of Salamanca is Skinner, *Foundations*, vol. II, Chapter 5. The most thorough work discussing the school's understanding of war, concentrating especially on Vitoria and Suarez, is E.B.F. Midgely, *The Natural Law Tradition and the Theory of International Relations* (London: Elek Press, 1975); see especially Chapter 2. Though I have learned much from Midgely's analysis, I differ from him on some points of interpretation.

[20] Pagden and Lawrence (eds.) *Vitoria: Political Writings*; Pagden, *Lords of All the World*; Pangle and Ahrensdorf, *Justice among Nations*.

[21] Vitoria, as was the custom of the day at Salamanca, has left us with two collections of texts: lectures on Aquinas' *Summa Theologiae* and the *Sentences* of Peter Lombard, on both of which he lectured every year at Salamanca, during his twenty-year tenure of the chair, and a set of 'Relectiones' – literally *Re-Readings* – delivered on more formal occasions and as commentaries on particular passages or problems in a text. *De Indis* was initially delivered as a *relection* at Salamanca in 1539, after a period of growing concern on Vitoria's part with both the practice and the justification of the actions of the Spanish crown in its New World colonies.

position is predicated on traditional questions of what becomes (during the process of this elaboration) what we now call the *jus ad bellum*, it in fact begins to create that part of the tradition we call the *jus in bello* as well.

The pivot on which this evolution hinges is what Johnson calls the problem of simultaneous ostensible justice. The traditional view, in earlier just war thinkers and still in much of the secondary literature, both historical and philosophical, is that it is plainly incoherent to talk of a war being 'just on both sides'. Aquinas, for example, is usually read as insisting that a just war is one fought in response to some fault, a view we have seen Vitoria agreeing with. Yet if this is the case, then clearly there cannot be justice on both sides; indeed, this is the traditional view: 'In the case of each of the prospective belligerents having a claim on something in dispute, there must be no war, and if one occurs, it is not just but unjust on both sides at once.'[22]

But the position in Vitoria in particular is far more complex than this. He suggests that the possibility of justice on both sides presents us with an ethical dilemma: 'if each side is just, neither side may kill anyone from the other and therefore such a war both may and may not be fought'.[23] One reading of Vitoria on this topic suggests that he counsels (as many later Catholic thinkers, for example Jacques Maritain, have also done) arbitration in these contexts. But, crucially, he also suggests that one has to make a distinction between *genuine* just cause and *believed* just cause, or what he calls, in a key passage in *De Indis*, 'invincible ignorance'. The relevant passage is as follows:

There is no inconsistency ... in holding the war to be a just war on both sides, seeing that on one side there is right and on the other side there is invincible ignorance ... the rights of war which may be invoked against men who are really guilty and lawless differ from those which may be invoked against the innocent and the ignorant.[24]

The point about this is that, as William Fulbecke makes clear,[25] it behoves people fighting a war to assume that those opposing them are

---

[22] This is Johnson's formulation, in Johnson, *Ideology, Reason and the Limitation of War*, p. 186. He is here citing and discussing a classic 'traditional' Catholic reading, Alfred Vanderpol, *La Doctrine Scholastique du droit de guerre* (Paris: Pedone, 1919).

[23] Johnson, *Ideology, Reason and the Limitation of War*, p. 187.

[24] Vitoria, *De Indis*, section III, 7. This passage is highlighted also by Johnson.

[25] See Johnson, *Ideology, Reason and the Limitation of War*, p. 189.

guilty of ignorance rather than genuine malfeasance; in other words, this passage emphasizes – and this is something Vitoria and Suarez both elaborate later in their work – that while *in truth* (i.e in the sight of God) there is no such thing as a war just on both sides, human knowledge is not up to judging this with any degree of accuracy. The natural implication is that in fighting a war, one should develop as many restraints as possible given that those who oppose you may not be guilty of genuine fault, but merely of invincible ignorance.

It is this that raises the significance of the *jus in bello* and begins the process of separating out the two parts of the tradition as we understand it today. Vitoria, for example, was very well aware of the significance of this. It is in Vitoria that we first find the development of the Augustinian notions of right intent and the existing contemporary restrictions via canon law and the customs of arms, taken together as a restriction on how we should understand who is legitimately a combatant. The *jus in bello*, in other words, grows out of the notion of non-combatant immunity, and it does so because, as we have already seen, for Vitoria a just war can only be to right a wrong done, and wrongs are not done by an innocent person and thus war cannot be waged on the innocent. In Vitoria (and his successors in the School of Salamanca) this places a premium on the limitation of destructiveness not merely for moral reasons but for epistemic ones: we do not know who is in the right. However, at the centre of this is the claim that, fundamentally, war can only be waged to avenge a wrong done and in that claim, as we shall see, lies the beginnings not of a restriction of the use of force – as clearly was Vitoria's intent – but of its expansion.

Working from the position established by the School of Salamanca, the *jus in bello* develops in leaps and bounds in the ensuing period, although hardly in a linear fashion. It is generally assumed that the two most important contributors after Vitoria and Suarez were the Dutch humanist, jurist and political actor Hugo Grotius (1583–1645) and the German philosopher Samuel Pufendorf (1632–94), and that this movement of thought reaches its climax in the thought of Emmerich de Vattel (1714–67).[26] It is unnecessary, in the current context, to offer a complete reading of these thinkers (nor would it be possible to do so in

---

[26] Again, good general discussions can be found in Pangle and Ahrensdorf, *Justice Among Nations*, and David Boucher, *Political Theories of International Relations* (Oxford University Press, 2000).

reasonable compass) but something I think does need to be said about the influence they had on the emerging shape of the tradition.

Grotius, for example, develops the arguments of his neoscholastic predecessors in various ways, especially with regard to the *jus ad bellum*, but significantly in the case of the *jus in bello* his views are somewhat less restrictive than Vitoria's had been, though he admits that charity (at least for Christians) should limit the manner in which wars are prosecuted.[27] Then also, Grotius's thought has rather more to say about the *jus ad bellum* than the *jus in bello*, though he also has a good deal to say about the latter. The principles of non-combatant immunity, and their root in the *jus gentium* rather than theological speculation – and thus their significance for the *jus in bello* – are carried much further, however, by Locke and then by Vattel, in whom the tradition very much in its modern form is very clear. Indeed, it is in Vattel that the kinds of distinction relating to non-combatant immunity and indeed other kinds of restrictions of war's destructiveness begin to emerge in recognizably modern form. For Vattel it is not merely what one might call the 'attitude of innocence' that matters but rather the social function an individual performs. What is also significant in these thinkers is the emphasis they place on the just war as righting a wrong – punishing wrongdoing – rather than chiefly limiting destructiveness. It is far more pronounced than was the case in the School of Salamanca and the reason I think is obvious – the growing resonance of the sovereign state and how one might understand it.

From *jus gentium* to the laws of war

The keys to the development of the *jus in bello* in its modern form, then, were the developments sketched above, but to that we should add also the changes in military tactics and technology that the modern period witnessed. As is well known, beginning in the seventeenth century European armies began to develop levels of organization and

---

[27] The key text is, obviously, *De Jure Belli ac Pacis*. For the most interesting and thorough recent treatment of Grotius's arguments in connection with war and international relations see Renee Jeffery, *Hugo Grotius in International Thought* (London: Palgrave Macmillan, 2006). A discussion of the material relevant to Grotius, Locke and Vattel can be found in Chris Brown, Terry Nardin and Nicholas Rengger, *International Relations in Political Thought: Texts from the Ancient Greeks to the First World War* (Cambridge University Press, 2002). See especially Chapter 6.

discipline unknown since Roman times and this, coupled with the accelerating pace of technological change, led to new strategies and tactics, new military institutions and processes, and, of course, new attempts to restrain war and new developments in the context of theorizing about both war and its restraint.[28] But there was already at hand the just war tradition as we have seen it emerge from the fifteenth and sixteenth centuries, with the *jus in bello* very much to the fore, and so it is hardly surprising that it was in the language of this tradition that much of the new context was put. It is worth adding here, to return to Oakeshott's argument that I sketched in Chapter 1, that it is precisely this context (and period) that Oakeshott sees as the 'chief nourishment of the belief that the state is an enterprise association'.[29]

To begin with, the changes to the development of the just war tradition were relatively mild. The eighteenth century, often seen as a period of 'limited war', of course saw the emergence of various different versions of the just war, most especially Vattel's as discussed above, but following the Napoleonic Wars more radical changes were made to the established *jus in bello*.

In particular, the growing significance of formal international law in the years after 1860 became central to the changing character of the *jus in bello*, but another significant departure was the issuing of general regulations to established armies, the most celebrated example being the General Orders No. 100 or the *Instructions for the Government of Armies of the United States in the Field* prepared and mainly written by Francis Lieber, at the invitation of General in Chief Henry Wager Halleck, during the American Civil War.[30] In both cases the concern springs initially from the problem of defining who are combatants and who are not, and of course it does so in the context of a civil war which requires a treatment of irregular warfare which had previously not been discussed (except in the occasional discussions of the ethics of

---

[28] For a thorough and fascinating survey of the evolution of military technologies, strategies and tactics in the modern period, see especially Geoffery Parker, *The Military Revolution: Military Innovation and the Rise of the West 1500–1800* (Cambridge University Press, 1996).

[29] Michael Oakeshott, *On Human Conduct* (Oxford University Press, 1975), pp. 266–74.

[30] See, for an excellent discussion, James Turner Johnson, *The Just War Tradition and the Restraint of War* (Princeton University Press, 1981).

siegecraft in medieval writing on the just war) and which gave rise to a considered discussion of duties owed to prisoners of war, a subject only cursorily treated by theorists such as Grotius, Pufendorf and Vattel. At roughly the same time, the gradual process of codification of international law – indeed what one might call the 'project' of international law itself – begins to take shape[31] – and this has pronounced effects on the *jus in bello* including the formal adoption of agreements limiting and banning certain classes of weapons or particular types of action.

Such attempts pre-dated the nineteenth century, of course, as Roberts and Guelff point out, citing as an example the 1785 Treaty of Amity and Commerce between the United States and Prussia, which 'concluded with two articles making explicit and detailed provision for observance of certain basic rules if war were to break out between the two parties. The first article defined the immunity of merchants, women, children, scholars ... and others ... the Second specified proper treatment of prisoners of war.' [32] The latter part of the nineteenth century, however, saw a great increase of this kind of provision, and the high-water mark was unquestionably the adoption of the 1899 and 1907 Hague conventions on the law of war.

Since that point, the 'laws of war' have expanded and developed with new conventions being adopted and new machinery being developed on a fairly constant basis. These developments became yet more central after the Second World War with the Nuremberg and Tokyo tribunals and the adoption in 1948 of the Universal Declaration of Human Rights and the Genocide Convention. After 1991, with the old Cold War deadlock removed, still more effective legal action seeking to restrain types of warfare was promoted culminating in the establishments of the ad hoc tribunals for Rwanda and the former Yugoslavia and then, in 1998, the creation of a permanent International Criminal Court, to mention merely the most prominent such attempts.[33]

---

[31] See the account offered in Martti Koskenniemi, *The Gentle Civilizer of Nations: The Rise and Fall of International Law, 1880–1960* (Cambridge University Press, 2003).

[32] Adam Roberts and Richard Guelff, *Documents on the Laws of War*, 3rd edn (Oxford University Press, 2000), p. 4.

[33] The best general treatment is Best, *War and Law since 1945*, though it does not include detailed discussions of the International Criminal Court.

By this point, however, the *jus in bello* had effectively become 'juridicalized' in a manner unforeseen by its creators in the sixteenth century. The *jus in bello* had moved from being seen as part of the *ius gentium* (law of nations) to being seen as the 'laws of war', part of a *ius inter gentes* ('law between nations'). Given the prevailing view of the character of law, this marked a very real change in the way in which the *jus in bello* was understood. Since I will return to it briefly in a moment, it might be worthwhile saying something about the significance of this distinction.

To explain this I should say something first about the origins of the term *ius gentium*. The root, of course, is Roman law. The Romans distinguished between *ius*, that is, customary law and *lex*, essentially enacted law. *Lex*, because it is enacted at a particular time and place, can be repealed or amended, but *ius* was part of what we would now call case law. Civil law governing relations between Roman citizens – specific allocation of rights and responsibilities – was therefore *lex*, but civil law governing relations between Romans and others, or between others generally, if under Roman authority, was a matter of *ius*. Hence the general term that came to be used for these kinds of discussions was *ius gentium* (law governing *gentes* – nations).[34]

By the early modern period – when as we have seen the key moves in developing the distinction between the *jus in bello* and the *jus ad bellum* were made – there was a widespread discussion of the appropriate relationship between the *ius gentium* and other parts of law, especially natural law, but it gradually became clear that there are two distinct meanings to the term *ius gentium* that did not always sit happily together; it is significant that among the first people to discuss this in detail was one of the most important thinkers in the history of the *jus in bello*, Francisco Suarez. Suarez insists that while *ius gentium* is used to refer to the common laws of individual states which are in accordance with similar laws elsewhere and thus 'commonly accepted', it *ought* only to be used for 'law which all the various peoples and nations observe in their relations with one another'.[35]

---

[34] For a more elaborate discussion of this point see Brown et al., *International Relations*, pp. 318–23.

[35] This reference is from Suarez, 'On Laws and God the Lawgiver', in his *Selections from Three Works*, trans. G.L. Williams (Oxford: Clarendon Press, 1944), cited in Brown et al., *International Relations*.

Gradually, during the latter part of the seventeenth century and in the eighteenth century this indeed is what happened. But even by Vattel's time, while the *ius gentium* was seen in this way, it was still seen also as part of the natural law, as being intimately connected with other aspects of law. Thus, Vattel's *Les Droits des gens* (The Law of Nations) contains discussions of matters internal to states as well as matters that would now be seen as matters of relevance to public law as well as to 'international' law as we understand it today. The real change – the change that marks, I suggest, the crucial difference – does not come until the nineteenth and twentieth centuries and the dominance of legal positivism, the growing significance of teleocratic conceptions of the state and an international law constructed in their image. It is to this that we must now turn.

The modern just war

Let me start here by emphasizing – the point is certainly not original to me – that the revival of the just war tradition in the second half of the twentieth century was one that had been in large part brought about by events in the world, rather than principally through intellectual reflection. Examples of this are legion. Consider (for example) the debates over the carpet-bombing of German cities in the Second World War (echoing, of course, the Germans' own practice earlier in the war), which led to the protests of Bishop George Bell on traditional just war grounds – such bombing could only be the deliberate targeting of the innocent – and, most important of all, of course, the Holocaust and its aftermath. Added to that were the Nuremberg and Tokyo tribunals and, in due course, the creation and (let us not forget) the use of nuclear weapons to end the war against Japan.[36] All of these

---

[36] This, in fact, led to one of the first sustained deployments of the just war tradition in post-Wittgenstein Anglophone analytic philosophy, in that Elizabeth Anscombe – student, translator and heir of Wittgenstein – wrote two papers in which she excoriated the decision to use atomic weaponry. A deeply devout Catholic, Anscombe drew in fact on very traditional just war arguments (as had Bell in the controversy over strategic bombing) but her status in the philosophical world made her arguments stand out. It was also helpful that the first of the papers – 'Mr Truman's Degree' – was in fact a response to the proposal that Oxford (where Anscombe taught at the time) should award Harry Truman – the US President who authorized the dropping of the atomic bombs on Hiroshima and Nagasaki – an honorary degree. The essays are reprinted in

events forced a rethink of the traditional view that states simply had a right to use force in defence of their interests, whatever they took them to be, which had been the standard view of international society at least from Vattel onwards.[37]

Initially, it was largely in the area of religious thinking on questions of war and peace that the tradition was most obviously and most consciously rethought, perhaps unsurprisingly. Protestant theologians, most notably Paul Ramsey and later James Turner Johnson, refined the traditional inherited categories and sought to deploy them in modern contexts. But in Catholic social thought too, where the tradition had long been prominent and, given the influence of Aquinas and the School of Salamanca generally, unsurprisingly so, the tradition was revived and discussed at length.[38]

In both these contexts, but perhaps especially in the Catholic context, as John Finnis has remarked, the tradition was not, fundamentally, legalistic.[39] It sought to retain the casuistic flexibility that had marked the work of the School of Salamanca. But it nonetheless existed in the context of an international order very different from the one confronted by Vitoria. While theologically inspired just war writing in the modern context confronts, as Oliver O'Donovan has rightly said, a pluralism that recognizes 'a multitude of peoples aware of themselves and asserting themselves in claims to absolute sovereignty', it is also in this context that the classic just war writers (he mentions specifically

---

volume III of G.E.M. Anscombe, *Philosophical Papers* 3 vols. (Cambridge University Press, 1981).

[37] For a discussion of the significance of this claim see, inter alia, Richard Tuck, *The Rights of War and Peace: Political Thought and the International Order from Grotius to Kant* (Oxford University Press, 1999), Pangle and Ahrensdorf, *Justice among Nations,* and Boucher, *Political Theories of International Relations.*

[38] See especially Paul Ramsey, *The Just War: Force and Political Responsibility* (New York: Scribner, 1968) and also his *War and the Christian Conscience: How Shall Modern War Be Conducted Justly?* (Durham, NC: Duke University Press, 1961). Ramsey's student James Turner Johnson is perhaps the person who has done most to explore the history of the tradition especially in *Ideology, Reason and the Limitation of War* and *The Just War Tradition and the Restraint of War,* but he has also illuminatingly discussed the content of the ideas; see *Can Modern War Be Just?* (New Haven: Yale University Press, 1984) and *Morality and Contemporary Warfare.*

[39] See Finnis's excellent account of the Catholic natural law tradition in 'The Ethics of War and Peace'.

Vitoria, Suarez and Grotius) look 'to the *ius gentium* to provide a bulwark against nationalist absolutism'.[40]

The problem, of course, is that the world, and the international system, has become far more marked by 'nationalist absolutism' in the centuries since the early modern period. And alongside that has developed the long and hugely complex process of secularization[41] which has – at least on the surface – created additional problems for a theologically framed just war tradition. It was therefore inevitable that, amongst other things, the renaissance of the just war tradition would also take explicitly secular forms. It is to this – and to one in particular – that I shall turn in a moment. But first I want to dwell briefly on the significance of the shift.

As a tradition of practical reasoning, the just war tradition was closely linked to related understandings of practical life in the late medieval and early modern periods, before such understandings were eclipsed by the rise of other powerful ways of relating theoretical reflection to practical activity and also, not incidentally, the rise of the modern state as a political form and what flowed from it (for example, in due course, the development of international positive law). In other words, in the late medieval and early modern periods the just war tradition was essentially a casuistical tradition, in which the resources of the tradition were deployed in specific contexts as seemed appropriate and reasonable and where balances between – for example – restraint and righting a wrong could be struck.

The gradual undermining of casuistical modes of practical reason in the seventeenth and eighteenth centuries was bound therefore to have an effect on the just war tradition and it duly did so. As Albert R. Jonsen and Stephen Toulmin have made clear in their study of the rise and fall of casuistry as a method of moral argument and reflection, it was the rise to prominence in the mid to late seventeenth century of modes of argumentation that took an essentially 'scientistic' form that consigned casuistry to an initially slow but increasingly rapid decline.[42] The rise to dominance in the modern world of notions that emphasize universally applicable moral rules by definition makes the kind of

[40] See O'Donovan, *The Just War Revisited*, p. 12.
[41] Among many important studies, a recent, and remarkable, analysis is Charles Taylor, *A Secular Age* (Cambridge, Mass.: Harvard University Press, 2007).
[42] Albert Jonsen and Stephen Toulmin, *The Abuse of Casuistry: A History of Moral Reasoning* (Berkeley: University of California Press, 1986).

moral reasoning prevalent in the medieval and early modern just war tradition – casuistical, particularist, case-based – extremely difficult.

In later work Toulmin has elaborated this process and offered a persuasive argument to the effect that the rise of these styles of reasoning, the evolution of modern science and technology, and the evolution of the modern states system are best seen as one movement of thought and practice.[43] A casuistical and particularist tradition was bound to have very considerable difficulty in accommodating itself to the dominant styles of moral reasoning of the modern age which became increasingly universalistic and rule-governed in the nineteenth and twentieth centuries. But at the same time, the evolution of positivist conceptions of law and, beginning in the mid nineteenth century, of the project of the 'codification' of international law (and especially of the 'laws of war') along positivist lines seemed to open up the possibility of an accommodation. Law after all, on the positivist understanding, is principally a system of rules which can be held to be universally valid within its own sphere.

But the rider to this, of course, is that (at least in origin) positivist conceptions of law were also tied to a particular model of the state and thus by accommodating itself to positivist law, the just war tradition also accommodated itself to the underpinning of that form of law, the state seen as the embodiment of 'command'. It is in that sense that 'modern just war' can rightly be seen as statist despite the obvious fact that in origin the just war tradition is not wedded to any particular concept of political form. Moreover, by yoking itself to this concept of the state the tradition also, *ipso facto*, yokes itself to the self-images of that state and its role and function. Inasmuch as the dominant (in the sense of being generally believed) modern conception of the state at least in most cases is teleocratic – a provider of goods and services, an active promoter of common purposes in many different contexts – then it is hardly surprising that the just war tradition will, perforce, accommodate itself to this image of the state, and of politics, more than to any other.

In the second part of this chapter I want to say something about the character of that revival and what impact it has had on the way in

---

[43] See, most especially, Toulmin's *Cosmopolis: The Hidden Agenda of Modernity* (University of Chicago Press, 1992), but also his more recent *Return to Reason* (Cambridge, Mass.: Harvard University Press, 2001).

which the tradition is understood and deployed. For it is in the context of this revival, I want to argue, that the entwining of the tradition with teleocratic conceptions of the state – and of politics more generally – is most visible. And it is in this entwining that the concerns that will occupy my next two chapters are most deeply rooted.

In order to do this, I shall divide the contemporary just war tradition into three distinct groups, which I shall term the juridical just war, the Christian just war and the cosmopolitan just war. To some extent these groups are an artificial construction, since many just war writers have feet in more than one camp. But the division has the merit of allowing me to focus on the ways in which the diversity and plurality of the tradition – which have always (as we have seen) been part of it and still are – to some extent mask the degree to which the tradition today is increasingly shaped by engagement with teleocratic assumptions, and thus also mask what (in my view) are the most problematic implications of that fact.

The juridical just war

I will begin with the juridical just war since it will be my argument that it is this version of the tradition that is the most significant, both academically and politically, and which, to a greater or lesser extent, has influenced the other versions of the tradition. I want to begin here by looking at the arguments of Michael Walzer, unquestionably the most influential academic writer on the just war in the twentieth century. Walzer has, of course, been one of the most influential general political theorists of the past forty years in Anglophone circles. He has written across a very wide range of topics in political theory and has also been very active as a public intellectual, co-editing the leading magazine of the American centre left, *Dissent*, for many years.[44] This

---

[44] Aside from *Just and Unjust Wars: A Moral Argument with Historical Illustrations*, 3rd edn (New York: Basic Books, 2000(1977)), Walzer's most influential academic studies have probably been *Spheres of Justice* (Oxford: Blackwell, 1983) and *Interpretation and Social Criticism* (Cambridge, Mass.: Harvard University Press, 1987) but earlier in his career he wrote on the political thought of the English Civil War (*Revolution of the Saints* (Cambridge, Mass.: Harvard University Press, 1965)), on the debates surrounding the French Revolution and the execution of Louis XVI (*Regicide and Revolution* (Cambridge University Press, 1974)) and produced many essays on various aspects of political thought and political thinking. Mostly these have been

combination of academic and political influence is unusual and partly accounts for the influence of many of his writings, including – perhaps especially – his writings on war.

In a symposium published to mark the twenty-fifth anniversary of the publication of *Just and Unjust Wars*, Michael Joseph Smith made the point that 'since its appearance the book has been a standard text at universities throughout the world – as well as at military academies including West Point'. He adds that 'I would ... name it without hesitation as the indispensable modern classic in the field. Most of the people I know who teach in this area would agree.'[45]

Indeed, I would too. So we can agree, then, that Walzer's book is certainly amongst the most influential books to have revitalized the just war tradition in the post-war period. It is, as Smith suggests, and as a host of other writers have testified, a magnificent book and contains within it some of the best just war writing of recent decades.

It is worth emphasizing one other thing. Walzer is not, of course, a legal theorist and so it might seem odd to ascribe to him juridical views on war. But what I mean by 'juridical' is not a narrow or black-letter legalism. Rather I want to emphasize that what I am calling the juridical just war is a just war account that takes the norms and conventions of the just war as themselves constitutive of the tradition and believes that there is no real need to refer to anything outside such norms or conventions. One might refer to it as the 'conventionalist' just war, except that in the cases of many who have followed Walzer, the formal juridical element is far stronger than it is in Walzer himself and so it seems fair to stay with the term 'juridical' for this set of readings of the just war in general.

The general argument of *Just and Unjust Wars* is well enough known to obviate the need for any kind of detailed summary of it so, instead, I want to concentrate here on two aspects of the book that have been crucial to its success but which have also, I think, deepened

collected as volumes of essays; see especially *Obligations: Essays on Disobedience, War and Citizenship* (Cambridge, Mass.: Harvard University Press, 1970) and *Thick and Thin: Moral Argument at Home and Abroad* (University of Notre Dame Press, 1994). Some of his most influential essays have recently been collected and edited by a Britain-based admirer, David Miller, as *Thinking Politically: Essays In Political Theory* (New Haven: Yale University Press, 2007).
[45] Michael Joseph Smith, 'Growing Up with *Just and Unjust Wars*: An Appreciation', *Ethics and International Affairs*, 11, 1997, 3–18, pp. 3–4.

the serious tension in the modern just war, in the context of the two assumptions that I suggested underpinned it: limitation of destructiveness on the one hand and elimination and/or punishment of wrongdoing on the other. These two aspects also display the increasing dependence of the modern just war in general on teleocratic notions of the state, and of politics more generally.

The first of these aspects is the way in which Walzer sets up his account of the just war in the first place. This has a good deal to do both with the origins of the book and Walzer's more general philosophical assumptions. In the preface to the original edition of *Just and Unjust Wars,* Walzer disarmingly tells us, 'I did not begin by thinking about war in general, but about particular wars, above all about the American intervention in Vietnam.' He adds that 'in those years of angry controversy, I promised myself that one day I would try to set out the moral argument about war in a quiet and reflective way ... I want to defend the business of arguing, as we did and as most people do, in moral terms.' He goes on:

> my starting point is the fact that we do argue, often to different purposes to be sure, but in a mutually comprehensible fashion: else there would be no point in arguing. We justify our conduct; we judge the conduct of others ... these justifications and judgments ... are ... a legitimate subject of study. Upon examination they reveal, I believe, a comprehensive view of war as a human activity and a more or less systematic moral doctrine, which sometimes, but not always, overlaps with established legal doctrine.[46]

This general argument seems to me to be right, in that it does, I think, chime with the way most people think about moral decision making in general and moral thinking about war in particular. Walzer is quite right also to say that the framework for moral thinking about war overlaps with, but is not reducible to, legal thinking about war and he is also quite right to say, as he does a moment later, that 'the proper method of practical morality is casuistic in character'.[47] This claim flows from his concern with what he calls 'the present structure of the moral world'[48] rather than with either possible ideal worlds (which are not ours and which, he suggests, are often the focus of philosophical attempts to understand morality) or the making of the moral world, which would involve detailed historical reconstruction of the just

---

[46] All the above quotations are from Walzer, *Just and Unjust Wars*, pp. xvii–xix.
[47] Ibid., p. xxii.   [48] Ibid., p. xix.

war tradition. I also think (as I am sure Walzer does, though he nowhere explicitly makes this point) that this way of reasoning about practical morality is precisely the way in which the just war tradition itself reasoned, from Ambrose and Augustine to the neoscholastics of the sixteenth century.[49]

The problem is that as Walzer moves into his *analysis* of his 'just and unjust' wars, these claims recede and a rather more programmatic account of the tradition takes their place. Most especially the way that he sets up the 'legalist paradigm' and the 'domestic analogy' in fact does the opposite of what his opening preface suggests it should do. In the first place he adopts, absolutely centrally, and from the beginning, the assumption that the principal agents of war are states, and thus he structures the legalist paradigm around his treatment of the 'rights' of political communities considered as (in the main at least) states. These rights, Walzer tells us, are merely the collective form of individual rights. However, he concedes:

The process of collectivisation is a complex one, [but] it is best understood ... as it has commonly been understood since the seventeenth century, in terms of social contract theory ... contract is a metaphor for a process of association and mutuality, the ongoing character of which the state claims to protect against external encroachment ... the moral standing of a particular state [therefore] depends upon the reality of the common life it protects and the extent to which the sacrifices required by that protection are willingly accepted and thought worthwhile.[50]

This way of thinking then generates, he argues, what he calls the 'legalist paradigm' which, however it might be slightly modified or reworked in practice (and he accepts that it would be), is the basic way we should ground and frame the just war tradition: 'It is', he tells us, 'our baseline, our model, the fundamental structure for the moral comprehension of war.'[51]

---

[49] This is, obviously, a large claim. And, of course, I am not suggesting that there are no differences between the original formulations of the tradition in Ambrose and Augustine and the School of Salamanca's version of it in the sixteenth and early seventeenth century. The point is merely to say that to all intents and purposes the general cast of the tradition for much of its existence into modern times was as a casuistic tradition of moral reflection not as a 'merely' juristic one. Of course that does not solve – as we shall see – a different problem, which is how Aristotelian the casuistry in question has to be.

[50] Walzer, *Just and Unjust Wars*, pp. 52–4.   [51] Ibid., p. 61.

Unavoidably, such a view sets up the just war as fundamentally state-based and connected with the language of rights as it has evolved and developed within modernity, and in particular, as we shall see in a moment, it connects the tradition centrally with a teleocratic conception of the state. However one interprets these facts, they incline the tradition to a more juristic and less casuistic reading than Walzer's opening remarks indicated was his intention. They do so for the simple reason that to structure an account of the tradition on the basis of rights language and social contract theory inevitably slots it into the form of modern political vocabulary that engages in 'rights talk' and what follows from that. Of course, in Walzer's own treatment of the just war as a whole, casuistic elements remain in place (most especially in his discussion of the *jus in bello* in parts 3 and 5 of *Just and Unjust Wars*) but they are, I think, to a large extent vitiated by the overall setting of the *jus ad bellum*. And, inasmuch as Walzer's text has been the most influential academic and secular treatment of the tradition, this way of thinking about the tradition has become gradually sedimented more generally in the wider intellectual culture.

It is worth emphasizing that this argument is echoed in the more general approach to politics manifested in Walzer's wider writings.[52] While he has always emphasized the importance of civil society and voluntary associations – families, clubs, unions and the like – and while he is an authentic pluralist of a very recognizable American type, he has also emphasized very strongly the centrality of what he calls 'democratic citizenship' as the glue that holds political community together, and the point of citizenship is the common purposes citizens have *qua* citizens. It is those that allow their citizenship to 'trump' their particular interests and engagements, and such a view of common interests (and goods) inevitably aligns Walzer with at least some versions of teleocracy.

There is one final point I want to make in connection with Walzer's recapture of the just war. Whatever might have been the case initially (and it is clear that Walzer's intention had always been, quite rightly, to try and look at the phenomenon of war as a general part of the human moral realm), the events in the world since the publication of Walzer's book have tended to foreground certain issues over others. As Walzer

---

[52] See especially Walzer, *Spheres of Justice and Politics and Passion: Towards a More Egalitarian Liberalism* (New Haven: Yale University Press, 2004).

himself notes[53] (and the comment is echoed in Michael Joseph Smith's reconsideration of *Just and Unjust Wars*)[54] the question of intervention (which had occupied only a small part of the original treatment) has become much more important, and in Walzer's treatment of intervention, while the statecentric and legalistic character of his account was dramatically obvious, his reluctance to countenance anything other than a very limited right of intervention looks like (and to some extent was, I think) a recognition of the abiding power of the tradition's primary task of limiting the destructiveness of war. However, Walzer's argument was also due to the strongly teleocratic form his conception of political community in general and the state in particular takes. In his recent writing, however, Walzer has given considerable ground to his critics on these issues and admitted a right of rescue rather more generous than his initial treatment allowed.[55] The point I want to make here, however, is that by understanding the state in the way that he does, a conception of the state as a purveyor of justice becomes almost impossible to resist, even when he would want to, as we shall see in more detail in Chapter 5.

Whilst Walzer has been the most influential figure in what I am terming the juridical just war, he has hardly been alone. But it is worth adding that many contemporary writers focus on the just war as *a way of asking questions about* the legitimacy of force rather than specifically *evaluating* the idea of the use of force per se. One finds aspects of this more recently in writers such as Matthew Evangelista,[56] Cian O'Driscoll[57] and Alex Bellamy, whose work I will take as representative here. Bellamy's *Just Wars: From Cicero to Iraq* is a major treatment of both the historical trajectory of the just war tradition and the dilemmas of that tradition in the context of contemporary wars.[58] It is

---

[53] See Walzer, *Just and Unjust Wars*, preface to 3rd edn, p. xi.

[54] See Smith, 'Growing up with *Just and Unjust Wars*'; cf. 'Perhaps no part of *Just and Unjust Wars* has inspired greater debate and controversy than its discussion of intervention' (p. 15).

[55] See especially 'The Politics of Rescue', in Walzer, *Arguing about War* (New Haven: Yale University Press, 2004).

[56] Matthew Evangelista, *Law, Ethics and the War on Terror* (Cambridge: Polity Press, 2008). For a fuller discussion of Evangelista's book see my review essay in *Perspectives on Politics*, 7, 2009: 937–9.

[57] Cian O'Driscoll, *Renegotiation of the Just War Tradition and the Right to War in the Twenty First Century* (London: Palgrave Macmillan, 2008).

[58] Alex Bellamy, *Just Wars: From Cicero to Iraq* (Cambridge: Polity Press, 2006).

divided into two parts. The first – 'Mapping the Just War Tradition' – is concerned with the development of the tradition historically from antiquity to the present. The second – 'Contemporary issues' – is concerned with the current shape of the tradition and with its approach to four important issues: terrorism, pre-emption, aerial bombing and humanitarian intervention.

Throughout the book, Bellamy sets out to show that the just war tradition has been, from its beginning, really not so much a single tradition but rather a broad intertwining of competing and collaborating traditions that are united simply by the task of trying to judge normatively acts of violence. The tradition, he argues, should fundamentally be seen as making claims about the legitimacy of particular acts of force in either *ad bellum* or *in bello* contexts. This claim is derived from Ian Clark's work on international legitimacy (also influential on O'Driscoll), where it is assumed that there are two approaches governing legitimacy which Clark calls 'substantive' – seeing acts as legitimate if they conform to certain rules – and 'procedural' – where the focus is on the manner in which decisions are reached. Clark, and in the current context Bellamy, opt for a version of the procedural account, that emphasizes that 'legitimacy claims are articulated and assessed by reference to three subordinate areas of norms ... legality, morality and constitutionality ... The just war tradition provides a legitimacy framework for encompassing three norms through its three main sub-traditions [namely natural law, or morality, positive law, or legality and realism, or constitutionality].'[59] This, then, provides the shape of the historical narrative that Bellamy undertakes in the first part of the book, tracing the evolution of these three traditions and the gradual intertwining of them into the modern just war tradition.

In his conclusion, Bellamy, argues that 'rather than being a theory or checklist used to determine whether a particular war is just or unjust, the just war tradition offers a framework that diverse communities use to debate the legitimacy of wars ... the tradition itself contains many competing ethical theories, each of which offers a different way of interpreting the legitimacy framework ... Viewed this way, the tradition poses a series of questions but provides few authoritative answers itself.'[60] By adopting the particular account of

[59] Ibid., p. 7.   [60] Ibid., p. 229.

legitimacy he does, Bellamy produces a very thoughtful narrative, emphasizing the disparate elements that go to make up the modern just war tradition. But there are two issues he does not really address.

First, this approach does not provide any method for assessing the truth claims of the tradition. By focusing on legitimacy as procedure, Bellamy – and much of the 'juridical' just war tradition in general, I suggest – dodges the question of how we are to understand the moral claims made in the tradition: how any of the claims, at any given point in time, have actual moral force. A substantive view of legitimacy would not have that luxury – legitimacy in terms of adherence to certain rules requires a reason for supposing such rules as having authority.

Second – and most important in the current context – Bellamy's just war account, like Walzer's, becomes tied up with certain conceptions of statehood and what (to use Chris Reus-Smit's phrase) the 'moral purpose of the state' should be seen to be.[61] And indeed it is here that the first point becomes most striking. For in the absence of a standard of judgement that could provide an assessment of the truth claims of the tradition – such as the traditional 'natural law' framing the tradition provided – it is almost inevitable that it will take on the moral colouring (as it were) of the institutions that provide legitimacy in its given context. In other words, in modern times, the state and the conceptions of politics dominant in the state. I will come back to the precise manner in which this occurs a little later on.

The Christian just war

To what extent, however, does this apply to what I will term here the 'Christian just war', that is to say accounts of the tradition that assert its theological or religious underpinnings? For it is worth saying that if the most generally influential version of the modern just war is what I have been calling the juridical just war, explicitly religious versions of the just war have by no means lost their power or influence.

---

[61] See Christian Reus-Smit, *The Moral Purpose of the State* (Cambridge University Press, 1999).

At least three very influential contemporary just war writers, Jean Bethke Elshtain, Oliver O'Donovan and James Turner Johnston,[62] write from explicitly religious premises and prior to Walzer, perhaps the most generally influential just war thinker of the twentieth century was Paul Ramsey, a Protestant theologian.

The question is whether these religious or theological commitments change the general shape of the way the tradition is understood and deployed. And here I think the short answer is that in some contexts they do, but in many they do not. The Catholic Church, for example, has continually upheld just war teaching in theory but over the last thirty years, during the pontificates of both John Paul II and Benedict XVI, has been markedly reluctant to admit to it in practice. I think that the reason for this is straightforward enough. Catholic social teaching, really from *Rerum Novarum* onwards, has been sceptical, sometimes heavily so, about state power. For the Church the contemporary state can only have derivative significance, and it is therefore extremely reluctant to admit the kinds of justification in general that states most usually give for their actions. This does not mean that the Church in general has become pacifist – the traditional logic of the just war still holds – but since contemporary international law and the general contextual setting of the contemporary use of force is shaped by the logic of state power – and state power moreover seen in terms of a teleocratic conception of politics – it does mean that the Church is likely to withhold general approval for particular actions taken in accordance with that logic.

Of course, other theological positions do not mandate or require adherence to Catholic social thought (though it is significant how close some, like Elshtain – by birth a Lutheran – are to them), but it is also, I think, significant that it is in contexts where a religious understanding of the polity is most obviously to the fore – for example in the United States – that the contemporary just war and teleocratic ideas about the

---

[62] We have already met O'Donovan and Johnson in Chapter 2. Elshtain, of course, is a very influential contemporary political theorist who, much like Walzer, has written about many aspects of contemporary local and global politics other than war. Her most significant writings on the just war are *Women and War* (Brighton: Harvester, 1987), *Augustine and the Limits of Politics* (University of Notre Dame Press, 1995), and *Just War against Terror* (New York: Basic Books, 2003). For an assessment of the latter in particular see my 'Just a War Against Terror? Jean Bethke Elshtain's Burden and American Power', *International Affairs*, 80, 1, 2004.

modern state have most obviously gone hand in hand. This has been perhaps especially marked after the 9/11 attacks and goes some way to providing an explanation of the manner in which just war thinkers sought to justify the US response. Witness, for example, Elshtain's powerful and characteristically eloquent apologia for her book *Just War Against Terror*:

I wrote this book because I have been provoked by much of what has been written and said about terrorism and our response to it; because September 11 2001 reminded me of what it means to be an American citizen; because I come from a small people, Volga Germans, who would have been murdered or exiled ... had they remained in Russia rather than making the wrenching journey to America ... because I am a woman who believes women must have scope to exercise their educated powers to the fullest; because I am a believer who believes that other believers have the same rights that I do ... because I also believe that with our rights come responsibilities, including the responsibility to reflect on the use of force and *whether it can ever be used to promote justice*; and because I share the commitment ... to a robust culture of democratic argument ... An image that crowds out many others in my mind is that of tens of thousands fleeing New York City by foot. As I watched and wept, I recalled something I had said many times in my classes on war: 'Americans don't have living memories of what it means to flee a city in flames. Americans have not been horrified by refugees fleeing burning cities.' No more. Now we know. (emphasis added)[63]

Note, in the emphasized passage, the reference to using force to promote justice, which is the characteristic theme, as I have suggested, of the modern just war entwined as it is with teleocratic conceptions of politics. In the rest of Elshtain's argument this connection is even more apparent. The two key chapters here are the last two, chapters 11 and 12. In these, Elshtain tries to argue not just that there is such a thing as a just use of force and that we have in the campaign in Afghanistan an example of it but also that it is a specific example of a special responsibility generated by great power and current circumstances, which puts together 'warmaking, peacekeeping and justice' in a very specific set of ways.[64] This claim, essentially Elshtain's version of the arguments I will consider in detail in Chapter 4, amounts to suggesting that the current context is especially dangerous and requires especially calibrated responses. There are a number of these. The first, again derived

[63] Elshtain, *Just War against Terror*, p. 7.   [64] Ibid., p. 158.

from Arendt, claims that states are central to democratic life in that states provide an environment that creates vibrant civil societies that are, in turn, connected to each other. Thus, 'states in which there is a democratic deficit are denuded of a flourishing civil society'. This weakens the otherwise pronounced tendency – Elshtain accepts it is clearly not a certainty – in international relations for the evolution of more democratic-rights-based communities. Rights are robust, however, only if they become part of the 'statutory armamentarium of states'.[65] The much-vaunted power and roles of non-governmental organizations, she argues, are *dependent upon* a culture of strong rights-protecting states and not a substitute for it. At the end of World War Two, Arendt had insisted that human dignity needed a new guarantee;[66] and rights are the guarantee, Elshtain argues, but then she asks, who will be the guarantor?

Her answer is stark and unambiguous. 'There is no state except the United States with the power and (we hope) the will to play this role.' For Elshtain, true international justice is defined as the 'equal claim of all persons to [have] coercive force deployed on their behalf if they are victims of one of the many horrors attendant upon radical political instability' and in this less-than-ideal world, absent an international body that could act as guarantor (and we *are* absent it) then

the one candidate to guarantee this principle is the United States, for two reasons: equal regard is the foundation of our own polity and we are the only superpower ... As the world's superpower, America bears the responsibility to help guarantee ... international stability, whether much of the world wants it or not. This does not mean that we can or should rush around imposing solutions everywhere. It does mean that we are obliged to evaluate all cries for justice and relief from people who are being preyed upon whether by non state enforcers (like terrorists) or by state sponsored enforcers. We, the powerful, must respond to attacks against persons who cannot defend themselves because they, like us, are human beings, hence equal in regard to us, and because they, like us, are members of states, or

---

[65] Ibid., pp. 161–2.
[66] Arendt's original claim is made in the first edition of *The Origins of Totalitarianism* (New York: Harcourt Brace Jovanovich, 1951). For an essay that argues a similar case to Elshtain's but in more detail, see Jeffrey Isaac, *Democracy in Dark Times* (Ithaca, NY: Cornell University Press, 1998), Chapter 4.

would-be states, whose primary obligation is to protect the lives of those who inhabit their polities.[67]

In later chapters I will come back to why I think such a view is so profoundly mistaken, but its significance in linking even the Christian just war with a strongly teleocratic conception of politics cannot, I think, be gainsaid.

The cosmopolitan just war

Neither the juridical just war nor the Christian just war necessarily changes the direction of a good deal of the extant tradition. Indeed, both see themselves as manifesting the central parts of what it is to be a tradition in the relevant sense and, as I have argued, do so in ways indebted to, and to some extent dependent upon, teleocratic conceptions of politics. But the third trajectory I want briefly to discuss here does rather more. It seeks, effectively, to take the tradition in what would be seen as a very different direction indeed: away from the statist assumptions that dominate the arguments of a Walzer, an Elshtain or even a Ramsey or a Johnson.

In calling this trajectory the 'cosmopolitan' just war, I mean to link it with cosmopolitan political theory more generally, on which it avowedly draws and to which it avowedly seeks to contribute. Of course, contributors to the cosmopolitan just war do not all agree with one another, but they do all seek to untie the close links that have bound the tradition to the state in dominant versions of the tradition. Writers who might be included under this rubric would include the aforementioned Shue and McMahan, David Rodin, Tony Coady, Cecile Fabre and, more tangentially but still important, Simon Caney and Toni Erskine, both writing from a broadly analytical philosophic perspective.[68] A rather different – and rather less

---

[67] Elshtain, *Just War against Terror*, pp. 168–70.

[68] For representative statements of their views on topics connected with just war, see Henry Shue and David Rodin (eds.) *Preemption: Military Action and Moral Justification* (Oxford University Press, 2007); Henry Shue and David Rodin (eds.) *Just and Unjust Warriors* (Oxford University Press, 2006); David Rodin, *War and Self Defence* (Oxford University Press, 2002); Jeff McMahan, *Killing in War* (Oxford University Press, 2009); C.A.J. Coady, *Morality and Political Violence* (Oxford University Press, 2008); Cecile Fabre, 'Cosmopolitanism, Just War and Legitimate Authority', *International Affairs*, 84, 5, 2008; Simon

analytical – cosmopolitan just war account can be found in the work of Patrick Hayden.[69]

Coady sets up the starting point of the cosmopolitan just war very well in his most recent book.

> My use of the expression political violence includes war as the primary instance of such violence but it is also meant to cover other violent activities that some would not include under the heading of war ... terrorism, armed intervention (for 'humanitarian' or other purposes), armed revolution, violent demonstrations or attacks by citizens aimed at less than the overthrow of their government and the deployment of mercenary companies or individuals.[70]

That is a view that would be broadly shared by other cosmopolitans. Moreover, they would also share the assumption that the justification for the use of force is not limited – as they argue traditional just war writing suggests it is – to 'legitimate political communities' but can be vested in groups of individuals or even individuals acting alone. The scholar who presses this point most thoroughly is Fabre, but the focus on individual responsibility for the waging of war is also heavily emphasized by McMahan and by Rodin (though, in an indication that not all cosmopolitan just war theorists would go this far, Shue notes some doubts about this).

The chief point here is that, unlike some in the juridical just war camp, for example, the cosmopolitan just war faction does try and engage in formal evaluation but tries to free such evaluations from what it sees as the unnecessarily restrictive limitations of requiring 'legitimate authority' where that is tied to specific forms of political community such as the modern state. Surely then, in cosmopolitan just war theorizing we might be seeing a rather different orientation in contemporary just war writing, one not wedded to the state – thus not perhaps to teleocratic conceptions of politics?

Caney, *Justice Beyond Borders: Towards a Global Political Theory* (Oxford University Press, 2005); and Toni Erskine, *Embedded Cosmopolitanism: Duties to Strangers and Enemies in a World of Dislocated Communities* (Oxford University Press, 2008).

[69] See especially Patrick Hayden, 'Security, Beyond the State: Cosmopolitanism, Peace and the Role of Just War Theory', in Mark Evans (ed.) *Just War Theory: A Reappraisal* (Edinburgh University Press, 2005).

[70] Coady, *Morality and Political Violence*, p. 3.

The crucial point to note here is that, for all the differences – real and not unimportant as they are – cosmopolitan just war accounts are essentially grounded in the way in which the tradition has been reformulated in the twentieth century. They do not, in other words, fundamentally change the manner in which the just war tradition has come to view the relationship between the punishment of wrongdoing (now increasingly seen as the elimination of injustice) and the restriction of the use of force. Indeed, as we will see in chapters 4 and 5, in some respects they push the tradition even further down the road of the permissive use of force. If we think back to the argument of Chapter 1, that is perhaps unsurprising. For in the twentieth – and now the twenty-first – century, teleocratic conceptions of politics do not apply to states alone but also to other forms of political agency including (for example) intergovernmental agencies such as the United Nations. The cosmopolitans wish to remove the state – or to find political agents more appropriate than the state – but they still see politics in the way that teleocratic understandings of the state suggest we should.

The parting of the ways

It is time to take stock. I have argued that the just war tradition, roughly from the sixteenth century onwards, has been uneasily saddled with a tension between the limitation of destructiveness and the punishment of wrongdoing. Whilst the initial development of just war doctrine emphasized the limitation of destructiveness, partly for moral and partly for epistemic reasons, the subsequent development of the tradition, especially the prevalence of the *jus in bello*, became increasingly prone to focus on the punishment of wrongdoing which – in the mid–late twentieth century – became in its turn chiefly associated with the promotion of justice or at least the elimination of gross injustice. I also argued that this is leading the tradition to adopt a more permissive attitude to the use of force.

In one sense, of course, this is merely to echo one of the longest-standing criticisms of the just war tradition as a whole: that it simply encourages rather than discourages the use of force and that it is, effectively, complicit with a ruinously expensive (in both material and moral senses) war system. This kind of complaint goes back at least (as we have seen) to Erasmus. To this can be added the modern concern that the *in bello* constraints, which effectively recognize and formalize the legality of at least some aspects of war fighting, clash with a presumed illegality of the use of force as such, which seems to be implied by some international agreements (for example, the Kellogg–Briand pact of 1928 and the UN Charter). As Roberts and Guelff point out,[71] however, neither of these two documents completely rules out resort to force and the whole point and thrust of the development of the *jus in bello*, as we have seen, has been to seek the implementation of the laws of war even in situations where there may not be a legitimate *ad bellum* reason. Furthermore it seems unlikely (to put it mildly) that the use of force by states, or other agents in world politics, would cease whether or not there is a just war tradition. Therefore I would suggest that in this context, at any rate, the tradition can be defended against its critics. One hardly needs the just war tradition to 'encourage' a practice that seems pretty permanently present anyway.

But it is also worth emphasizing a second criticism often made with respect to the evolution of the laws of war since the middle of the nineteenth century: that they are effectively a sliding scale, constantly playing a game of catch-up with new developments in military technology. The role of submarines in both the First and the Second World Wars is an example that has been often discussed here. To sink merchant shipping was deemed to be against the laws of war and yet no punishment was visited on the perpetrators and the rules were not basically changed. There is, I think, something to this, and it might be added that the requirements of framing particular instances of law may often also run the risk of having formal rules that are disobeyed without sanction since the very specificity necessary will require close attention to the particularities of whatever is involved (a particular weapons system, for example). Allied to this is the obvious fact that the *jus in bello* acknowledges rules such as military necessity that permits the overcoming of such restraints on force as may exist. At one level this criticism merely points out the inherent difficulty of restraint in an environment of extremes which few, if any, just war theorists would deny, and the fact that such judgements are inherently difficult and often messy does not imply that they cannot or should not be made at all. I might add that the force of this criticism also rather depends on how the notion of a rule, in this context, is understood. On some understandings of what is involved in rulebound behaviour the

---

[71] See Roberts and Guelff, *Documents*, p. 28.

criticism may have some weight, but on others it most certainly does not; a lot will stand or fall on how you understand the character of the rules in question.[72]

It is significant in this regard that much of the debate over the character of the contemporary just war has again – as it did in the fifteenth and sixteenth centuries – turned on arguments on what we might call the *jus ad bellum*, rather than the *jus in bello*. We have seen that the distinction grew out of the attempt by Vitoria to deal with the question of simultaneous ostensible justice and his suggestion that we assume a stance of ignorance rather than one of malevolence on the part of our adversaries. In the early renderings of this view in the sixteenth and seventeenth centuries, however, this view was combined with the general concerns of what was rapidly becoming the *jus ad bellum* in a manner that sought to do justice to both. The distinction was then largely a secondary one and the manner in which the judgements were made blended custom, precedent, formal agreements and experience in almost equal measure. This is what Johnson means, I think, when he suggests that the just war tradition between the fifteenth and the seventeenth centuries becomes 'non-ideological' – as opposed to the 'ideological' form it had taken during the religious wars that preceded this period.[73]

However, one might characterize this change in a rather different way: the reason for the change, one might say, lies less in the character of the just war tradition itself, but rather more in the manner in which law itself was being understood, in turn reliant on an understanding of the relation between law and political regime type. As Koskenniemi has argued,[74] the project of international law was very much in keeping with both the progressive liberalism and the legal positivism that were largely dominant in the mid to late nineteenth century and that were then to have a central role in shaping the way that the juridicalizing of the *jus in bello* took place. In this respect, one might say that the casuistic, flexible and open discourse of the *jus in bello* from its infancy up until (roughly) the time of Vattel became much more constrained and hemmed in by a legal positivism that gave to it an 'ideological'

---

[72] For further elaboration of this point, see Anthony Lang Jr, Nicholas Rengger and William Walker, 'The Role(s) of Rules: Some Conceptual Clarifications', *International Relations*, 20, 3, 2006, 274–94.

[73] See Johnson, *Ideology, Reason and the Limitation of War*, p. 261.

[74] In *The Gentle Civilizer of Nations*.

character it had up to that point avoided. Of course the *content* of the ideology was very different – a liberal, progressivist, positivistic one, rather than a theological one that had been the justification for religious war – but its effect was not dissimilar. Rather than allowing the *jus in bello* to *balance* competing demands and competing claims, it tended to force the *in bello* constraints into one particular shape: that of modern, positive international law and of the state forms that have given birth to that idea.

But as I have already pointed out, while those state forms are usually classified by regime type – as liberal, autocratic or what have you – there is often an elision between the logic associated with a particular regime and the logic that should be associated with a particular mode of association. Not only does this cast doubt on theses like the democratic peace thesis but it has, as we shall see, a pronounced impact on the way in which the just war tradition and conceptions of the contemporary liberal democratic state interact. The way in which the just war tradition is imagined as part of the modern social imaginary of war, in other words, is shaped by its embedding in a dominant (in the sense of widely accepted) 'enterprise association' and teleocratic understanding of the modern state and states system. When that understanding is confronted with a set of concerns that seem to offer clear and obvious instances of injustice to oppose, the tension that has always been at the heart of the just war tradition between limiting destructiveness and punishing wrongdoing is pushed, I suggest, to breaking point. In extreme cases, and as we shall see in a moment we face, and are likely to face many such, we may even have reached the parting of the ways.

4 | *Force for good?*

Now days are dragon-ridden, the nightmare
Rides upon sleep; a drunken soldiery
Can leave the mother, murdered at her door,
To crawl in her own blood, and go scot-free;
The night can sweat with terror as before
We pieced our thoughts into philosophy,
And planned to bring the world under a rule,
Who are but weasels fighting in a hole.

     Yeats, 'Nineteen Hundred and Nineteen'

The renaissance of the just war tradition in the second half of the twentieth century was, as I remarked in the previous chapter, as much a feature of reactions to the political world as to intellectual inquiry on its own, World War Two, Vietnam and so on. And in the 1980s and, especially, the 1990s a still different set of 'events' – the Gulf War, Rwanda, Bosnia, Kosovo, 9/11 and after – produced reflections crucial both to contemporary thinking about international relations and the role of modern states in international relations and to the understanding and deployment of the just war tradition. In this chapter and the next, therefore, I want to offer an interpretation and at least a provisional assessment of where the entwining of teleocratic conceptions of politics and the modern just war tradition has led us. Although I shall certainly engage in some criticism of the arguments I will discuss, that criticism will be largely 'immanent': I will save the more general assessment of why I see it as so problematic and what, if anything, can be done about it for the Epilogue.

The end of the Cold War of course produced a good deal of rhetoric, not all of it insincere, about the possibility of a new beginning in international relations. The first President Bush's call for a 'new world order' is much derided,[1] but it is as well to remember that he was

---

[1] See the full text of the speech available online via Wikisource.

hardly alone at the time in thinking that the end of the Cold War threw up genuine opportunities which could be built on to create a much fairer and more just global order.[2] In particular, the opportunity appeared to exist to strengthen the international rule of law and to go back to something like the framework, both legal and political, that (it was widely believed at least)[3] the original creators of the United Nations had wanted and expected after the Second World War.[4]

This was predicated on one obvious and central assumption. If the 'international community' was effectively to build a fairer and more just world, it had to start with the elimination of the most obvious and egregious challenges to such a world. Chief amongst these, of course, were physical brutality and oppression, practised by the strong against the weak. This would have to be stopped. Such actions would not always require lethal force – sometimes they might be achieved through diplomacy, sometimes by coercive, but non-violent, sanctions – but in the background there would have to be the possibility of the use of force to enforce compliance with international norms or, in other words, it would require 'intervention' in international relations.

Of course, 'intervention' as an issue has not exactly been absent as a question discussed by jurists, philosophers and, indeed, political actors for much of the modern period. Indeed, at one level the notion of 'intervention' is itself a necessary corollary of the so-called 'Westphalian' states system.[5] A system predicated upon a rule of

---

[2] See, for some sample views: Lori Fisler Damrosch and David J. Scheffer (eds.) *Law and Force in the New International Order* (Boulder: Westview, 1991); Anthony Clark Arend and Robert J. Beck, *International Law and the Use of Force* (London: Routledge, 1993).

[3] For a rather more sceptical view of the intentions and objectives of the framers of the founding documents of the United Nations (a view which I would largely share) see Mark Mazower, *No Enchanted Palace: The Ends of Empire and the Ideological Origins of the United Nations* (Princeton University Press, 2009).

[4] This argument is made in a good deal of the literature of international relations and international law published in the late 1980s and early–mid 1990s. In other words, before the horizon began, once more, to darken. See, for example: Adam Roberts and Benedict Kingsbury (eds.) *United Nations, Divided World* (Oxford: Clarendon Press, 1988); Geoff Berridge, *Return to the United Nations: UN Diplomacy in Regional Conflicts* (London: Palgrave Macmillan, 1990).

[5] Debates about how best to characterize the 'Westphalian' states system are now legion, of course. Very differing, but equally stimulating accounts can be found in Martin Wight, *Systems of States* (Leicester University Press, 1977), Stephen Toulmin, *Cosmopolis: The Hidden Agenda of Modernity* (University of Chicago Press, 1992).

territorial integrity must take violations of that rule extremely seriously and thus the so-called 'rule of non-intervention' became one of the central norms of the Westphalian system, despite the manifold and regular violations of that principle in the history of international relations from the seventeenth century to the present,[6] and thus, inevitably, discussions of intervention have been an equally permanent feature of the international system. In particular, the *fact* of intervention was often contrasted with the – to some – idealized legal status of non-intervention as an ordering principle of international relations.

In the mid 1980s, conscious of this dilemma, Hedley Bull argued that intervention would be easier to justify if it were, in some sense, *collective* intervention. This view of intervention explicitly draws upon the allegedly 'Grotian' tradition in international theory that Bull himself had done so much to explicate.[7] Christian Wolff, for example, writing in the seventeenth century, remarked that intervention is acceptable only when it is carried out by the *civitas maxima*. Similarly, Bull argues:

Ultimately we have a rule of non-intervention because unilateral intervention threatens the harmony and concord of the society of sovereign states. If, however, an intervention expresses the collective will of the

[6] One finds discussions of the principles of 'legitimate intervention' in many of the most influential thinkers of the sixteenth, seventeenth, eighteenth and nineteenth centuries, for example Vitoria, Suarez, Grotius, Pufendorf, Wolff, Leibniz, Vattel, Hume, Kant, Hegel and Mill. See, for example, the selections and commentary included in Chris Brown, Terry Nardin and Nicholas Rengger (eds.) *International Relations in Political Thought: Texts from the Ancient Greeks to the First World War* (Cambridge University Press, 2002). The classic modern treatment of non-intervention is R.J. Vincent, *Non-Intervention and International Order* (Princeton University Press, 1974). For the 'organized hypocrisy' of the Westphalian system see Stephen Krasner, *Sovereignty: Organized Hypocrisy* (Princeton University Press, 1999).

[7] See Hedley Bull, 'The Grotian Conception of International Society', in Herbert Butterfield and Martin Wight (eds.) *Diplomatic Investigations* (London: Allen and Unwin, 1966) and Bull, Adam Roberts and Ben Kingsbury (eds.) *Hugo Grotius and International Relations* (Oxford University Press, 1986). For an elaboration and critique of Bull's view see Edward Keene, *Beyond the Anarchical Society: Grotius, Colonialism and Order in World Politics* (Cambridge University Press, 2002). A radically different view of Grotius is presented by Richard Tuck in *The Rights of War and Peace: Political Thought and the International Order from Grotius to Kant* (Oxford University Press, 1999). The most thorough and enlightening investigation of the 'Grotian tradition', and both Grotius's and Bull's relation to it, is Renee Jeffery, *Hugo Grotius in International Thought* (London: Palgrave Macmillan, 2006).

society of states, it may be carried out without bringing that harmony and concord into jeopardy.[8]

Despite the long pedigree of this view, the general position of modern international relations and (from the nineteenth century) international law down to the end of the Cold War was that intervention could only be justified in the most specialized and narrowly defined circumstances. Coercive military intervention, for example, is forbidden under articles 2 and 51 of the United Nations Charter. This prohibition was elaborated in the Declaration on Friendly Relations Between Nations of 1970. Of course, during the Cold War there were many interventions, variously justified,[9] but the general legal and political position did not change.[10]

For many, however, the end of the Cold War changed this. Within a couple of years of the end of the Cold War, Yugoslavia collapsed as a coherent polity and the civil war which followed raised profound questions within and beyond Europe about whether outsiders should intervene, either to stop the slaughter or perhaps to give aid to those caught up involuntarily in the crossfire. These questions reached their apogee after the massacre in 1995 of over 8,000 men at Srebrenica in Bosnia and then, even more appallingly, in 1994, by the horrific genocidal slaughter in Rwanda, wherein at least 800,000 men, women and children were massacred. Very quickly, year on year, moreover, yet more names were added to the litany of horror: Somalia, Kosovo, Sierra Leone, northern Iraq, Timor-Leste (East Timor) and so on.

These events gave rise to debates which ran throughout the 1990s and continue to this day. For many, such events should be understood as something distinct and different in the history of international

---

[8] Bull's reference is to Wolff's *Ius Gentium* (Halle, 1754), the philosophical basis of which – though Bull does not cite this – can be found in his *Philosophia Practica Universalis*, 2 vols. (Halle, 1736–9). Bull's argument is contained in the introduction to Hedley Bull (ed.) *Intervention in World Politics* (Oxford University Press, 1984). See also Brendan Simms and D.J.B. Trim (eds.) *Humanitarian Intervention: A History* (Cambridge University Press, 2011).

[9] See, for a characteristically acute discussion, Philip Windsor's chapter 'Superpower Intervention', in Bull (ed.) *Intervention in World Politics*, pp. 45–66.

[10] For discussions of legal views surrounding practices of intervention see, for a general overview, Antonio Cassese, *International Law* (2nd edn) (Oxford University Press, 2004). See also Chapter 15 of Rosalyn Higgins's celebrated Hague Curatorium lectures published as *Problems and Process: International Law and How We Use It* (Oxford University Press, 1993).

relations. Mary Kaldor and others have suggested that they should be seen as manifestions of a new category in the long history of human violence; they were 'new wars', as she famously and influentially put it,[11] and they created a new dynamic for conflict for which the old categories would no longer be sufficient. In particular, such situations created 'complex humanitarian emergencies' – conflict-related humanitarian disasters involving 'a high degree of state and institutional breakdown and social dislocation and … requiring a system wide response from the international community'.[12] In this respect, the old question of intervention – which we might term 'Westphalian intervention' – becomes subsumed into a rather different question, concerning intervention to respond to *these kinds* of situations: a 'humanitarian' intervention.

It is the literature, and to some extent the practice, of so-called 'humanitarian intervention' that profoundly augments the already noted predilection of the modern just war towards the punishment of wrongdoing – now seen also as the elimination of injustice – and which goes hand in hand with a particular reading of the state as an enterprise association united around a notion of the common good and an idea about 'enlightened government'. Before turning to the questions of intervention and preventive war, therefore, I want to elaborate a little on this, since it will underpin a good part of my argument in this section of the book.

'Humanitarian' intervention: framing a debate

Here, of course, the literature over the last couple of decades has exploded and it is continuing to increase at an exponential rate. Some in these debates have suggested that they can trace the gradual emergence of a 'norm of humanitarian intervention' in international

---

[11] The canonical statement is Mary Kaldor, *New and Old Wars: Organized Violence in a Global Era* (Cambridge: Polity Press, 2007). See also Herfried Münkler, *Die Neuen Kriege* (Reinbek: Rowohlt, 2004) and Paul Gilbert, *New Terror, New Wars* (Edinburgh University Press, 2003).

[12] See Mark Duffield, *Global Governance and the New Wars: The Merging of Development and Security* (London: Zed Books, 2001), p. 12. See also Michael Barnett and Thomas G. Weiss (eds.) *Humanitarianism in Question: Politics, Power, Ethics* (Ithaca, NY: Cornell University Press, 2008).

society;[13] others, perhaps a trifle more cautiously, have noted the emergence of ethical, political and legal dilemmas *surrounding* moral reasons for intervention in these kinds of context without suggesting anything like a settled norm has emerged.[14] But the debates such claims (and such events) generated could not be avoided. Coupled with wider developments in the international system, for example the continued expansion of the 'human rights revolution' that produced, in 1998, the statute of the International Criminal Court and the British House of Lords Pinochet judgment, much international opinion coalesced around a doctrine, first proposed in 2001 and finally adopted by the UN in 2005: the so-called doctrine of a 'responsibility to protect' (R2P).[15] Whilst some considered this little more than Western liberal

[13] The best-known and most well-developed elaboration of the international society version of this case is Nicholas J. Wheeler, *Saving Strangers: Humanitarian Intervention in International Society* (Oxford University Press, 2000).

[14] See, for early and influential discussions, Stanley Hoffmann, *The Ethics and Politics of Humanitarian Intervention* (Notre Dame: University of Notre Dame Press, 1996), Michael Joseph Smith, 'Ethics and Intervention', *Ethics and International Affairs*, 1989, Ian Forbes and Mark Hoffman (eds.) *Political Theory, International Relations and the Ethics of Intervention* (Basingstoke: Macmillan, 1993) and Michael Walzer, 'The Politics of Rescue', in his *Arguing about War* (New Haven: Yale University Press, 2004). Very good general discussions can be found in Deen Chatterjee and Don Scheid (eds.) *Ethics and Foreign Intervention* (Cambridge University Press, 2003), Eric Heinze, *Waging Humanitarian War: The Ethics, Law and Politics of Humanitarian Intervention* (New York: State University of New York Press, 2009), Jeff Holzgrefe and Robert Keohane (eds.) *Humanitarian Intervention: Ethical, Legal and Political Dilemmas* (Cambridge University Press, 2003), Anthony J. Lang, Jr (ed.) *Just Intervention* (Washington, DC: Georgetown University Press, 2003), Terry Nardin and Melissa Williams (eds.) *Humanitarian Intervention* (NOMOS XLVII) (New York University Press, 2005) and Jennifer Welsh (ed.) *Humanitarian Intervention and International Relations* (Oxford University Press, 2004).

[15] A detailed and important first-hand account of the emergence of this idea – though also (perhaps excusably) justificatory – is Gareth Evans, *The Responsibility to Protect: Ending Mass Atrocity Crimes Once and For All* (Washington: Brookings, 2008). An equally important take on its current provenance can be found in Louise Arbour, 'The Responsibility to Protect as a Duty of Care in International Law and Practice', *Review of International Studies*, 34, 3, 2008, 445–58. A thorough overview of the issues involved can be found in Alex Bellamy, *Responsibility to Protect: The Global Effort to End Mass Atrocities* (Cambridge: Polity Press, 2009). A set of eloquent responses to Arbour's article can be found in *Review of International Studies*, 36, December 2010.

handwringing, or even a new form of imperialism, and insisted on the traditional prerogatives of state sovereignty and a firm rule of non-intervention,[16] others saw it as something much more positive. As Charles Beitz suggests in his important study of human rights, 'violations or threatened violations of [human rights] standards ... might reasonably be taken as a justification for remedial or preventive action by outside agents'. He continues, 'One need not deny that international humanitarian action has a longer history to recognize that these facts mark a watershed in the history of global normative order.'[17]

As we will see a little later on, it is indeed the linkage of *remedial* with *preventive* action, which Beitz so tellingly foregrounds here, that has done so much to generate contemporary ideas about preventive war. However, it is worth closing this section by briefly mentioning a corollary of the growing debate about humanitarian intervention. This is the veritable avalanche of literature (and policy, indeed) dealing with the *consequences* of such interventions, and in particular to the dynamics of what are often called 'post-conflict situations' or, what some thinkers in the just war tradition are calling the *jus post bellum*.[18] Here the debates have tended to concentrate around the *possibilities* of genuinely 'democratic' 'peace-building' strategies in post-conflict situations – such as for example, state-building or legal strategies[19] – the

---

[16] See, for example, the dissenting voices noted in Alex Bellamy, 'R2P and the Problem of Military Intervention', *International Affairs*, 84, 4, July 2008, 615–39.

[17] See Charles Beitz, *The Idea of Human Rights* (Oxford University Press, 2009), p. xi.

[18] Good early discussions here include Richard Caplan, *A New Trusteeship? The International Administration of War Torn Territories*. Adelphi Paper no. 341. London: IISS. The most detailed discussion is probably Ralph Wilde, *International Territorial Administration: How Trusteeship and the Civilizing Mission Never Went Away* (Oxford University Press, 2008) and the most historically and theoretically acute, William Bain, *Between Anarchy and Society: Trusteeship and the Obligations of Power* (Oxford University Press, 2003). To some extent these discussion grow out of earlier literatures of so-called 'state failure' – see, for example, William Zartman (ed.) *Collapsed States: The Disintegration and Reestablishment of Political Authority* (Boulder: Lynne Rienner, 1995).

[19] See, for example, Robert Keohane, 'Political Authority after Intervention: Gradations of Sovereignty', pp. 275–98, and Michael Ignatieff, 'State Failure and Nationbuilding', pp. 299–321, in Holzgrefe and Keohane (eds.) *Humanitarian Intervention*, and the exponentially expanding literature of 'state building'. Very thoughtful general studies include Francis Fukuyama, *State-Building: Governance and World Order in the 21st Century* (Ithaca, NY:

critique of so-called 'liberal peace building',[20] and the *ethical dilemmas* involved in post-conflict situations.

I shall want to return to all of this towards the end of this chapter. However, with the background established, let me now turn to the debates about humanitarian intervention themselves.

Debating humanitarian intervention

Here it is worth saying at the outset that there are multiple strands that go to make up such advocacy and it would be impossible in one chapter to discuss them all equally. Instead, I want to highlight what I take to be major positions in each case. The paradigm case of what I will call the minimalist case for humanitarian intervention is found in the work of Michael Walzer. As we saw in Chapter 3, the essential premise of Walzer's overall argument is a derivation of the rights of political communities from the rights of individuals: 'the duties and rights of states are nothing more than the duties and rights of the men who compose them'.[21] For Walzer, as we saw, the process by which such a derivation takes place is a very complex one and is best understood in terms of social contract theory. He argues that:

The moral understanding on which the community is founded takes shape over a long period of time, but the idea of communal integrity derives its moral and political force from the rights of contemporary men and women to live as members of an historic community and to express their inherited culture in forms worked out among themselves.[22]

This implies that instances of states' rights, for example territorial integrity, derive from this same complex process involving individual rights. Therefore they are subject to the vicissitudes of the common life.

Cornell University Press, 2004) and Stephen Krasner, 'Addressing State Failure' (with Carlos Pascual), in *Foreign Affairs*, 84, 4, 2005.

20 This, again, is an exponentially expanding field; especially in Europe. For good discussions from a variety of perspectives, see Oliver Richmond and Jason Franks, *Liberal Peace Transitions: Between Peace Building and State Building: A Model Argument with Historical Illustrations*, 3rd edn (Edinburgh University Press, 2009).

21 Walzer, *Just and Unjust Wars* (New York: Basic Books, 2000(1977)), p. 53. He is quoting, with approval, the international lawyer John Westlake.

22 Walzer, 'The Moral Standing of States: A Response to Four Critics', in Charles Beitz et al. (eds.) *International Ethics* (A *Philosophy and Public Affairs* Reader) (Princeton University Press, 1985), p. 219.

This form of argumentation leads Walzer to see the international order as equivalent in important respects to the domestic order. Walzer adopts, in short, the 'domestic analogy' and what he calls the 'legalist paradigm'.

This combination of the domestic analogy and the legalist paradigm leads Walzer to adopt a strict principle of non-intervention which nevertheless can be vitiated in circumstances, 'where the ban on boundary crossings ... does not serve the purposes for which it was established'.[23] There are three such circumstances, he suggests: secession, counter-intervention in the context of civil war, and cases of massacre and genocide. Thus, for Walzer, intervention is justified ethically if it represents the spirit of the ban on boundary crossings enshrined in international law as the principle of sovereignty even though it appears to violate the letter of that principle.[24]

In the 1990s Walzer's position shifted a little, though not substantively. 'The presumption against intervention is strong', he wrote in 1994, 'but ... nonintervention is not an absolute moral rule: sometimes what is going on locally cannot be tolerated.'[25] He was willing to accept that there were times when the international society, and perhaps states themselves, should adopt what he called a 'politics of rescue', recognizing, of course, that 'the politics of rescue is certain to be complex and messy'.[26] Perhaps the most important shift in his view, however, occurred in the likely timescale of legitimate interventions. As he himself puts it: 'On the standard view of humanitarian intervention (which I adopted when writing *Just and Unjust Wars*) the source of the inhumanity is conceived as somehow external and singular in character: a tyrant, a conqueror or usurper or an alien power set over against a mass of victims.' But what, he asks, 'if the trouble is internal, the inhumanity locally or widely rooted, a matter of political culture, social structures, historical memories, ethnic fear, resentment and hatred? Or what if the trouble follows from state failure, the collapse of any effective government?'[27] In these cases, he suggests:

two forms of long lasting intervention, both associated in the past with imperial politics, now warrant reconsideration. The first is a kind of trusteeship, where the intervening power actually rules the country it has

[23] Walzer, *Just and Unjust Wars*, p. 90.
[24] This puts Walzer fairly close to Bull's 'Grotian' view, of course.
[25] Walzer, *Arguing about War*, p. 69.   [26] Ibid., p. 71.   [27] Ibid., p. 70.

rescued, acting in trust for the inhabitants, seeking to establish a stable or more or less consensual politics. The second is a kind of protectorate, where the intervention brings some local group or coalition of groups to power and then is sustained only defensively, to ensure there is no return of the defeated regime or the old lawlessness and that minority rights are respected; Rwanda might have been a candidate for trusteeship; Bosnia for a protectorate.[28]

He concludes his argument here with an admonition that he is not abandoning his earlier position.

Despite all that I have said so far I don't mean to abandon the principle of non-intervention – only to honour its exceptions ... the norm is not to intervene in other people's countries, the norm is self determination. But not for these people, the victims of tyranny, ideological zeal, ethnic hatred, who are not determining anything for themselves, who urgently need help from outside. And it isn't enough to wait until the tyrants, the zealots and the bigots have done their filthy work and then rush food and medicine to the ragged survivors. Whenever the filthy work can be stopped, it should be stopped, and if not by us, the supposedly decent people of this world, then by whom?[29]

If Walzer represents something of a minimalist position, then probably the most influential kind of contemporary advocacy of humanitarian intervention is what I will call 'solidarist' interventionism. This has been adopted by both academic and political figures. The powerful case for humanitarian intervention made by Nick Wheeler in *Saving Strangers*, for example, falls into this category. Wheeler's argument is, in fact, very carefully made and heavily nuanced: he is well aware of the obstacles that stand in the way of a robust solidarist intervention-ism. But, as he puts it in his conclusion:

it is no good being shocked by television images of atrocities or starvation, since what is required is we all do something to end these and stop them recurring ... [I]n the Bosnian and Rwandan cases, Western state leaders believed that public opinion was not prepared to pay the price ... to end these atrocities. Had they judged their policies of limited engagement in Bosnia and non-intervention in Rwanda were likely to lead to a moral outcry at home and that public opinion was prepared to accept the human as well as the financial costs of intervention, politicians would have found it much more difficult to ignore the voice of solidarism in foreign policy decision making. Governments are notoriously unreliable as rescuers but where else

---

[28] Ibid., p. 76.   [29] Ibid., p. 81.

can we turn to save those who cannot save themselves? At present it is only states that have the capabilities to fly thousands of troops halfway round the globe to prevent or stop genocide or mass murder. The challenge then for those working in human rights NGOs, universities and the media is to mobilize public opinion into a new moral and practical commitment to the promotion and enforcement of human rights. This change in moral consciousness will not guarantee intervention when it is morally required. What it will do is to heighten awareness on the part of state leaders that they will be held accountable if they decide not to save strangers.[30]

Politically, the best-known advocate of 'solidarist' interventionism is probably Tony Blair. In his speech given before the Economic Club of Chicago on 24 April 1999,[31] Blair outlined what he saw as a new approach to international relations as a whole but with very specific implications for the use of force. He predicated it on the operation in Kosovo, of which he had been one of the architects, but he then went on to try to articulate a more general case based on that specific one:

The most pressing foreign policy problem we [in the West] face is to identify the circumstances in which we should get actively involved in other people's conflicts. Non-interference has long been considered an important principle of international order. And it is not one we would want to jettison too readily ... But the principle of non-interference must be qualified in important respects. Acts of genocide can never be a purely internal matter. When oppression produces massive flows of refugees which unsettle neighbouring countries then they can properly be described as 'threats to international peace and security'. When regimes are based on minority rule they lose legitimacy – look at South Africa.

Obviously this argument needs to have a set of considerations about when to intervene. He lists five:

First, are we sure of our case? ... Second, have we exhausted all diplomatic options? ... Third, on the basis of a practical assessment of the situation, are there military operations we can sensibly and prudently undertake? Fourth, are we prepared for the long term? ... And finally, do we have national interests involved? The mass expulsion of ethnic Albanians from Kosovo demanded the notice of the rest of the world. But it does make a difference that this is taking place in such a combustible part of Europe.[32]

---

[30] Wheeler, *Saving Strangers*, p. 310.
[31] Full reference can be found at www.number10.gov.uk/Page1297.   [32] Ibid.

These were clearly significant considerations, and they read especially interestingly from the perspective of someone writing after the 'interventions' in Afghanistan and Iraq.[33] Nonetheless it is striking how close to much of the academic advocacy of a right (or norm or duty) of humanitarian intervention this is.[34]

Perhaps the most full-blown version of a doctrine of humanitarian intervention, however, has emerged in the now very voluminous cosmopolitan literature on international relations and international law, and especially in what we might call the 'human rights' cosmopolitanism that is very much the engine room of this set of claims.[35] Allen Buchanan, for example, has suggested that we should see the state as an instrument of justice, and that if we do then among the duties that creates is a duty of enforcing justice (or eliminating injustice) in egregious cases of oppression or exploitation beyond the boundaries of the state concerned.[36] David Luban, a persistent critic of Walzer, argues a very similar case. For Luban:

A state (or government) established against the will of its own people, ruling violently, may well forfeit its right ... even against a foreign invasion ... [thus] it would appear that in such a case intervention is justified even in the absence of massacre or slavery.[37]

[33] It does not look as if the then prime minister consulted his 1999 speech again before deciding to intervene in Iraq, whatever might have been said about Afghanistan.

[34] This is perhaps not as surprising as it seems since, by all accounts, a good deal of Blair's speech was culled from ideas suggested to him by the distinguished British scholar Sir Lawrence Freedman, who has broadly supported what we might call a relatively moderate solidarist version of the argument for humanitarian intervention.

[35] By 'human rights' cosmopolitanism I mean to distinguish cosmopolitans like Simon Caney, Thomas Pogge and Allen Buchanan from those like Onora O'Neill who, while certainly cosmopolitan in their general orientation, have a marked (and often Kantian-derived) suspicion about the assertion of rights over and above duties or obligations. For good expositions of contrasting views see, for example, Simon Caney, *Justice beyond Borders: Towards a Global Political Theory* (Oxford University Press, 2005), Thomas Pogge, *World Poverty and Human Rights* (Cambridge: Polity Press, 2003), Allen Buchanan, *Human Rights, Legitimacy and the Use of Force* (Oxford University Press, 2010) and Onora O'Neill, 'The Dark Side of Human Rights', *International Affairs*, 80, 1, January 2004 and *Bounds of Justice* (Cambridge University Press, 2000).

[36] See Buchanan, *Human Rights, Legitimacy and the Use of Force*, Chapter 9.

[37] D. Luban, 'The Romance of the Nation State', in C. Beitz, L. Alexander and T. Scanlon (eds.) *International Ethics: A Philosophy and Public Affairs Reader* (Princeton University Press, 1985), p. 242.

Elsewhere in the same essay he is even more explicit:

Human rights accrue to people no matter what country they live in and regardless of history or tradition. If human rights exist at all they set a moral limit to pluralism ... moreover [rights] are crucial to us – as Walzer points out they are deeply connected with our notions of personality and moral agency.

In other words, on this view, intervention is not merely a right; under certain circumstances it is a duty. It is not simply extreme cases, such as genocide and massacre, but any violation of socially basic human rights which justifies, perhaps necessitates, intervention. Luban suggests that the 'romance of the nation state' vitiates the real force of Walzer's commitment to intervention on humanitarian grounds. It is Walzer's subscription to the 'morality of states' which leads him into a pluralistic relativism that defeats the ends for which it was brought into being, namely the existence of the common life and the possibility of moral agency.

It is obvious, then, that within the literature on humanitarian intervention – and I have only scratched the surface here – there is a wide range of views. Nevertheless, two crucial assumptions are shared, I think, across the debate. In the first place, 'we' – and I will come back to that term in a moment – have duties to intervene under certain circumstances not for reasons of material interest (or at least not for these alone) but for humanitarian ('ethical') purposes and, second, 'we' have these purposes because 'we' are the kinds of communities where these purposes have weight.

As we will see, there is a logical corollary to both of these claims, and both of them fit like a glove into that combined idiom of teleocratic belief I mentioned a moment ago. But before getting to that, I want to turn to the most recent extension of this logic: the idea of preventive force.

From intervention to preventive war

As we saw in Chapter 3, for most of the modern period, the just war tradition set its face against the idea that force can legitimately be used against anticipated future threats – what is usually referred to as 'preventive war' – whilst permitting, in certain very specialized circumstances, the use of force to ward off or defeat an imminent

attack – which I will refer to as 'pre-emptive war'. While there were
some in the early modern period who challenged this view – perhaps
most obviously Gentili[38] – and while, outside the tradition, notions of
preventive war were plentiful – though not always under that name[39] –
by and large the consensus against preventive war has held and sur-
vived the changes that in other respects, I have argued, have altered the
character of the tradition greatly. That consensus seems now to be
fraying, however, and fraying precisely amongst those who might have
been expected to sustain it, that is to say those who support and
advocate the role of the rule of law – including the moral rules of the
just war tradition – in international affairs.[40]

In many respects the same logic that we above saw driving a more
permissive notion of intervention – for 'humanitarian purposes' – is at
work in the growing resonance of arguments in favour of preventive war.

[38] See, especially, Alberico Gentili, *De Jure Belli* (1598). A good recent discussion
of Gentili's argument can be found in Larry May, *Aggression and Crimes
against Peace* (Cambridge University Press, 2008), pp. 75–8.

[39] One can find many discussions in ancient writings on war and politics of what
would today be called 'preventive war'. Thucydides has much of importance to
say in the context of his rehearsal of various arguments for and against
particular instances of war in portions of the *History of the Peloponnesian War*.
Aristotle too has interesting comments (largely negative) on the tendency of
societies in his own day to fight first and ask questions afterwards (see, for
example, his discussion of war and the virtues in the *Nichomachean Ethics*
1177b10), though he accepts in good naturalist style that there might be some
contexts in which this is the appropriate thing to do ('appropriateness' being
an important category of virtue for Aristotle, of course). It is also possible that
part of Aristotle's reputed coolness towards Alexander's campaigns had
something to do with the fact they were undertaken for ignoble reasons. While,
as we saw in Chapter 3, Roman custom on the declaration of war was very
formal, there was also a good deal of military practice that looks suspiciously
'preventive'; a good discussion, though controversial, can be found in Edward
Luttwak, *The Grand Strategy of the Roman Empire* (Baltimore: Johns Hopkins
University Press, 1976). Among more modern writers Machiavelli, both in
The Prince and *The Discourses* and in the *Art of War*, argues preventive war is
both logical and necessary – and is quite clearly, in his own mind at least,
echoing Roman ideas and practice here. See Felix Gilbert's excellent discussion
in 'Machiavelli: The Renaissance Art of War', pp. 11–31 in Peter Paret (ed.)
Makers of Modern Strategy (Oxford: Clarendon Press, 1986). One can also find
many discussions of preventive war in the realpolitik literature of the
seventeenth and eighteenth centuries.

[40] As the previous note makes clear, and as I have had occasion to remark on
many occasions earlier in this book, there have been many critics of this view,
but it is the slippage in the ideas of those previously not critical that is my chief
concern here.

This is the crucial difference between earlier 'defences' of preventive war – such as Gentili's – and the contemporary debate. And what has *increased* the perceived requirement for the international community (or at least certain members of it) to develop a doctrine of justifiable preventive war? Precisely the logic of the United States' reaction to 9/11, and all that it has brought in its train, which we examined in Chapter 1, coupled with the growing arguments about the normative force of humanitarian intervention. Let us look at the detail of the arguments themselves.

Arguments for a doctrine of justifiable preventive war

Both immediately after the 9/11 attacks (in for example the 2002 National Security Strategy) and subsequently, in many speeches and official pronouncements, President Bush's administration elided the traditional distinction between preventive and pre-emptive war, and while talking the language of pre-emption made it perfectly clear that they meant that the United States would act 'preventively' if it decided that was in its interests. As President Bush remarked in an address at Fort Bragg in 2005, 'This nation will not wait to be attacked again. We will take the fight to the enemy ... there is only one course of action against [those who subscribe to this murderous ideology]: to defeat them abroad before they attack us at home.'[41]

However, central though the reaction of the Bush administration was to the growing interest in notions of preventive war, I shall not spend much time on their accounts of it here. Partly this is simply because the administration's formal defence of its position, inasmuch as there was one, was hardly marked by interpretive nuance or subtlety – hence the rather clumsy elision between pre-emption and prevention that has characterized the articulation of their position[42] – but it is also because that particular administration – or at least leading members of it – made little secret of its contempt for such moralistic niceties as the just war tradition.

[41] See the 'Address to the Nation on the War on Terror from Fort Bragg, North Carolina', Weekly compendium of presidential documents, 41, 26 (28 June 2005), cited in Michael Doyle, *Striking First: Preemption and Prevention in International Conflict*, ed. Stephen Macedo (Princeton University Press, 2008).
[42] Well discussed – and criticized – in Matthew Evangelista, *Law, Ethics and the War on Terror* (Cambridge: Polity Press, 2008), pp. 103–29.

What is most significant, as I say, in the current vogue of thinking about preventive war is not the reaction from sceptics about the just war tradition or the laws of war, but rather the reaction of those who might in general terms be seen as supporters. Over the past few years a wide range of writers otherwise committed to the rule of law in international affairs, or to the just war tradition, or both, have begun to suggest that, while the manner in which the Bush administration articulated it was clearly mistaken – and possibly deeply damaging – the instinct that the changing circumstances of contemporary conflict warrant revisiting the notion of preventive war is correct, and that as a result we need to think how we can work in a notion of preventive war to our thinking about legitimate force.

As this implies, there are a range of writers I might look at here, and I certainly do not have the time to look at them all. My strategy, therefore, is to focus on those who have developed what I take to be the strongest position in defence of a notion of legitimate preventive war, from the standpoint of an otherwise clear commitment to the international rule of law and/or the just war tradition.[43] For this chapter, I will take those writers to include, principally, Robert Keohane, Allen Buchanan, David Luban and Michael Doyle, with briefer roles played by Philip Bobbitt and Henry Shue. Let me begin with the arguments presented by Buchanan and Keohane.

Amongst the earliest arguments in favour of a newly developed conception of preventive war was an article co-authored by Allen Buchanan and Robert Keohane in 2004,[44] where they argued that 'within an appropriate rule governed, institutional framework that is designed to help protect vulnerable countries against unjustified interventions without creating unacceptable risks of the costs of inaction, decisions to employ preventive force can be justified'.[45] In the course of their argument they identified four contemporary positions on the use of force which they term the just war blanket prohibition, the legal

---

[43] Of course, there are some who meet these criteria and who also provide powerful and interesting arguments that I do not discuss in the detail their ideas warrant. Personal predilection at some point has to trump even-handedness, or this book would be even longer than it already is. *Mea culpa.*

[44] See Allen Buchanan and Robert Keohane, 'The Preventive Use of Force: A Cosmopolitan Institutional Proposal', *Ethics and International Affairs*, 18, 1, 2004, 1–22.

[45] Ibid., p. 1.

status quo, the national interest (the standard realist line that states do what they will), and the expanded right of self-defence (essentially the Bush administration's position as articulated in the 2002 National Security Strategy). All of these views are insufficient, they argue, for the changed circumstances of the contemporary world, and so they propose a fifth, a cosmopolitan institutional view, predicated on a commitment to the human rights of all persons. Such a commitment, they argue, manifestly justifies the permissibility of force to prevent 'presently occurring' massive human rights violations (and this has already been accepted by international actors, for example in the context of the Kosovo intervention in 1999). They then suggest that there is, therefore, a prima facie argument for the permissibility of force to prevent massive violations of basic human rights. They stipulate that this argument applies not to any possible harms but to 'situations where there is a significant risk of sudden and very serious harms on a massive scale' and they add that 'such a risk is inherent in weapons of mass destruction but not exclusive to them. Genocides may also erupt suddenly.'[46] With the moral permissibility of preventive force thus established, Buchanan and Keohane move on to discuss two risks inherent in such action and how to meet them. The first risk is self-interest masquerading as concern for the common good, which could lead to unjustifiable decisions, and the second is that preventive action could undermine existing beneficial institutional norms constraining the use of force. The rest of their article consists in a set of institutional proposals to address these dangers. They do not suppose that 'we … [can] … reduce the risk of unjustified preventive action to zero but we can lower it sufficiently so that preventive action can become a more useful tool of policy'.[47] The suggestions they make are all interesting, but since my main concern here is precisely with the foundational claim – that we need and can develop a moral case for preventive war – I will defer them for the moment.

To some extent, these arguments are paralleled by those of Philip Bobbitt, in his recent *Terror and Consent*.[48] Bobbitt argues that the evolution of the international system into a market state system (from a

---

[46] Ibid., p. 5.   [47] Ibid., p. 10.

[48] See Philip Bobbitt, *Terror and Consent: The Wars for the Twenty First Century* (London: Allen Lane, 2008).

nation-state system),[49] along with the technological shifts that the past few decades have witnessed, has generated a new dynamic of terror where the possible risks of the use of (say) weapons of mass destruction (WMD) on market state societies are now so high that methods of interdiction and prevention akin to classical accounts of preventive war must be considered. It is worth pointing out that Bobbitt is a powerful supporter of the rule of law; indeed he argues further that the rule of law and strategic reality must be brought further into congruence with one another – picking up here an argument from his earlier book *The Shield of Achilles*[50] – and that this is an additional reason why we need to rethink the idea of preventive war.

A third writer who has developed a similar case is David Luban, whose critique of Walzer's 'casuistry' we met earlier.[51] Luban's version of the case is perhaps the most restrictive of those under consideration but he is still prepared to accept the logic of 'preventive war' under certain very specific conditions, to wit, 'where the distant threat involves weapons of mass destruction' and where the putative possessor is a 'rogue state' 'whose ideology and past history of violence, combined with its current hostile intentions and weapons program make it likely that it plans to launch an attack when it acquires the capacity'.[52] His desire to restrict this concession is shown, however, by the fact that, for Luban, permission to launch preventive war is (in his terms) 'nonproxyable': 'only the state that is actually the target of the emerging threat can launch war to forestall it'.[53]

As Luban admits, this notion has echoes of the position that John Rawls famously adopts in *The Law of Peoples*.[54] Here, Rawls argues that what he calls outlaw states are those states willing to use war to secure their instrumentally rational (but not because of that *ex hypothesi* reasonable, or justified *in toto*) interests. Luban agrees with

[49] I cannot forbear to add that Bobbitt's 'market state' is, to all intents and purposes, a 'marketized' version of an enterprise association model of the state.

[50] Philip Bobbitt, *The Shield of Achilles: War, Peace and the Course of History* (London: Allen Lane, 2002).

[51] Luban has developed his argument to date in two articles: 'Preventive War', *Philosophy and Public Affairs*, 32, 2004, 207–48, and 'Preventive War and Human Rights', in Henry Shue and David Rodin (eds.) *Preemption: Military Action and Moral Justification* (Oxford University Press, 2007), pp. 171–201.

[52] See Luban, 'Preventive War and Human Rights', p. 172.   [53] Ibid., p. 173.

[54] Rawls, *The Law of Peoples* (Cambridge, Mass.: Harvard University Press, 1999).

this, except he thinks that it is too restrictive: such states might pursue irrational, not just rational, goals through war and thus he prefers his more expansive definition, which then underpins his conceptions of legitimate preventive war.[55]

Perhaps the most developed argument to date along similar lines, however, can be found in Michael Doyle's Tanner Lectures, delivered at Princeton in 2006 and now published.[56] As Stephen Macedo says in his Introduction, 'the task that Doyle has set for himself in these essays is no less than to articulate the conditions under which preventive war is justified and to specify workable and useful criteria that ought to be recognized by the international community to guide, constrain and assess resort to preventive war'.[57] Doyle himself repeats the claims of Bobbitt, and Buchanan and Keohane, to wit that 'both international law, as it is currently formulated, and the Bush doctrine of prevention are inadequate for today's global security environment'[58] – thus critiquing (in Buchanan and Keohane's terms) the legal status quo and expanded right of self-defence arguments. His argument proceeds roughly by suggesting that in the current security environment, the 'legal status quo' (as expressed through international law and institutions such as the UN Security Council) does, in fact, require a legitimate doctrine of prevention but doesn't have one. In particular he suggests that the adoption of the doctrine of 'responsibility to protect' in 2005 built on earlier practice of the Council to engage 'preventively', on the basis, for example, of Chapter VII of the UN Charter.[59] As he puts it 'The UN charter authorizes the Security Council to prevent but we should not write the Security Council a blank check. It needs a jurisprudence of prevention. Moreover, the council will sometimes fail to behave responsibly. We then have to decide when a state can justifiably engage in unilateral preventive self defence before international law would currently allow.'[60]

---

[55] Jeff MacMahan, David Rodin, Susan Uniacke and some others have all criticized Luban's formulations, in one way or another. His second essay on the topic was in large part a response to their objections.

[56] Doyle, *Striking First*, pp. 3–96.   [57] Ibid., p. xvi.   [58] Ibid., p. 6.

[59] For a not too dissimilar reading of 'responsibility to protect' see Arbour, 'Responsibility to Protect'.

[60] Ibid.

In his second essay, Doyle outlines four 'standards for prevention' that could provide a 'jurisprudence of prevention'. Let me briefly identity each in turn. They are:

- lethality, which 'identifies the likely loss of life if the threat is not eliminated'
- likelihood, which 'assesses the probability that the threat will occur'
- legitimacy, which 'covers traditional just war criteria of proportionality, necessity and deliberativeness of proposed responses' and, finally
- legality, which 'asks whether the threatening situation is itself produced by legal or illegal actions, and whether the proposed remedy is more or less legal'.[61]

Doyle is insistent that 'building on just war theory, I argue all four standards are necessary to justify prevention',[62] and the rest of his argument consists of an elaboration of these standards set against the criteria of past (and in one instance future) cases of actual (or possible) preventive war. As with Bobbitt, and Buchanan and Keohane – and in this respect unlike Luban whose insistence on the nonproxyable character of legitimate preventive war effectively rules it out – a great deal of attention is paid to the institutional infrastructure that could be developed to facilitate such a doctrine. Indeed, in Doyle's case the legality requirement is even more systematically discussed than in the others, and he adds that the overall set of standards that he proposes should be seen as multiplicative not additive.

This simply means, for him, that 'if one standard measure is at zero, no preventive action is justified. Combined, they provide guides for determining when prevention is justified.'[63] It is worth quoting him at length to see how he envisages this working:

First, if a threat is not imminent, and hence uncertain, it can still be likely enough that, when the lethality is taken into account, it is as dangerous as a threat justifiably pre-empted ... Second, acquisitions of destructive capabilities by law abiding states, whatever their ideology, should not be considered sufficient evidence to justify preventive measures. Third, the greater the lethality and likelihood of an attack by a threatening regime, the less egregious its violations of international law must be in order to justify

[61] All quotations taken from Doyle, *Striking First*, p. 46.   [62] Ibid., p. 47.
[63] Ibid., p. 63.

prevention. And fourth ... the less the lethality and likelihood of the threatened attack, the greater the weight that should be placed on both the legality of the threatening regime's actions and any potential international response.[64]

The similarity of these categories to those articulated by Buchanan and Keohane and to some extent hinted at by Bobbitt does not really need elaborating. One can find many other similar arguments. One final example must stand for many. Henry Shue recently put forward a similar argument in which, at the end, he also gives four 'tentative necessary conditions for a justified early military action':[65]

1 it must be limited to the effective elimination, including the prevention of the return, of the danger that justifies it;
2 it must be undertaken only when military action is urgent;
3 it must be based on well-verified, solid intelligence collected by a highly competent agency; and
4 it must be substantively multilateral, that is based on principles justifiable on the basis of reasons broadly acceptable internationally.[66] (This is an obvious difference from someone like Luban for whom, one supposes, this would be anathema.)

Again, the similarity is striking, even though Shue qualifies his conditions rather more than Doyle does by insisting that they are 'incomplete and utterly minimal' and 'extremely difficult to satisfy'.[67]

The real point of all of the above, I want to insist however, is the extent to which writers such as Doyle, Buchanan and Keohane, Luban, Bobbitt, and Shue – all well-known supporters of the laws of war and committed to institutional restraints on the use of force – are prepared to countenance an extension of the scope of the use of force beyond anything that the just war tradition has historically countenanced. We have seen this gradual stretching of the scope of 'legitimate force' before, both in the case of humanitarian intervention and in the wider debates after 9/11, and in its most baleful form we will see it in Chapter 5 in the deployment of notions of supreme emergency.

---

[64] Ibid.
[65] Henry Shue, 'What Would a Justified Preventive Military Attack Look Like?' in Shue and Rodin (eds.) *Preemption*, pp. 226–46.
[66] Ibid., p. 245.   [67] Ibid., p. 246.

Assessing the arguments

In a moment I want to turn to the mutual relationship of what I called (in Chapter 1) the 'enlightened therapeutic' state and the arguments I have just discussed. But first, I think it would be useful to say something about how we might evaluate arguments about both humanitarian intervention and preventive war on their own terms, since I would like to suggest that even if we do broadly accept the claims they make about the changing circumstances of global security – and I will return in a moment to whether we should – there are very good reasons for not developing a doctrine of justifiable preventive war and for being very suspicious about many (if not all) claims for humanitarian intervention. I should emphasize, however, that this does not imply, by definition, that there are no instances of actions taken to prevent an obvious wrong being legitimate. I shall come back to this seeming paradox in the Epilogue. In general, I think we might offer three kinds of responses to these arguments: pragmatic, ethical and epistemological.

Pragmatic responses

To begin with here, I think that it is worth dwelling on the obvious fact that much of the weight of the arguments both about humanitarian intervention and, especially, preventive war rests on the possibility of the institutionalization of the moral framework outlined. This is most ambitious in the cosmopolitan framework outlined by Buchanan and Keohane, but Doyle too suggests that *central* to the idea of a justifiable doctrine of preventive war is an institutional setting in which the justifications could be heard, weighed and judged, and in much of the literature of humanitarian intervention, as we saw (especially, for example, in claims about 'responsibility to protect'), the possibility of effective institutionalization is also central. But, short of a world state with sovereign powers,[68] who is to enforce judgement on major powers if there is disagreement (as famously there was in the case of

---

[68] It is not insignificant, I think, that interest in the idea of a world state has risen again – after almost a fifty-year hiatus – in tandem with debates on the use of force post-9/11. For a good survey of recent arguments see Campbell Craig, 'The Resurgent Idea of World Government', *Ethics and International Affairs*, 22, 2, 2008, 133–42.

Iraq)? The United Nations Security Council is after all – as currently constructed – a *forum* for sovereign powers not a *replacement* of them, and sovereign powers, as we know, jealously guard their sovereignty.[69] Thus, how will these mechanisms work to guarantee that states will not abuse the institutional processes set up to establish 'humanitarian interventions' or 'justifiable preventive wars', as they have many times already done with other aspects of existing institutional processes? States are, after all – at least some states and possibly most states – part of the problem; is it really appropriate to suppose they could suddenly become the solution?

An additional point might be that in creating an institutional process for justifiable preventive war, even in the very careful way in which Doyle, and Buchanan and Keohane suggest, one might create what amounts to a system of perverse incentives to create circumstances where the institutional process will be used. In his first article advocating a limited right of preventive war, Luban himself makes this point, calling it 'the self fulfilling prophecy problem',[70] and it is one of the reasons why he insists that his notion of legitimate preventive war should be limited not only to the state under threat but also to a certain kind of threat (WMD). We can certainly easily conceive of what he means. Think of how some Palestinians might reason about the existence of Israel in terms of Doyle's four conditions. On past form it would certainly not be unreasonable for Palestinians to think that on Doyle's lethality principle there will be high continuing loss of Palestinian life if the threat (Israel) is not eliminated and high likelihood that the threat (Israeli use of force against Palestinian forces or territory) will occur. Palestinians could easily develop a case for a proportional, necessary, deliberated, and military response, and as far as legality is concerned, how should one understand the 'legality' of either side's views in this most intractable of problems, where both sides routinely break agreements, drag their feet, and exercise high levels of just plain mendacity in their dealings with one another and outsiders as well? The point of course is not to take a stand on the merits of the argument but rather to show how

---

[69] This is related to the sceptical arguments advanced by Richard Tuck in his response to Doyle's arguments, though I am putting it slightly differently. See Doyle, *Striking First*, pp. 119–28.

[70] See Luban, 'Preventive War' and 'Preventive War and Human Rights', p. 172.

easy it would be to develop a case for 'preventive war' in many different sorts of circumstances, once the bar is lowered.

Ethical responses

The next set of problems strike deeper still. Almost all of the writers I cited above pay homage to, or assert that they are drawing on, the just war tradition (or both) but also accept, of course, that the tradition has, latterly at least, not had much time for notions of intervention and even less for preventive war.[71] They therefore are keen to emphasize that their suggested modifications to contemporary theory and practice are compatible with the just war tradition. How reasonable is this claim?

To assess it, let me consider Buchanan and Keohane's critique of what they term the 'just war blanket prohibition argument' against preventive war.[72] The first objection they consider is from those who would argue that the 'crucial point about preventive force ... is ... [that] it is directed toward someone who has not committed a wrong. Thus preventive action violates the rights of its target.'[73] Their response to this objection is to say that 'there is, trivially, a right not to be attacked unjustly. But to assume that this includes the right not to be attacked unless one has already committed, or begun to commit, a wrongful harm is to beg the question at issue – namely whether preventive force can ever be justified.'[74] As they have stated it, this is fair enough, as far as it goes, but it does not, I think, go very far. A just use of force, according to even modern versions of the tradition, would require that several conditions be met if it is to be plausibly presented as legitimate. The reason why preventive force cannot meet these conditions may *contingently* have something to do with the claim that a preventive use of force will be attacking an 'innocent' – that is to say not wrongdoing – party but this *is* a contingent argument not

---

[71] A partial exception is Wheeler, who does not refer to the tradition and who, in some places, indicates he shares aspects of the general 'English school' scepticism about it, that I touched on in Chapter 2.

[72] For a very interesting critique of their position, on parallel but different lines to the one presented here, see Steven Lee, 'A Moral Critique of the Cosmopolitan Institutional Proposal', *Ethics and International Affairs*, 19, 2, 2005, 99–107. See Buchanan and Keohane, 'Reply to Steven Lee: Justifying Preventive Force', in the same issue, pp. 109–11.

[73] Buchanan and Keohane, 'The Preventive Use of Force', p. 6.   [74] Ibid.

a necessary one. The just war criterion that would principally limit preventive war is a different one, namely last resort. By definition, a *preventive* use of force could not be a 'last resort'. And, of course, the prohibition in the tradition is on the *use of force*, not on the idea of preventive action per se.

And it is perhaps worth emphasizing here that in many cases, in both discussions of humanitarian intervention and preventive war, there is often an elision of *action* and *force*. The just war tradition has no prohibition at all on many types of intervention or preventive *action* – up to and including political, legal and/or economic sanctions – it only prohibits preventive force, because it assumes that force should always be the last resort not only because it is intrinsically bad (because it must require killing) but also because of its unpredictability.

Another objection Buchanan and Keohane consider is the claim that:

> prevention carries special risks that are not present in the case of armed responses to actually occurring attacks ... even if preventive action would be morally justified when certain highly ideal conditions were satisfied, it does not follow we should replace current restrictions on preventive force with a more permissive rule ... it is not enough to show, the objector would conclude, that there are some circumstances in which preventive action would be morally justified. If these cases are few – and if there is significant risk that those contemplating preventive action may err in determining whether those circumstances will obtain – then perhaps preventive action should be prohibited altogether.[75]

Their response to this objection, however, is to argue that it is fatally incomplete.

> It overlooks the fact that acceptable risk reduction can be achieved not only by a blanket prohibition but also by a more permissive rule embedded in an appropriate institutional framework. Indeed a blanket prohibition comes at a high cost, since it rules out action to prevent massive violations even when the costs of prevention are very low and the likelihood of its success is very high.[76]

Again, the problem here is partly that they mischaracterize, I think, both the reason for the just war tradition's hostility to the idea of preventive war – its abhorrence of the idea of war in general – and the manner in which it should be understood. But in this case I would also call in aid the pragmatic concerns I mentioned above. Buchanan

[75] Ibid., p. 8.   [76] Ibid.

and Keohane are resting their response to this objection in part on the claim that their institutional proposals – as I have said, rather more ambitious than Doyle's – can deliver the goods of 'risk reduction' better than an outright ban, but I have already argued that I think this is very questionable absent a much more robust institutional mechanism than we currently have in place, and indeed – as I shall argue in a moment – I would be sceptical about their prospect of success even if such a robust institutional mechanism were present. They make an additional point that a blanket ban also weakens other forms of preventive action – such as coercive diplomacy – since without the possibility of preventive force, coercive threats will be 'less credible', but frankly, I simply do not see how this is supposed to follow. If state A says to state B that it will intervene in state B's attempt to suppress group C if state B oppresses group C with military force, I do not see how the mere fact of the lack of a formal doctrine of preventive war will make state A's statement any less credible. Either state B will take state A's claim seriously – in which case it will factor it into its decision making – or it will not. Whether it does so will depend on many factors: its history of relations with state A, its assessment of the political conditions in state A, the interests that might be at stake (spoken or unspoken), and a whole host of other factors. The lack of a formal doctrine of justifiable preventive war to me does not seem likely to be very high up the list.

Epistemological responses

Let me now turn to the epistemological reason I have for supposing doctrines of humanitarian intervention and even more of justifiable preventive war to be very problematic. Buchanan and Keohane have effectively already raised this in the above discussion, and conceded that there is a problem, albeit one they think can be addressed by their institutional proposals. But fundamentally the problem is not one about institutions, but rather one about individuals and the knowledge they can or should be able to possess, and what they can or should do with that; in other words it is a question of both epistemology and judgement. As Buchanan and Keohane put it, in the tones of the objection they seek to reject:

The prima facie moral argument for preventive action asserts that preventive action may be undertaken to remove or mitigate a wrongfully imposed dire risk. However for a dire risk to lead to harms, a long causal series of events must typically be completed. Even if the probability of each event in the series is high, the probability of the harm will be much lower … furthermore if events are uncertain – that is probabilities are unknown – it is impossible to calculate precise probabilities.[77]

To which, I am tempted to respond, it always is. Not merely because of the long 'causal chain' – I am leaving aside the question as to whether this is a very helpful way of considering human agency in any event – but also because events are always uncertain and projected ones even more so than any other sort. The just war tradition, as I pointed out in Chapter 3, has always been very sceptical not only about human motivation but also about human reasoning capacities: not that we cannot reason, but we cannot expect too much of our reason. It is no accident that the tradition's first great thinker, Augustine, was also a profound sceptic about reason. One of the major problems with a good deal of contemporary just war theorizing, as I suggested in Chapter 3, is precisely the attempt to replace Augustinian scepticism with a much more 'rationalist' approach to the tradition. An additional advantage of the existing prohibition is that it at least requires *actual* harms before we act; thinking we know harms are on the way is all too easy but may be mistaken; but then, if we have taken 'preventive action', we have let the genie of war out of its bottle and will have the devil's own time putting it back.

'Enlightened therapeutic' agents, intervention and preventive war

All of the above set to one side the initial claim that led to the argument about justifiable preventive war in the first place. How plausible, then, is the claim that the contemporary 'global security environment' presents a new set of challenges that requires us to develop a justifiable notion of preventive war? I have already argued[78] that general claims of this sort, made often enough in the post-9/11 environment, are overstated and exaggerated when they are not clearly false, but does this also hold in the context of preventive war?

In important ways, I think it does. Most of the writers I have cited above make the lynchpin of their arguments the changing relationship between weapons of mass destruction (chiefly nuclear, but also perhaps chemical and biological) and the possibility of their use by 'rogue'

[77] Ibid.   [78] See Chapter 1.

regimes or substate groups, arguing that this new relationship profoundly changes the character of possible pre-emption, as it may make
detection of what Doyle calls 'active preparation' much more difficult
than it has perhaps been traditionally (and it was difficult enough
then). Of course, none of this rules out other possible measures to deal
with specific problems. Doyle discusses dissuasion through non-
forcible prevention, denial and deterrence as possibly effective strategies in many cases, but he adds that 'today's more salient threats do
not appear to be fully amenable to such traditional counterstrategies.
Preventive responses that involve unilateral armed attack or multilateral enforcement measures may be necessary.'[79]

Yet if we look at the kinds of cases that are usually seen as instanti-
ating 'today's more salient threats', we come down, effectively, to one:
'terrorism' – I put this term in quotation marks to indicate a question
about the term and its usefulness, at least in the current context. It is a
notorious truism, of course, that there is no agreed scholarly definition
of 'terrorism',[80] that most discussions of 'terrorism' adopt explicitly
political understandings (that is to say, understandings that are used
and deployed by political actors for political reasons), and that there is
a great, and in particular in times of real tension, very obvious impre-
cision in the use of the term even when these two observations are
borne in mind. But my chief concern about the term is rather at right
angles to this. To put it as delicately as I can, I am unclear how the term
'terrorism' helps us, either normatively or even analytically. If the point
of the discussion is normative – that is to say asking questions about
the moral (or other normative) justification for this or that instance of
political violence, then the term 'terrorism' adds nothing since the
answer (if, indeed, answer there can be) will be of the form '*This*
instance of political violence is morally/normatively legitimate/illegit-
imate for reasons xyz.' Calling instance A of political violence 'terrorism' is simply irrelevant in this context. Even very thoughtful scholars
of the ethics of force can get caught up in this particular paradox.
Tony Coady, for example, whose work I referred to in Chapter 3,

---

[79] Doyle, *Striking First*, p. 21.
[80] For discussions of the issues surrounding this see Paul Wilkinson, *Terrorism
versus Democracy* (New York: Frank Cass, 2001), Bruce Hoffman, *Inside
Terrorism*, 2nd edn (New York: Columbia University Press, 2006), and Louise
Richardson, *What Terrorists Want: Understanding the Terrorist Threat*
(London: John Murray, 2006).

understands terrorism as 'the deliberate targeting of non-combatants for political purposes'[81] (he is followed in this by some others, for example Alex Bellamy).[82] But surely, this cannot be exhaustive. It may well be (I would agree, in general terms, it would be) monstrous deliberately to attack civilians for political purposes, but one then has to have a conception of non-combatant or 'civilian' that all could accept. Are we to infer from Coady's definition that if somebody 'genuinely' believed that all Western citizens are collectively guilty for the alleged crimes of their governments – as some jihadists are said to, for example – then targeting them would not be 'terrorism' because, at least in their own minds, such an attack would not be on non-combatants? This hardly seems plausible, in which case it is surely better to do without the notion of 'terrorism' altogether.

If the purpose of the discussion is rather to describe a particular action or class of actions, either in terms of the intention of the agents or the class of actions to which the actions belong, then any term used has, surely, to be adopted as a strictly descriptive term across all possible, or plausible, instances of its use. Some prominent scholars have, for example, suggested that 'terrorism' is a 'strategy', a technique; essentially one that is designed to use fear and terror to achieve political objectives.[83] But then all instances of the technique must fall under the descriptor. Nuclear deterrence was openly predicated upon fear and terror, and so if this 'technique' is terroristic, all states that advocated or relied on deterrence were, by definition, 'terrorists'. Yet this conclusion is not generally drawn and so, again, I fail to see what the use of the term adds to our scholarly inquiry. One certainly can, of course, write a history of a group that explicitly sees itself as a 'terrorist' group (something that most groups so designated do not do) and say interesting things about their use of the term and what they mean by it and one can also trace the uses to which such a term is put in contemporary politics, but that is about the extent of the usefulness of the term.

In which case, surely, it is difficult to see how it can be used to justify the possible need to resort to preventive war. Doyle argues that

---

[81] C.A.J. Coady, 'The Morality of Terrorism', *Philosophy*, 60, 1, 1985, 47–69.

[82] In Alex Bellamy, *Just Wars: From Cicero to Iraq* (Cambridge: Polity Press, 2006), Chapter 7.

[83] This definition is especially associated with some of the 'founding figures' of terrorism studies, for example Paul Wilkinson and Brian Jenkins.

scholars who have written on these topics – he cites, for example, Graham Allison[84] – have argued that the possibility of 'nuclear terrorism' requires a preventive – and cooperative and multilateral – strategy, in other words just the kind of strategy that Doyle is himself seeking to develop. But the point here is that the question we have to deal with is surely the use of preventive force, not of prevention in general. As Doyle himself admits, many states and even some substate groups can be dealt with in relatively traditional ways, and where they cannot it is not clear that preventive force would deal with them either, at least in ways that would not make the cure worse than the disease. It may well be true that groups such as al-Qaeda have much more interest in acquiring and using weapons of mass destruction than groups like the IRA, but to use 'preventive force' against al-Qaeda would simply mean striking them before they had struck anyone, on the assumption that they were going to (using force against al-Qaeda now, after they have attacked, hardly counts at all as 'preventive', though of course it is open to be judged in other ways), and in this respect the justification would, in principle, exist for any group that threatens the state. Doyle's reasoning would, it seems to me, certainly have legitimated the British government attempting a 'preventive strike' against the Provisional IRA after the split with the original IRA. But, of course, this kind of strategy is not remotely new; it has existed, in all probability, since the beginnings of organized violence. The only thing that is new about it is the attempt to legitimize it, and in this context, I do not see how the changed circumstances add anything of substance to the world we have always known.

In other words, I am far from convinced that anything has changed in the 'global security environment' that would require or legitimate a new 'doctrine of preventive war'. But one thing does seem to have changed: there is an increasing desire to relax the prohibitions that currently exist on the use of force coming from those who have traditionally been keenest to see the use of force restricted. If this desire is successful it will, I think, create very serious problems for the coherence of the just war tradition in the contemporary world and also indeed for the ideas that liberal internationalists (such as Buchanan, Keohane and Doyle) have traditionally supported both in their own

---

[84] In Graham Allison, *Nuclear Terrorism: The Ultimate Preventable Catastrophe* (New York: Times Books, 2004).

countries and in the wider international society. I cannot think that if they look hard at this they would welcome either.

Conclusions

The attempt to restrict war is always going to be, at least to some degree, a rush for fool's gold (as perhaps some other chapters in this book have suggested). And even if it is not, the reality of the practice of preventive war in the history of international politics – or at least wars that might be deemed 'preventive' – by both states and by non-state actors might mean that whatever might be true more generally, the attempt to constrain this practice is equally likely to run into the sand. One might also suppose that since the agents all our advocates of preventive war are relying on to guarantee the 'institutional processes' of validating justifiable preventive war are states – which, as I have already remarked, are more usually part of the problem – we would be very foolish to suppose that anything other than 'business as usual' in the international system is likely to ensue.

But none of these claims would come as a surprise to any of the major thinkers of the just war tradition from antiquity to the early modern period. It is their scepticism about human beings, not any belief in their inherent nobility, that fed into the just war tradition in the first place. The tradition was necessary because human beings and human societies were the way they are, torn between conflicting demands, moral and practical. No serious just war thinker expected war to be abolished – few excoriated it more than Augustine – but therefore we have to learn how to think about it, how to reason in the light of it, what to think and how to understand, given the reality of war. As I have said, I think that the tradition is close to both pacifism and realism in its unflinching way of confronting the fact that human beings do behave like this, and probably always will, but it is also properly realistic in its acceptance that human beings being torn between the ethical and the practically necessary is not all there is to human beings or human societies.

That is where I think the contemporary shift away from this 'dark-souled' element of the just war tradition towards, relatively speaking, a more rationalist and more optimistic assessment both of the proclivities of individuals and groups, including states, and of our ability to create and set up institutional procedures that can manage a permissive attitude to the use of force, is so problematic. It is not that Doyle, Luban, Bobbitt, Buchanan or Keohane are anything other than genuinely committed to thinking through ways in which human beings might be able to regulate their collective affairs more benignly, more effectively, and with less likely violations of the things we hold most dear, or that their efforts to do so are not marked by scrupulous intellectual honesty and very considerable power. They have the sense that we need to rethink aspects of the way we think about the use of force, by states and by other groups, and I agree with them. But because they are predicating this rethinking on a belief that the world of international politics has changed in important ways – that it has changed in kind, rather than just in degree – and that the required response means the institutionalization of common purposes, they are taking that rethinking in a profoundly problematic and teleocratic direction.

In *Murder in the Cathedral*, his wonderful meditation on the dilemmas of moral and practical action, and of the temptations of both temporal and spiritual pride, T.S. Eliot puts into verse a sense of the danger that hovers over much human action. 'The last temptation is the greatest treason', Eliot writes. 'To do the right thing, for the wrong reason.' It is, of course, right to try to rethink how we might understand and confront those tendencies in our world that threaten the possibilities of lives lived free from artificially imposed fear or oppression. But to do so by opening the door to more permissive uses of force when so many of the tendencies in the international system are already pushing in that direction, and to weaken the restraints, however limited, however partial, of traditions of thought such as the just war tradition is surely to risk succumbing to the 'greatest treason'. This applies not merely to the use of force 'internationally'; it applies also to the use of coercive force per se. For such a way of thinking goes hand in hand with one other prominent trajectory in the contemporary use of force that is antithetical both to the just war in any of its traditional guises and to the notion of civil politics itself: the idea of supreme emergency.

5 | *Supreme emergency*

Listen to what they did.
Don't listen to what they said.
What was written in blood
Has been set up in lead.

Lead tears the heart.
Lead tears the brain.
What was written in blood
Has been set up again.

The heart is a drum.
The drum has a snare.
The snare is in the blood.
The blood is in the air.

Listen to what they did.
Listen to what's to come.
Listen to the blood.
Listen to the drum.
James Fenton, 'Blood and Lead'

In 1977, H.L.A. Hart published an essay in the *Georgia Law Review*. 'The Nightmare and the Noble Dream' essayed a characteristically brilliant interpretation of twentieth-century American legal theory suggesting that the whole body of United States jurisprudence was focused on the question of how to respond to the reality of judges striking down democratically validated legislation on constitutional grounds.[1] One response – the nightmare – was to assert versions of a totally

---

[1] 'American Jurisprudence through English Eyes: The Nightmare and the Noble Dream', *Georgia Law Review*, 11, 5, 1977, 969–90. I am not the only one, of course, to recognize the fecundity of Hart's title. The phrase also became the subtitle of Nicola Lacey's excellent biography *The Life of H.L.A. Hart: The Nightmare and the Noble Dream* (Oxford University Press, 2006).

unconstrained indeterminacy in law, a position adopted in varying ways and to varying degrees, Hart thought, by the early twentieth-century American legal realists, by Deweyesque pragmatists and, more recently, by the critical legal studies movement. The leading alternative – the noble dream – assumed a complete legal determinacy, with resources being found within law for a consistent set of legal principles informing judges' decisions and, indeed, the law itself. Among the leading representatives of this view, Hart thought, were Roscoe Pound (and, one might add, though Hart did not, Lon Fuller), but the chief contemporary representative – and Hart's chief target in the essay – was the judicial prescriptivism of Ronald Dworkin.

My concern in this chapter, of course, is not with Hart's essay or with US legal theory, but rather with an idea which has become increasingly prevalent in the years since 2001, though it is certainly not without antecedents in previous periods. In the version I shall want to consider here, I shall call it the argument from 'supreme emergency'. That term has been most searchingly discussed in recent times by Michael Walzer, and I shall indeed turn to his understanding of the term in a moment, but I should emphasize that my use of the term covers rather more than Walzer's does, though his understanding is also central to it, for reasons I will elaborate a little later on.

It is in this context that Hart's essay – or at least his title – becomes useful. For I think that in the contemporary discussions of supreme emergency we can see something similar to the dichotomy Hart describes. I want to suggest that, for the modern just war in general, supreme emergency exists as a kind of 'noble dream', a suspension of the rules that somehow still supports them and one which is constrained by the spirit (if not the letter) of the laws. Perhaps the paradigm case of this argument is outlined with unmatched clarity by Walzer, but a rather different though still related version of it, I suggest, can be found in some other prominent contemporary just war writers, for example Jean Bethke Elshtain.[2]

However, for many it is not a dream but a 'nightmare'. For those who think this, as we saw in Chapter 2, what we face – perhaps especially what we face now – is the radical indeterminacy of threat and response brought about by the changing character of the threats and the danger

[2] In, respectively, *Michael Walzer, Just and Unjust Wars: A Moral Argument with Historical Illustrations*, 3rd edn (New York: Basic Books, 2000(1977) and Jean Bethke Elshtain, *Just War Against Terror* (New York: Basic Books, 2003).

they create and which issues in the assumption that because there *is* such an emergency, the 'rules', whatever they are, no longer apply and must be remade or completely set aside. For those who think like this – for example Richard Posner, and at least many of those who crafted the jurisprudence of the Bush administration in the early twenty-first century – the just war tradition is at best an irrelevance, at worst a positive hindrance to the successful exercise of power. And the 'rules of war' in the twenty-first century will have little or no place for it.

In fact, however, I will argue that these conceptions are interdependent in that both are dependent on a 'strong' reading of the centrality of the modern teleocratic state as the *sine qua non* and that, inasmuch as they are, they tend to incline in the same direction, much to the detriment of any meaningful deployment of the just war tradition. Indeed, in many respects, and extending the argument of Chapter 4, the entangling of the just war tradition with the teleocratic state creates what I shall suggest is an ultimate *reductio ad absurdum* for the tradition: it is in the context of the notion of supreme emergency that the tradition's essential incompatibility with the idea of the teleocratic state is most manifest.

My argument in this chapter thus falls into three broad parts. In the first, I shall look at some recent attempts to deploy 'nightmare' versions of this argument in the context of the so-called war on terror and suggest both some specific reasons why they are each individually problematic and also one general reason why they are all so. Then, second, I shall consider what I take to be the most important contemporary formulations of the 'noble dream' version of the supreme emergency argument in the just war tradition, and examine their strengths and weaknesses. I will suggest both that such arguments represent the most convincing cases for some deployment of the idea of supreme emergency and that if they cannot be sustained (as I shall argue they cannot) then the 'nightmare' version cannot be either. In the third part, I will suggest what the persistence of the arguments – in the light of that failure – tells us about the politics of war, the character of the state, and the just war tradition in our own time. Finally, and as a precursor to the Epilogue, I shall offer a thought about how we might react to this.

The nightmare

To begin with, then, I want to pick up the threads of the argument outlined in Chapter 2. The context in which certain kinds of 'supreme emergency' argument have been made in recent years is obvious: it is the aftermath of 9/11.[3] While there was already considerable interest in notions of 'catastrophic risk' or 'laws of fear' in more general terms,[4] these ideas both fed off, and were fed into, both academic and practical debates surrounding 9/11. As we saw in Chapter 1, in both the United States and within the United Kingdom especially, wholly new legislative and executive powers have been deemed to be warranted – for example the creation of the whole apparatus of homeland security in the US,[5] and the new anti-terror laws and new potential crimes such as are suggested in the government's recent anti-hate-speech legislation in the UK.[6]

In all these cases, the 'enabling' argument has been a version of the one I discussed (and criticized) in Chapter 1 – that the situation we face is new, and it is new because the political community – the state – has to face a distinctively new set of threats with possibly incalculable consequences. This claim was already nested in an existing set of concerns about growing 'catastrophic' risks and how we should think about them and respond to them. From the mid 1990s onwards there has been a veritable cottage industry of work that argues that human beings both face a range of potentially catastrophic risks and are not thinking very clearly (if indeed at all) about how to reduce or manage them.[7]

As we saw, this 'new' situation has led some to champion very extreme responses to the 'new' threats: in the recent context, very substantial restrictions of liberty and the overturning of some of the assumptions on which existing international (and in many cases

---

[3] See the full discussion in Chapter 2.

[4] See, for example, Corey Robin's excellent *Fear: The History of a Political Idea* (Oxford University Press, 2004); Cass Sunstein, *Laws of Fear: Beyond the Precautionary Principle* (Cambridge University Press, 2005); Richard Posner, *Catastrophe: Risk and Response* (Oxford University Press, 2004).

[5] For the remit and mission of the Department of Homeland Security see the Executive Order under which it was established: www.whitehouse.gov/news/ releases/2001/10/20011008-2.html. For an assessment of its achievements since then see the RAND Corporation report 'The Department of Homeland Security: The Road Ahead', January 2005.

[6] Racial and Religious Hatred Act 2005. For an overview of British legislative and organizational responses to 9/11 see Bradley W.C. Bamford, 'The United Kingdom's "War Against Terrorism"', *Terrorism and Political Violence*, 16(4), Winter 2004, pp. 737–56

[7] For a (very small) sample, see John Leslie, *The End of the World: The Science and Ethics of Human Extinction* (London: Routledge, 1996) and Posner, *Catastrophe*.

domestic) law was thought to be based. Perhaps the highest-profile case was the defence (or redefinition at least) of what was previously thought to constitute torture and the sense (and from many different angles) that some attention needed to be given to this since it was an inevitable feature of this 'new' situation. Most notoriously, perhaps, the Harvard Law scholar Alan Dershowitz argued for the incorporation of torture into US law under specific circumstances through the creation of what he called 'torture warrants'.[8]

Dershowitz's defence of this claim is couched in terms of a by-now-familiar form of rhetorical philosophical argument: the so-called 'trolley problem', first developed by Philippa Foot in the context of medical ethics and then, more famously, by Judith Jarvis Thompson.[9] Dershowitz's version is as follows:

The classical hypothetical case involves the train engineer whose brakes become inoperative. There is no way he can stop his speeding vehicle of death. Either he can do nothing, in which case he will plough into a busload of schoolchildren, or he can swerve onto another track, where he sees a drunk lying on the rails. (Neither decision will endanger his passengers.) There is no third choice. What should he do?[10]

Of course, a number of things might be said about this form of argument. First, it seems at least pertinent to remark that such hypothetical examples are used because they have the 'alleged' merit of focusing on the specifics of choice and abstracting from real contexts. In keeping with the rather stylized manner in which such 'choice situations' are introduced, actual reference to anything that might smack of the 'world out there' is ruthlessly exorcized. Some time ago Robert Goodin provided a powerful (and very funny) critique of this kind of reasoning,[11] but apparently people have not been listening, given the prevalence such arguments have today. Surely, as he suggests,

---

[8] See Alan Dershowitz, *Why Terrorism Works: Understanding the Threat, Responding to the Challenge* (New Haven: Yale University Press, 2003). See also the discussions in Sanford Levinson (ed.) *Torture: A Collection* (Oxford University Press, 2005).

[9] Judith Jarvis Thompson, 'The Trolley Problem', *Yale Law Journal* 94, 1985, 1,395–415. Philippa Foot, 'The Problem of Abortion and the Doctrine of Double Effect', *Oxford Review*, 5, 1967, 5–15.

[10] Dershowitz, *Why Terrorism Works*, p. 132.

[11] See Robert E. Goodin, *Political Theory and Public Policy* (University of Chicago Press, 1982). See his critique of the *Philosophy and Public Affairs* 'Thought Experiment' on pp. 8–12.

it is at least as plausible to suppose that the process of abstraction in fact makes understanding what is at stake in real choice impossible, for it is precisely the contexts that shape the choosing. Second, the choice situation is structured in such a way that the relevant agent – here the train engineer – *literally* has no choice but to do something. Yet in real-world contexts it is unlikely to be the case that anyone (politican, activist, citizen, or what have you) will be in quite that position.

In the contemporary post-9/11 context, however – again as we saw in Chapter 1 – the argument is endlessly repeated that we are faced with a 'devil's alternative', a choice between two evils, and all we can do is to choose the lesser evil. This argument has been pressed by many in the post-9/11 context, including authors as otherwise different as Dershowitz, Michael Ignatieff and Jean Bethke Elshtain.[12] Indeed, such a claim, made in varying ways and different forms, has been central to many issue areas in the post-9/11 context.

There is in many of these arguments (thought certainly not all) a certain whiff of impatience with what some see as unnecessarily finely grained ethical distinctions which are simply out of place in the kind of conflict we ('in the West') now find ourselves in. A not atypical attitude to these developments is that expressed by Richard Posner in his contribution to Sanford Levinson's excellent *Torture: A Collection*. 'Only the most doctrinaire civil libertarians', Posner writes, '(not that there aren't plenty of them) deny that *if the stakes are high enough*, torture is permissible. No one who doubts that should be in a position of responsibility' (emphasis added).[13]

But such claims, of course, beg a number of questions. When (and how) can we determine when the stakes *are* high enough? What indeed might the 'stakes' be said to be? And just who, exactly, are the relevant 'we' here? Who is empowered to make such a decision? Posner's essay indicates the most usual answer to these questions, of course. It is to those in 'positions of responsibility' that such decisions fall. They decide what the stakes are, and when they are high enough to warrant

---

[12] Not all of these arguments are necessarily versions of supreme emergency, though most come close. In addition to Dershowitz, see Michael Ignatieff, *The Lesser Evil: Political Ethics in An Age of Terror* (Princeton University Press, 2004) and Jean Bethke Elshtain, *Just War against Terror* (New York: Basic Books, 2003). See also the argument I developed against Elshtain in Chapter 4.

[13] Levinson (ed.) *Torture*, p. 295. Posner is here partly agreeing with (though also criticizing) Dershowitz's arguments about torture.

the kinds of decision that might legitimate torture. But there is, of course, a suppressed premise here. For states seen as I suggested (in Chapter 1) modern states should be seen, only one way of understanding such a state – the teleocratic one – could conceivably warrant such decisions – and even that way of understanding such a state does not *automatically* legitimate them. In other words, we are still required to find a moral justification for taking the kinds of decisions Posner seems to suggest are (in the circumstances) obvious.

Moreover, there are many reasons, I think, why believers in 'liberal' states at least should be very hesitant to do so even if they subscribe to a broadly teleocratic view of such a state. These reasons have been made very clear recently by a number of scholars who have examined the arguments that Posner and others have given. To give a flavour of this let me turn to the arguments of two such writers who are, I think, especially pertinent.

In his essay 'A Life of Fear'[14] George Kateb provides an acute and powerful (if perhaps a little overwrought) critique of the general trajectory of the George W. Bush administration in terms of the erosion of civil liberties and the magnification of the power of the state. 'Great Power', he says, 'magnifies its opponents in order to justify using its strengths.'[15] He particularly concentrates on the 'National Defence Strategy of the United States of America' document, adopted in March 2005, and subjects it to withering critique:

Intrinsic to [its] mentality is an almost total disregard of the moral cost of violent means to achieve political ends ... the document ... wants 'global freedom of action' an amazing aspiration if you think about it for a minute. This is one version of pure politics ... a politics of action and augmentation for its own sake ... There is a fatal lack of moderation where every great danger is felt as an even greater opportunity ... [and thus] the long term motives behind the erosion of civil liberties and the practise of torture and degradation now come into sight. A society in which civil liberties are abridged *accustoms its people to put an inflated sense of safety or security above all other considerations and to do so on a regular basis* ... the state of emergency becomes the normal condition [and in] a state of emergency traditional kinds of restraints on, and inhibitions of, the state are weakened or dissolved.[16] (emphasis added)

[14] George Kateb, *Patriotism and Other Mistakes* (New Haven: Yale University Press, 2006), Chapter 4.
[15] Ibid., p. 89.   [16] Ibid., p. 90.

A different way of framing an essentially similar argument is offered by Bonnie Honig. In the Introduction to her powerful study *Emergency Politics* she observes that, in the current post-9/11 context, much political and legal theory focuses on questions of justification:[17]

> what may we do in response to emergency? ... What justifies the suspension of civil liberties? Under what conditions can sovereign power declare emergency, legally suspend law? ... When is it permissible to torture, detain without habeas corpus rights, deport, use rendition or invade another country?[18]

It is not Honig's intention to suggest that these are unimportant questions. Far from it. But she does want to rehearse a concern about what it is that *democratic* theorists do when they raise them.

> One worry is that we contribute to the very account of sovereignty that we mean to oppose ... we move the terrain for debate away from the critical questions of how emergency (re)produces sovereignty ... and how democratic actors can respond otherwise [onto] instead questions of when do the facts justify the (newly constrained or proceduralized) decision and what sort of decisions are justifiable at all.[19]

I want to suggest that Kateb and Honig are correct to assume that the invocation of emergency itself is part of the central problem not only because it is meant to justify extreme measures but also because such measures – and the invocation of emergency itself – become, in time, normalized. But here I want to add that the problem is perhaps even deeper than they suppose, for it is written deep in the heart of the teleocratic conception of the modern state. Indeed, in a certain sense, as we saw in Chapter 1, the condition of 'emergency' associated with the permanent threat of war is the default setting of a state considered as an association of this kind.

Thus it is perhaps not surprising that in circumstances where it is believed (however erroneously) that the threats arising from changed constellations of forces are as severe as some clearly believe, the 'emergency' setting will trump all other considerations. And clearly this is what happened in the minds of some, at least, after 9/11. But the fact

---

[17] Bonnie Honig, *Emergency Politics: Paradox, Law, Democracy* (Princeton University Press, 2009). Kateb is a co-dedicatee of the book, so it is perhaps not surprising that they are arguing along the same lines.
[18] Ibid., p. 1.   [19] Ibid., p. 2.

that they assume it (perhaps sincerely) is not in itself a justification. And, as the arguments of Kateb and Honig make clear, the dangers inherent in such a path, for liberal states at least, far outweigh any benefits that might accrue, even if the argument that justifies such moves in the first place were correct; which, as I have already argued, it is not. Which is why, I think, such arguments have been widely understood as profoundly problematic, even by those who make them. They cannot resist, so to say, a bad conscience, even though they do not let it stop them.

The noble dream

The bad conscience might vanish if it could be argued that, in fact, such decisions were ethically justifiable, even if still, in certain respects at least, problematic. It is this position, I fear, we find in a good deal of writing in the modern just war tradition. On the face of it, this would seem absurd for surely, it might be said, such arguments could not be made in the just war tradition. And indeed, on the surface, this would be paradigmatically true. The above argument is, after all, a modern version of an ancient argument, one essentially predicated on a much-quoted Latin tag, *inter arma, silent leges,* 'in time of war, the laws are silent'.[20] There is a good deal of discussion of such arguments in the literature of war from medieval times to our own.[21] But the just war tradition in general has always set itself against such arguments. As I pointed out in Chapter 3, citing Oliver O'Donovan, the tradition is nothing but 'a proposal for doing justice in the theatre of

---

[20] Remember that brief discussion of the *Bellum Romanum* in Chapter 3. An exhaustive discussion of the character, effectiveness and sustained power of the Roman idea of war can be found in Edward Luttwack, *The Grand Strategy of the Roman Empire* (Baltimore: Johns Hopkins University Press, 1979). See also note 13.

[21] General treatments of the character of war in the medieval period are plentiful. Two good collections are Maurice Keen (ed.) *Medieval Warfare: A History* (Oxford University Press, 1999) and Jim Bradbury (ed.) *The Routledge Companion to Medieval Warfare* (London: Routledge, 2004). An excellent account of the general significance of the Crusades – including ideas about holy war (influential on the modern notion of supreme emergency) – is Norman Housley, *Contesting the Crusades* (Oxford: Blackwell, 2006). A standard text for consideration of modern warfare is, of course, Peter Paret (ed.) *Makers of Modern Strategy* (Oxford: Clarendon Press, 1986).

war' and as such does not accept that there are 'emergency' situations that could set 'justice' aside.

So how does the principle become lodged within contemporary just war writing, and how significant is it that it is so lodged? The answer to the first part of the question, I think, is straightforward enough and implied by the argument of Chapter 3. It is principally through the example and the argument of Michael Walzer, who insists that the central issue in thinking about war is the protection of a certain conception of political community. As we saw in Chapter 3, Walzer is, in so many ways, the lodestar of the 'secular' just war and he is so in this context also. The answer to the second part of the question is, however, a bit more complicated. It is unquestionably true that many contemporary just war thinkers reject Walzer's arguments about supreme emergency. However, as I shall seek to argue, they do so in ways that do not damage the main thrust of his case and in this context, leave the *case for* the 'supreme emergency argument' essentially open, even if they reject the particular arguments Walzer himself makes, and this is enough to open the tradition to underwriting the overriding of the moral rules it exists to uphold, or in other words opens it to the charge of flat contradiction. Indeed, I will go further and suggest that it is in the arguments over the possibility (or not) of supreme emergency that the central dilemma facing the modern tradition is made most explicit. This will concern me at the end of this chapter.

Walzer's supreme emergency

To begin with, however, we should see how Walzer frames his argument, how, in other words, he tries to embed the supreme emergency argument in the architecture of the modern just war. Walzer develops the idea of supreme emergency, of course, in the context of spelling out 'the war convention' – as we saw in Chapter 3, this corresponds roughly to Walzer's version of the traditional *jus in bello* – and specifically as a precursor to his discussion of perhaps the most problematic aspect of that (for him): the question of nuclear deterrence. He suggests that the idea of supreme emergency is, in fact, a compound of two conditions both of which must be present if the idea of supreme emergency is to be (justifiably) invoked – danger and imminence:

[Supreme emergency] is defined by two criteria, which correspond to the two levels on which the concept of necessity works: the first has to do with the imminence of the danger and the second with its nature. The two criteria must both be applied. Neither one by itself is sufficient as an account of extremity or as a defence of the extraordinary measure extremity is thought to require ... can a supreme emergency be constituted by a particular threat – by a threat of enslavement or extermination directed against a single nation? Can soldiers and statesmen override the rights of innocent people for the sake of their own political community? I am inclined to answer this question affirmatively, though not without hesitation and worry ... [but] danger makes only half the argument; imminence makes the other half.[22]

Walzer illustrates this thesis with two detailed examples, both cases where the central principle of the *jus in bello* – non-combatant immunity – was intentionally violated. The first is the case of the strategic bombing of German cities by the British between 1940 and 1943 (which he argues could be seen as a context in which supreme emergency was legitimately deployed) and the second, the decision to drop atom bombs on Japan (which he argues cannot really be seen as a case of supreme emergency and was therefore doubly a crime). The reasons why the one was a case of supreme emergency which could therefore justify setting aside the rules of war and the other could not are complex but deserve some attention since they go to the heart of the justification Walzer wants to offer for the idea of supreme emergency.

In the British case, Walzer's argument depends on the claim, disputable of course but nonetheless very widely believed at the time, that the possibility of German victory in 1940–1 seemed real and that a German victory, given the character of the Nazi regime, was an appalling prospect, perhaps the most appalling prospect imaginable. Walzer is here drawing on a well-known earlier argument of his,[23] to wit that a Nazi victory would have been the worst thing imaginable and that, in order to defeat it, almost anything would be permissible. As he puts it in *Just and Unjust Wars*:

it does seem to me that the more certain a German Victory appeared to be in the absence of a bomber offensive, the more justifiable was the decision to launch the offensive. It is not just that such a victory was frightening, but also that it seemed in those years very close; it is not just that it was close, but also that it was so frightening. Here was a supreme emergency,

22 Walzer, *Just and Unjust Wars*, pp. 252–5.
23 See Walzer's well-known essay 'World War II: Why This War Was Different', *Philosophy and Public Affairs*, 1, 1, 1971.

where one might well be required to override the rights of innocent people and shatter the war convention.[24]

The corollary of this, of course, is that when the two things diverge, the idea of supreme emergency loses its hold. Walzer argues that while the bomber offensive *was* justified when Britain stood alone, by 1942 – when other military options had become available – it no longer was. Similarly, he argues that Truman's decision to drop atom bombs cannot be seen as a case of supreme emergency – though it is often portrayed as such – since the determining condition – that which made the choice either dropping the bomb or possibly suffering unimaginably large casualties on both sides – was not a fixed and appalling possibility (as in the case of a German victory) but rather a relatively easily removable policy – the Allied policy of unconditional surrender – so the twin poles of supreme emergency were not both present in this case.[25]

Eleven years after the publication of *Just and Unjust Wars*, Walzer returned to the question of supreme emergency in a lecture.[26] In this, he recognized the seeming paradox of asserting the *fact* of moral rules – he never suggests that the rules vanish – whilst at the same time saying it is a responsibility for the community to override them in certain very specific circumstances. He suggests, however, that this paradox is a paradox we have to live with. Indeed, he grounds the reality of the paradox in the fact that a community must do – sometimes – what individuals are rightly forbidden from doing in order to secure what he terms a community's 'ongoingness'.[27] Citing Burke's famous description of the political community as a contract between 'those who are living, those who are dead and those who are yet to be born', Walzer argues that such a

commitment to continuity across generations is a very powerful feature of human life, and it is embodied in the community. When our community is threatened, not just in its present territorial extension or governmental

[24] Walzer, *Just and Unjust Wars*, p. 259.

[25] American military planners estimated that Operation Olympic – the invasion of Japan – would cost at least 1 million US battle deaths and many more Japanese deaths, both military and civilian.

[26] 'Emergency Ethics'. First given as the Joseph A. Reich Sr Distinguished Lecture at the Air Force Academy and published by them, later included in Michael Walzer, *Arguing about War* (New Haven: Yale University Press, 2004).

[27] Walzer, *Arguing about War*, p. 43.

structure or prestige or honour but in what we might think of as its *ongoing-ness*, then we face a loss that is greater than any we can imagine, except for the structure of humanity itself. We face moral as well as physical extinction, the end of a way of life as well as a set of particular lives. And it is then that we may be driven to break through the moral limits that people like us normally attend to and respect.[28]

Walzer accepts that this is a radically 'communitarian' position and accepts also that this might be counted as an argument against communitarianism, 'For if we didn't value the community (however we conceive of community: people, nation, country, religion, common culture) in this intense way we might fight fewer wars and face fewer emergencies.' He adds, however, 'this is only to say that life would be safer without emotional entanglements. The statement is obviously true but not very helpful.'[29] Walzer insists that we do value community in the way he suggests we do, and that therefore supreme emergency as he describes it is a necessary corollary of that commitment. He concedes (and I shall come back to this later) that 'the strongest argument against supreme emergency is that it makes a fetish of the political community' but he insists that this is not to be understood as the state.

'The state' is nothing more than *an instrument* of the community, a particular structure for organizing collective action that can always be replaced by some other structure. The political community (the community of faith too) can't be similarly replaced. It consists of men, women and children living in a certain way and its replacement would require either the elimination of the people or the coercive transformation of their way of life. Neither of these actions is morally acceptable. But the reason for this unacceptability has nothing to do with fetishism. The political community is not magical, not mysterious ... it is a feature of our lived reality, a source of our identity and self understanding ... Moral communities make great immoralities morally possible. But they do this only in the face of a greater immorality ... and only at the moment when this attack is near success and only insofar as the immoral response is the only way of holding off that success. We can recognize a moral community by its respect for that reiterated word 'only'.[30] (emphasis added)

This claim is at the roots of Walzer's defence of the idea of supreme emergency, but as we shall see in a moment, it can only be sustained if the idea of community in question is, in fact, understood in a certain

[28] Ibid.   [29] Ibid., pp. 44–5.   [30] Ibid., pp. 49–50.

(teleocratic) way. However, for the moment let us see how the wider community of just war writers have responded to Walzer's arguments.

Criticisms of Walzer, but not of 'supreme emergency'?

As I remarked above, Walzer's general arguments on supreme emergency have not been met with anything like universal agreement from other just war thinkers. So how can I meaningfully suggest that the modern just war tradition opens itself to supreme-emergency-type arguments? In the first place, I happily accept that a large number, perhaps a majority, of contemporary just war thinkers do not agree with Walzer's formulation of the argument, indeed are profoundly critical of it. Nevertheless, crucially, I think that the criticisms they develop of it are, so to say, specific to Walzer's *arguments* and not to his general position. In other words, the *reason* why Walzer makes the arguments he makes is not disputed by most of his critics, only the specifics of his particular arguments in defence of them.

Of course, in the space available I cannot look at every possible line of criticism, so rather I want to focus on what I take to be three especially significant sets of criticisms, represented in turn by Joseph Boyle, Brian Orend, and Tony Coady. To begin with Boyle, he has made clear in a searching interrogation of Walzer's original arguments in *Just and Unjust Wars* that there are at least two ways of reading his arguments on this topic.[31] On the first reading, the basic assumptions underlying the claim are fundamentally consequentialist. As such they threaten to trump every other consideration (as consequentialist moral arguments usually do). As Boyle puts it, 'If the constraints of supreme emergency still allow a justification of terror bombing, as well as an inferred justification of nuclear deterrence, then it seems hard to fix the limits as stringently as Walzer wants.'[32]

This argument has been put to Walzer before, of course. David Luban, as we saw in Chapter 3, suggested many years ago that the danger in Walzer's 'casuistry' is that it effectively adopts a 'sliding scale' attitude to moral judgement; as the conventions change, in

---

[31] See Joseph Boyle, 'Just and Unjust Wars: Casuistry and the Boundaries of the Moral World', *Ethics and International Affairs*, 11, 1997, 83–98.
[32] Ibid., p. 93.

response, say, to technological development, moral judgements do as well, and that this effectively tips the argument into consequentialism.[33]

Boyle suggests, however, that this consequentialist reading is not one that meshes with the emphasis Walzer gives in the book on rights, with considerations of utility playing only a secondary role (it is also worth noting that Walzer expressly dismisses a consequentialist reading of his position in his 'Emergency Ethics' lecture). And so he is disposed to understand Walzer's claims about supreme emergency in a different way. This is simply to see them as 'genuinely tragic'. 'Although required, they are wrong; *pecca forbiter* ('Sin bravely') as a Lutheran might prescribe.'[34] This way of thinking, Boyle suggests, explains in a way that consequentialism cannot Walzer's sense that wrong is still done in such cases (for consequentialists, of course, it simply is not the case that wrong is done, if the action undertaken was the best in the circumstances).

Boyle thus suggests that this second way of reading Walzer's claim about supreme emergency certainly seems truer to Walzer's more general position than the previous consequentialist one. Yet both, he thinks, leave a gap at the same place. Simply put, the gap lies in the inability of Walzer's argument to stipulate how we should choose between possible actions: neither on utilitarian calculations nor on principled ones. 'Even after all moral considerations have been made,' Boyle remarks, 'one can only choose randomly between opposing demands or be guided by non-rational considerations like feelings. Calculation and intuition are replaced by volition and desire.'[35]

Why might this matter? It matters for Boyle, of course, since he wants to assert both that consequentialism fails as an ethical standard (a view he thinks he shares with Walzer) *and* that there is a plausible alternative in the form of a rationalistic deontology such as that proffered by Alan Donegan,[36] which is importantly different from Walzer's 'tragic', existential view of human moral choice, in that it can offer reasons for (or against) this or that course of action and does

---

[33] See David Luban, 'Just War and Human Rights', *Philosophy and Public Affairs*, 9, 2, 1980, 161–81.

[34] Boyle, 'Just and Unjust Wars', p. 97.   [35] Ibid.

[36] Alan Donegan, *The Theory of Morality* (University of Chicago Press, 1977). Boyle also sees this immanent in the 'new natural law theory' developed by himself, Germain Grisez and John Finnis. See, for example, Grisez, Boyle and Finnis, *Nuclear Deterrence, Morality and Realism* (Oxford University Press, 1987).

not have to fall back on 'volition or desire'. What Walzer seems to be arguing, by contrast, is that however central the 'rules of war' must be for our thinking about war in general, there are cases – like Britain in 1940 – that stand outside them and where the rules therefore can be overridden since the danger posed is so great and so imminent that anything could be justified in opposition to it.

Yet here, if this conclusion is to be generally upheld, then it must surely be predicated on seeing the survival of political community *as such* as central, rather than simply seeing the opposition of one state at one time as a necessary and just opposition to a particularly vile form of political community, namely Nazi Germany. In other words if there is a defensible argument about supreme emergency that is not specific to a particular moment in time or a particular historical situation but is generalizable – as a part of the just war tradition – then it must be the case, for Walzer, that the character of the moral world as such allows for a reasoned overriding of the rules. But if this is the case – if, in other words, what allows for the overriding of the 'usual' moral rules is a particular kind of threat to political community as such, which you might call an existential threat – then it is the safety of the political community, and not the rules of the moral world, that determines whether or not one adheres at any given moment to the rules. Moreover, this surely must apply *ex hypothesi* to any or all political communities, not merely to 'moral' ones (as Walzer rather obliquely suggests in his 'Emergency Ethics' lecture).

Brian Orend has provided some of the most powerful recent critical arguments against Walzer's conception of supreme emergency. In both a recent book and a recent essay, he charges Walzer with both radical inconsistency and muddled argument and details a range of problematic aspects to Walzer's arguments.[37] Yet at the end of the day, he does not deny the *fact* that there can be supreme emergencies, only that Walzer's way of framing them is adequate. For Orend, a supreme emergency takes us beyond morality:

From the moral point of view, a supreme emergency is a moral tragedy. A moral tragedy occurs when, all things considered, each viable option you

---

[37] Brian Orend, *Michael Walzer on War and Justice* (Montreal: McGill-Queen's University Press, 2001), and his 'Is There a Supreme Emergency Exemption?' in Mark Evans (ed.) *Just War Theory: A Reappraisal* (Edinburgh University Press, 2005).

face involves a severe moral violation ... From the prudential point of view, a supreme emergency is a desperate, Hobbesean struggle for survival and as a matter of fact any country subjected to it will do whatever it can to prevail.[38]

In other words, for Orend, as for Walzer, the fact of 'communities' – countries, in Orend's usual locution – leads to the inevitable fact of supreme emergencies. Orend concludes:

I do believe that the victim country, supposing its supreme emergency measures to succeed, owes its citizens and the international community a full public accounting after the war for what it did and why it did it. But that's all – no war crimes trials, no shaming, no symbolic handwringing. It was forced to do terrible things in order to survive.[39]

Here too, then, the most important fact seems to be the centrality of the political community. It is this – and nothing else – that accounts for and warrants (Orend would not, of course, say *justifies*) supreme emergency.

But are there no just war thinkers that would challenge this? The short answer, of course, is that there are. Let me take, as one representative figure here, C.A.J. Coady. In an important article and in a recent book, Coady outlines a distinctive position on morality and political violence.[40] Specifically in the current context, Coady takes Walzer to task for his alleged 'statism' and argues that there is no good reason (even on Walzer's own grounds) why if 'states' 'enjoy supreme emergency licence other groups should not'. But Coady adds:

As the name suggests, the supreme emergency story ... gets its persuasiveness from the idea that its disruptive power to override profound moral prohibitions is available only the rarest of circumstances. Any broadening of the reach of these circumstances tends to reduce the rarity value of the exception and hence increase the oddity of the idea that it can be right to do what is morally wrong.[41]

Thus, he argues, we are faced with a choice – an acceptance of a sliding scale of 'supreme emergencies' where all groups (potentially) could

---

[38] Orend, 'Is There a Supreme Emergency Exemption?' pp. 148–9.
[39] Ibid., p. 151.
[40] C.A.J. Coady, 'Terrorism, Morality and Supreme Emergency', *Ethics*, 114, 2004, 772–89, and his *Morality and Political Violence* (Oxford University Press, 2007).
[41] Coady, 'Terrorism, Morality and Supreme Emergency', p. 787.

claim them – which way lies moral and political chaos – or a decision to apply it to no agent at all and to say that the rules simply must be adhered to, the choice he suggests we should adopt.

Here, finally then, we appear to have found a theorist who rejects supreme emergency, reasserts the traditional just war insistence on the inviolability of the moral rules, and does not accept the 'statist' claims that have dominated the most influential versions of the modern tradition. However, while this is not a wholly inaccurate reading of Coady's position, it is also not wholly satisfactory either.

Coady's approach, as Christine Chwaszcza points out in an acute review of one of his books, hovers between a focus on individual moral obligations and a certain kind of realist consequentialism. As Chwaszcza puts it:

is it really sensible to frame [just war] in terms of personal integrity and to transform the responsibility for determining the justice of warfare into a question of individual virtues and vices? [Also] since Coady seems to agree that basic human rights of individual persons constitute a valuable source of claims for justice, he faces the problem that the restoration of respect for people's human rights can require the use of force against those who violate them.[42]

The problem, of course, is who is to exercise such force? It must be some sort of political community, presumably – though not necessarily a state – but if so then we are back to the kinds of claims that might be made for such political communities which could include (and if you are Walzer or Orend *would* include) a claim for a supreme emergency exemption under some circumstances. It is not that Coady agrees to this, exactly, it is simply that on the arguments as he presents them, he simply cannot (in practice) oppose it.

One might say, of course, that some other cosmopolitan just war thinkers we looked at in Chapter 3 would do so, but even there, as we saw, the strength of the argument for a purposive, justice-oriented political community (again not necessarily the state, as conventionally conceived) would push certainly secular versions of cosmopolitan just war theory into something very like a 'supreme emergency exemption' if certain conditions were met. The logic would be the same as Walzer's even though the specific agents, and the specific defences of such an agent's actions, would not.

[42] http://ndpr.nd.edu/review.cfm?id=13429.

Supreme emergency and teleocratic politics

We have reached the crux of the argument I want to present in this chapter. Both versions of the supreme emergency argument I have presented here depend for their plausibility on the existence and justificatory power of a strong purpose-oriented form of political community. In earlier chapters, I suggested that this form is chiefly visible, in the European tradition at least, in what, following Oakeshott, I called a teleocratic understanding of the modern state. That is, I think, clearly visible in the 'nightmare' versions of the argument given above. But in the context of the 'noble dream' version, Walzer, and some others (Coady, for example, and the cosmopolitans), might want to retort that the teleocratic conception of politics does not apply to them as they are not asserting a particular version of the state at all – that states and communities are *different* kinds of agents for them and that they are making an argument predicated on the idea of a strong community, but not at all on any given account of the state.

How are we to respond to this? In the first place, I think Walzer's claim that the state 'is nothing more than *an instrument* of the community, a particular structure for organizing collective action that can always be replaced by some other structure' is deeply, and at every level, implausible. Walzer wants to separate out the idea of the 'community' from particular institutional structures that manifest the will of that community. But the community cannot be said to *have* a will unless there are processes and institutional structures that can express it. Some of these – particular institutional arrangements et cetera – may indeed be contingent and replaceable, but is Walzer really suggesting that the idea any community possesses of the office and purpose of government per se is one such? As I argued in Chapter 3, Walzer's own general philosophy has a very clear understanding of how a community in the generic sense can have such a conception and does not assume that these two things are easily separable at all.[43]

---

[43] See for example Walzer's discussion in Chapter 4 of *Politics and Passion: Towards a More Egalitarian Liberalism* (New Haven: Yale University Press, 2004) where he points out that 'state and civil society resemble the chicken and the egg. No significant move toward greater equality has ever been made without state action but states don't act in egalitarian ways unless they are pressed to do so by … civil society' (p. 83). See also his discussion of membership and citizenship in *Spheres of Justice* (Oxford: Basil Blackwell, 1983).

Of course, there are forms of 'community' that do not possess such conceptions but those forms of community are not the kind with which Walzer is really concerned. He says, after all, that 'The *political* community is not magical, not mysterious ... it is a feature of our lived reality, a source of our identity and self understanding' (emphasis added). Indeed; and as such – as a 'political' community – it has a sense of institutionalized form, which includes ideas about the state, which *non*-political communities (the local chess club, the cricket team, the membership of Amnesty International) will not have. Walzer, as we saw in Chapter 3, has for a long time been criticized as succumbing to the 'romance of the nation-state', but even if this particular charge is not entirely fair, to suggest that the state and the political community do not converge in important – and non-separable – ways is not plausible at all.

If Walzer is vulnerable to this charge, what about some of the others I discussed? Perhaps they escape more easily. Not really. Orend talks about countries rather than communities but is much less worried whether this makes him a 'statist' and seems to accept something like a 'tragic' version of the nightmare case. Coady and the cosmopolitans present the most obvious challenge, on the surface, and I think it is true that certainly for some of them there is a real attempt to escape from the strictures of the nation-state as conventionally conceived. The problem, however, is what is supposed to replace it. Most cosmopolitans argue for some version of what Simon Caney has termed a 'cosmopolitan political programme – in which there are democratic supra-state institutions charged with protecting people's civil, political and economic rights'.[44] But there are perhaps two considerations that might be mentioned here. The first is to ask, as with any set of political institutions, what should (and would) be done if such an order were under existential threat – the kind of threat some believe contemporary Western states are under. There are reasons – perhaps best displayed in some versions of classical natural law theory – why one might say (and mean) *fiat iustitia ruat coelum*, 'let justice be done though the heavens fall', but without the kind of transcendental warrant that natural law in its classical form provides it seems unlikely that many would say that.

---

[44] Simon Caney, *Justice Beyond Borders: Towards a Global Political Theory* (Oxford University Press, 2005), p. 149.

In that case, the 'supra-state institutions' would themselves end up with a version of the supreme emergency exemption.

Moreover, they are very likely to do so if the second consideration is borne in mind. This is simply to repeat that the teleocratic mode of understanding government is not tied directly to the institutions of the nation-state. As I remarked earlier, Oakeshott himself pointed out in a brief note that the post-1945 development of the United Nations should be conceived of in specifically teleocratic ways.[45] While this obviously involves teleocratic conceptions of the state it also goes beyond that – the relevant 'state' is simply considered to be the world community as a whole, conceptualized as a project of 'world management'. Indeed, I would suggest that the teleocratic mode of understanding the role of government has been given a very powerful further push – as if one were needed – by the dominant perceptions of various processes of globalization so perhaps this is hardly surprising.

In other words, given the dominance of teleocratic conceptions of the role of government and given further the logic inherent in such conceptions, it is hardly surprising that 'supreme emergency exemptions' are part and parcel of contemporary conceptions of war for modern, 'liberal' states. I will turn in the Epilogue to why I think this is a problem generically for conceptions of international order, but for now let me turn to why I think it is a particular problem for the just war tradition.

Against supreme emergency

If we bear in mind what I suggested about the tradition in Chapter 3, the basic reason for my concern will be obvious. The general interpretation I offered of the tradition there drew firmly on Oliver O'Donovan's view that we should see the tradition neither as 'a theory' nor as about 'just wars', but rather as 'a proposal for doing justice in the theatre of war'.[46] Notwithstanding the ambiguities inherent in the tradition that Chapter 3 also pointed out, the idea of 'overriding the rules' is simply nonsensical. The tradition is, in a very important sense, *constituted by and through* its 'rules', and they cannot be 'trumped' or overridden by any particular social or contextual

---

[45] See Oakeshott, *On Human Conduct* (Oxford: Clarendon Press, 1975), p. 313, n. 1.
[46] Oliver O'Donovan, *The Just War Revisited* (Oxford University Press, 2003), p. vii.

circumstance. That, indeed, is what it means, I think, to see the just war tradition – as Walzer at least claims to do – as a casuistic tradition.[47] Any given action – the bombing of German cities, for example – would have to be examined in the context of the 'rules' – which are not merely laws, and nor are they fixed, but they certainly have a centre of gravity around a common set of precepts. 'Political communities' may have a *putative* right of defence under these precepts, for example, but such a right is always conditional on other precepts being met and is never absolute.

Walzer's 'communitarian' position – a position derived from a teleocratic conception of politics in general – effectively seeks to make political communities absolute in a way that the tradition simply cannot accept. And this, I would suggest, not only drives a coach and horses through the general strategy Walzer uses in the rest of *Just and Unjust Wars* – which is to emphasize casuistry, context and the circumstances of judgement – but also runs the risk of simply denying what the just war tradition in general is most at pains to emphasize and thereby failing in his expressed aim of 'recapturing' the just war for moral and political theory. In the specific cases he discusses – the bombing of German cities, the decision to drop the atomic bomb, and the structures and strategies of nuclear deterrence – a seriously casuistical just war theory could argue the toss about each of the decisions without any recourse to notions of supreme emergency. The only function that doctrine fulfils is simply to permit political communities to *override the constraints of the tradition* in specific contexts.

Let me close these remarks by elaborating on just one aspect of this argument. The just war tradition, I have said, as a tradition is constituted by and through the rules that it develops. These rules include what we would call the 'laws of war' (or now 'international humanitarian law') but are not limited to them. As Walzer himself says, what he calls the 'war convention' consists of 'articulated norms, customs, professional codes, legal precepts, religious and philosophical principles and reciprocal arrangements'.[48] Yet recognizing this seems to me to carry two implications.

---

[47] For a discussion of the sense of casuistry as a general practice that supports this interpretation see Albert R. Jonsen and Stephen Toulmin, *The Abuse of Casuistry: A History of Moral Reasoning* (Berkeley: University of California Press, 1986).

[48] Walzer, *Just and Unjust Wars*, p. 44.

To begin with, it suggests that our judgements about war are never *merely* legal judgments; that we cannot reduce our judgements about the legitimacy of this or that instance of the use of force to the question of whether it was (or is) 'legal'. In the contemporary context this implies that questions about (for example) the legitimacy of the war in Iraq, either in general (*jus ad bellum*) terms or more specific (*jus in bello*) senses, might begin with discussions of its legality but that is the beginning of the discussion not the end. Moreover, it may be that our judgement determines an instance of the use of force to have been 'legal' (but illegitimate) or the reverse. It is precisely in this 'casuistic', case-based way that the tradition should offer its interpretation of events, and in that respect contemporary public international law, important though it unquestionably is, is only a small part of the story and cannot be assumed in advance to trump the other parts. Here, if we return to Hart briefly, lies the challenge to the kind of jurisprudence that sees law as either a nightmare or a noble dream. Hart's version of analytical jurisprudence sought to do neither and while I would not agree with the formal content of Hart's concept of law, I certainly agree that he was right to see law differently from either version of US legal theory.

The second implication is simply that, just as international law cannot be assumed to trump other aspects of the constitution of judgement, the *deus ex machina* of the (teleocratic) state, as Walzer's bearer of rights and value, cannot be supposed to do so either. Political communities, on the reading of the just war tradition advanced in Chapter 3, do not have an *intrinsic* right of self-defence only a *stipulative* one, and even if such a right is granted, other criteria have to be met for an act of self-defence to constitute a legitimate act of force. But if this is so, then there can never be a meaningful deployment of the idea of 'supreme emergency' because *if* a certain act is deemed legitimate one does not need to invoke special reason to justify it and if it is *not*, it is simply gratuitous special pleading to argue that 'the rules' do not apply.

Walzer opened *Just and Unjust Wars* by trying to refute the idea that *Inter arma silent leges*. He was, I think, right to do so and his reformulation of the just war tradition has quite properly been among the most influential treatments of the political theory of war in our time. For this reason it is, I think, doubly worrying that by deploying a notion of supreme emergency that depends on a very particular conception of the moral priority of a particular political community (the teleocratic state) he runs the risk of undermining his theory at its core – the casuistical character of the human moral world. For it is precisely the point of the tradition, as he rightly stresses, to assert that the laws – the rules – are not silent in time of war; they speak with the force they have always had. They address the political communities that would invoke them as much as the agents who act for them and as such it is not open to those communities under any circumstances simply to set aside the rules to which they cleave; that is why the 'rules' are as they are. In that sense, as Cicero once said, and in order to end as we began, with a Latin tag: *etiamsi tacent, satis dicunt*, 'even if they are silent, they say enough'.

Epilogue: a choice not a destiny

Little children have known always
What Plotinus taught the wise,
That the world we see, we are:
Kathleen Raine, *Living with Mystery*

The main argument of this book has been that the intertwining of the teleocratic conception of the modern state and the post-sixteenth-century just war tradition has produced, in the modern reworking of the just war, a conception of 'legitimate force' that, at least in principle, is much more permissive than is usually supposed. It is permissive to the extent that, rather than acting as a restraint on the use of force by states, or indeed by other agents, it can act as a facilitator, even a driver, *for* such use. In the specific context of international order after the Cold War, and especially after 9/11, I have suggested that such a permissive conception of force has had extremely malign consequences and that, notwithstanding the always changing contexts of international politics in the twenty-first century, such malign consequences show every sign of remaining in place and perhaps becoming ever more parlous as the century continues.

Again, I emphasize that this is a *trajectory*, albeit one with deep roots in the history of European political thought and which has become, and is becoming, ever more dominant. But even if I am right to point to this trajectory, it might be said, I have said nothing in general terms to justify my claim that such a trajectory should be seen as, in itself, intrinsically problematic. Perhaps there are occasions or contexts in which it might be – such as the situation post-9/11, for example – but surely that is a contingent, not a necessary, reality. In other words, yes, in the aftermath of 9/11 especially perhaps, tendencies that existed within teleocratic conceptions of politics were pushed into damaging and self-defeating forms, but that does not, by definition, impugn the trajectory itself.

In this Epilogue I want to consider this general charge. I shall repeat that, in fact, the growing power of teleocratic politics is, indeed, a choice, not a destiny. That is, we are not obliged to make it. But at the same time, I want to suggest why, if we do make it – as we certainly have been doing to an ever-increasing extent over the past century or so – I think that the trajectory is so profoundly mistaken and will (not just might) have the kinds of consequences I have sought to lay out above and others that might be more disastrous still, and why, therefore, I think we should reject such a choice.

To get a better purchase on what is at stake in this general claim, I want to begin by considering two possible ways of responding to what I have argued here, both of which are well represented in the contemporary literatures of politics and international relations and indeed in the practices of contemporary politics and international relations as well. Let me take each in turn.

A realistic world?

The first response might run something like this. On my own argument (in Chapter 1) the character of international order itself has not changed dramatically, at least in kind, over the past century or so, whatever some more alarmist arguments might suggest. Yes, we are living in a globalized world and, yes, technological change has made enormous differences in certain areas but as far as the logic of international politics in general is concerned these are largely epiphenomenal changes and so in general the world of international politics is no more 'uncivil' now than it has generally been: it was always an 'anarchical society' (at best) and it remains so. In which case, the excesses of the past few years in terms (for example) of the denial of civil liberties in the context of the post-9/11 world, or the push from the 1990s onwards for 'humanitarian interventions' should be seen as just that: excesses, from the worst aspects of which major actors in world politics are already rowing back.

Moreover, it might be said, the very geopolitical changes I talked about in Chapter 1 would surely suggest that the tendency towards a more permissive use of force I have been concerned with in general is surely now less present, at least in modern liberal states, especially after the debacle of the Bush interventions of the early 2000s. Moreover, whatever might be the attitude that prevails towards the use of force in (say) the People's Republic of China – fairly robust on all the available evidence – it would hardly be affected by any alleged trajectories in the just war tradition since the Chinese elite probably have very little time for that tradition in any event. So again, whether or not we are moving into a period of more or less conflict, the alleged changes I have traced in modern Western conceptions of the justification of the use of force are hardly likely to make much difference.

This challenge would chiefly come, of course, from those of a generally 'realist' persuasion, though that term covers, I think, a multitude of sins.[1] It might also come from those who adopt a broadly 'pluralistic' account of international relations (to use the language of the so-called English school) and even from some liberal thinkers as well.[2] From whatever direction it appears, however, it effectively suggests that my argument, even if plausible at the level of intellectual history or political theory, no longer represents a reasonable understanding of the shape of the contemporary international order and the likely threats to (or within) it and so is (at best) old news.

If truth be told, I have some sympathy with this view. I obviously agree that international politics has not changed anything like as much as some would suppose – or at least in the ways that they suppose – and it is manifestly the case that those who are unsympathetic to the just war tradition – such as the Chinese political elite, but of course by

---

[1] Discussions of realism are a drug on the market and I do not want (here) to get involved in the new theology of distinguishing between various different kinds – 'classical', 'neo-classical', 'structural', 'defensive', 'offensive' and so on. Contemporary realists who would (I imagine) take the kind of line I am outlining here would include Kenneth Waltz, *Theory of International Politics* (Reading, Mass.: Addison-Wesley, 1979) and John Mearsheimer, *The Tragedy of Great Power Politics* (New York: Norton, 2000). An interesting and similar non-European view would be Yan Xuetong. See especially his essays gathered in Daniel Bell (ed.) *Ancient Chinese Thought, Modern Chinese Power* (Princeton University Press, 2010). See also my discussion of realism in *Dealing in Darkness: The Anti-Pelagian Imagination in Political Theory and International Relations* (London: Routledge, in press).

[2] I am thinking particularly of, for example, Robert Jackson in *The Global Covenant* (Oxford University Press, 2000) and James Mayall, *World Politics: Progress and Its Limits* (Cambridge: Polity, 2000). Liberal thinkers who might think like this might include those I have elsewhere described as 'dystopic' liberals, writers like Raymond Aron, Judith Shklar and Stanley Hoffmann. See my contribution 'Realism Tamed or Liberalism Betrayed: Dystopic Liberalism and International Order', in R. Friedmann, K. Oskanian and R. Pachacho (eds.) *After Liberalism* (London: Palgrave, in press).

no means only them – are hardly likely to incline further towards the use of force (or indeed away from such use) by any changes in it. Inasmuch as the world is moving into a more 'multipolar' order (as the jargon has it) wherein the 'West' will be much more on a par with 'the rest' than perhaps has been the case over the last couple of hundred years, that clearly will have an impact.[3]

However, this argument, plausible though it is as far as it goes, does not in fact go very far. It is unquestionably the case that, in the short term at least, Western governments are unlikely to be proselytizing for 'humanitarian interventions' in the manner of Mr Blair after Kosovo; both for geostrategic and for fiscal reasons and despite all the rhetoric associated with 'Responsibility to Protect' and so on (more on which in the next section) there very well may be, as Jennifer Welsh has recently suggested, a swing away from conceptions of 'sovereignty as responsibility' and towards a more traditional 'sovereignty as equality' view.[4] But there is no getting away from the fact (I would argue) that Western governments and the international institutions that still, to a very large extent, bear the intellectual imprint of European political thought unquestionably think generally largely in teleocratic terms and also (as we have already seen in some detail) think of the use of force in teleocratic terms. The justifications offered for the 2011 intervention in Libya make the point very forcibly.

In other words, the trajectory I have mapped out above is still present and, indeed, if we look at a lot of the work recently done both in the academy and in the wider public intellectual community, it is becoming *more* deeply entrenched not less.[5] It still casts (I would argue) a baleful shadow over the way in which we understand our liberties within our own societies and still offers the possibility (however much that possibility is not currently being picked up) of an expansive – sometimes at least semi-imperial – use of force, convinced of the rightness of its cause. The fact that such ideational claims will often be congruent with perceptions of Western interests will merely strengthen the temptation to accede to them.

The problem here is, as I have insisted from the beginning, the *growing* dominance of the teleocratic conception of politics not its

[3] I do not, by the way, endorse this claim. I merely say, conditionally, if it is the case then clearly it will have an impact.
[4] See Jennifer Welsh, 'Implementing the "Responsibility to Protect": Where Expectations Meet Reality', *Ethics and International Affairs*, 24, 4, 2010.
[5] This was, of course, the argument of chapters 4 and 5.

existence as such. Inasmuch as this understanding of political association was 'balanced' (we might say) by its opposite 'nomocratic' pole,
its full implications while observable were rarely fully realizable. But
that is decreasingly the case. Moreover, and perhaps more significantly
still, many other states – and other actors altogether – effectively think
in teleocratic terms, whatever their relation to the history of European
political thought. Indeed, inasmuch as the modern state in all its various
forms is one of the 'gifts' of the European political experience to
world politics, one might say that the logic of statecraft that has been
globalized and the particular form that logic has tended to take is,
effectively, teleocratic.[6]

In this sense, I would argue that the trajectories I have identified here
will, if not checked or reversed, lead to a profound *deepening* of the
uncivil condition that international politics already resembles but with
the political context within many societies thrown into the mix as well.
In these contexts Robert Kaplan's prediction a decade or so ago about
a 'coming anarchy' might not be all that far off the mark, except that
for him it was an inevitable direction; for me, it is an avoidable
trajectory.[7]

The necessity of teleocracy?

I began Chapter 1 by remarking that one general view of the human
condition over the past century or so has been, in however chastened a
fashion, an optimistic one. The second response I want to consider here
is in many ways, I think, an offspring of that view. Overall, it is
probably the most influential view current in the West and it has
powerful advocates elsewhere as well, certainly among leading international institutions, although of course it is a view which comes in
many shapes and sizes and with many shadings and varieties. The
argument of these critics would concentrate on the fact that, as they
see it, I have not given aspects of the trajectory I trace their real due.
Yes, 'teleocratic' styles of politics that I draw attention to might, in
some contexts, be susceptible to corruption or excess, but crucially
they are also part of an important shift in international political

[6] This would, of course, require a much fuller argument to substantiate properly.
I hope to provide such an argument in future work.
[7] See, Robert D. Kaplan, *The Coming Anarchy: Shattering the Dreams of the Post
Cold War World* (New York: Random House, 2000).

sensibilities – perhaps of political sensibilities more generally – towards a recognition that the international community must take a more proactive role in certain areas of global life than it traditionally has done. Global order and good global governance require a more co-ordinated set of responses, at least on certain issue areas, than the classic 'system of states' model of international order has provided or can provide, and therefore a more purposive international system, at least in principle, is not a bad thing at all.

After the disasters of the past few years, for example, who could doubt that we *have* to regulate – at least in some respects and to some degree – the global economy, and that the forms such regulation will take (and setting to one side the arguments about forms of regulation) will (and will have to be) to some extent purposive.[8] And, more germane to the main themes of this book, surely we need a system for managing international security problems that can react when necessary to large-scale threats, so we *need* regional associations that can share the heavy lifting in particular contexts, and a strengthened and robust international security architecture at the global level; and again, such a framework will have to be teleocratic in essence, in that it will have to be rooted in a notion of common goals and purposes to which all members of the international community feel attached. And perhaps most significant of all, we *need* to be able to address the large and growing challenges that cannot be met by any one country acting alone – climate change, environmental degradation, cross-border issues of many kinds and so on, and in order to do this we will need an institutional structure that has, shares and mobilizes behind the kind of common purposes we have as a species.[9]

The point is (my critics might well say) *only* a teleocratic vision, a vision of politics that does put the resources of the relevant community, be it state, regional or global, behind the necessary common purposes we must have, has any chance of doing this. And only if we do have

---

[8] The literature on the crash of 2007–8 and its implications is already huge and getting bigger by the day. I cannot possibly offer any real thoughts on it here. A good short guide, very well written and thoughtfully argued, is Andrew Gamble, *The Spectre at the Feast: Capitalist Politics and the Politics of Recession* (London: Palgrave, 2009).

[9] See, for example, the arguments developed by Thomas Weiss in *What's Wrong with the United Nations and How to Fix It*, 2nd edn (Cambridge: Polity Press, 2012).

such a vision can we expect the slow civilizing of the 'uncivil condition' that is, and has been, the default understanding of international politics for most of its history. So if I want to avoid the deepening of the uncivil condition that I suggested might be the fate of an unmediated international order in response to the challenges mentioned above, then it is to some form of teleocratic politics – some form of politics that stresses our *common* purposes and our *common* engagements, not our diverse and different ones – that I must turn. As Andrew Hurrell, in one of the most sophisticated and thoughtful articulations of this position, puts it:

The conservative ideal, embodied in the work of Hayek and Oakeshott, that political life should be concerned only with limited procedural rules governing coexistence, cannot be satisfactorily applied to the conditions of global political life in the twenty first century which *require the identification of substantive collective goals and the creation of institutionalized structures of governance to implement them.* (emphasis added)[10]

Leaving aside the question of whether it is entirely appropriate to yoke Oakeshott and Hayek together in this way,[11] or whether the forms of nomocratic politics that might be opposed to teleocracy are best seen as merely 'limited procedural rules governing coexistence',[12] it is clear that the vast majority of commentary on contemporary global order would broadly agree with Hurrell, without necessarily sharing the particular nuances of his argument (and probably without sharing his moral and intellectual capaciousness either). Many, indeed, would go much further. Critical theorists such as Andrew Linklater,[13] as well as

---

[10] Andrew Hurrell, *On Global Order: Power, Values and the Constitution of International Society* (Oxford University Press, 2007), p. 298. It is worth pointing out that Hurrell is very far from being an uncritical supporter of teleocracy. In many respects he has affinities with the 'pluralist' version of the Realistic response above.

[11] My own view is that it is not, in that Hayek, although advocating a minimal and procedural order, did so for instrumental reasons almost wholly at variance with Oakeshott's understanding. It is also broadly 'progressive' which, again, Oakeshott's is not. An illuminating contrast between the two, emphasizing Hayek's progressivism and Oakeshott's belief that progress was a 'dangerous, insensitive and intrusive delusion', can be found in Maurice Cowling, *Religion and Public Doctrine in England* vol. III: *Accommodations* (Cambridge University Press, 2004). See especially p. 499.

[12] Again, I don't think they are, certainly not in Oakeshott's case.

[13] Perhaps most obviously in Linklater, *The Transformation of Political Community* (Cambridge: Polity Press, 1997).

advocates of cosmopolitan democracy such as David Held[14] (and certainly many of the cosmopolitan just war theorists we examined between chapters 3 and 5), would argue that Hurrell's broadly liberal internationalism does not go anything like far enough, that it gives too much ground to the realists and the pluralists. But still they would all agree that there is no way back from a broadly teleocratic conception of politics (at all levels) if we are to address the challenges that face us.

Some indeed would even go as far as to suggest that what the challenges of the contemporary period require is the evolution of a world state. It is a remarkable feature of the past few years that this idea, largely quiescent since a brief flurry at the end of the Second World War, has been taken up with increasing vigour by advocates from a number of different perspectives, and given the scale of the challenges the international order faces it is perhaps not surprising.[15] But even if we do not go this far, the 'transformation of political community', to borrow the title of one of Linklater's books, must essentially be about the construction of 'forms of political community which promote universal norms which recognize cultural claims and demands for the reduction of material inequalities' and which in turn 'have a unique role to play in bringing about the transformation of international relations'.[16] And this process must in its turn be fundamentally teleocratic.

In this context, they would also surely add that the trajectory I have identified in the just war tradition is a source of hope, not a reason for despair. What, they might reasonably argue, *should* we do in the event of genocide or the fact or the possibility of large-scale mass killing? Surely under some circumstances preventive war *will* be better than the alternatives, and the richness of recent just war writing gives us ample material to construct ways of assessing and evaluating the use of such

[14] Originally in Held, *Democracy and the Global Order* (Cambridge: Polity Press, 1995), but also in many subsequent works.

[15] See, for revealing discussions, Campbell Craig, *Glimmer of a New Leviathan: Total War in the Realism of Niebuhr, Morgenthau and Waltz* (New York: Columbia University Press, 2003), Daniel Deudney, *Bounding Power: Republican Security Theory from the Polis to the Global Village* (Princeton University Press, 2007), Alexander Wendt, 'Why a World State Is Inevitable', *European Journal of International Relations*, 9, 4, 2003, 491–542 (note that Wendt's argument is expressly and very strongly teleological) and Weiss, *What's Wrong with the United Nations*.

[16] See Linklater, *Transformation of Political Community*, p. 220.

force whether by states, regional agencies, the UN, private security firms or anyone else. If we have, as at least in theory we now do have, a responsibility to protect, surely we should *exercise* that responsibility? For that purpose the 'new just war' is surely extraordinarily helpful.[17]

The problem with these arguments, powerfully made and clearly well intentioned though they very often are, is they simply do not establish what they need to establish: the *necessity* of teleocracy. Rather, they amount to variously disguised forms of teleocratic advocacy. As Michael Oakeshott points out in a particularly waspish section of *On Human Conduct*:

> The disposition in favour of teleocracy which [some] represent as a recent emergence has been a feature of the European political consciousness for more than five centuries and it received its definitive expression three hundred years ago in the idea of 'enlightened government' ... Of course it is true that there have been secular changes in modern European history which have favoured teleocracy (notably the demands of modern war) ... but the notion that there is an irresistible trend in Modern European history towards teleocratic government and we are now offered the choice between teleology and disaster belongs only to the seedy rhetorical outfit of an unconfident teleocrat.[18]

His point, I think, is simply to emphasize as I have done from the beginning that while teleocracy is (obviously) a real, and exclusive, conception of politics there is no 'necessity' that dictates its adoption. It is a choice we can make (and increasingly have been making) but not a required direction.

What's wrong with teleocracy?

That raises the obvious question: why not adopt it? The more subtle advocates of teleocracy discussed above would argue I think that they are not saying that teleocracy is simply inevitable. Rather they would

---

[17] The literature on 'R2P' as it is now known has become, in a stunningly short time, immense and it is growing all the time – a sure sign of its rhetorical power, if nothing else. Good and non-hysterical accounts can be found in Gareth Evans, *The Responsibility to Protect: Ending Mass Atrocity Crimes Once and For All* (New York: Brookings, 2008) and Alex Bellamy, *Responsibility to Protect: The Global Effort to End Mass Atrocities* (Cambridge: Polity Press, 2009).

[18] *On Human Conduct* (Oxford: Clarendon Press, 1975), pp. 322–3.

argue that their case is a conditional one: *if* you want to have a reasonable chance of solving the problems that confront a globalizing world, then some version of teleocracy is really the only game in town; teleocracy is to be chosen for the benefits it brings. But this, then, surely invites us to consider the losses it entails as well. In this last substantive section I want to do just this and to suggest why I think we should view teleocratic politics with suspicion.

To begin by returning to our main concern in this volume, I want to emphasize that nothing I have said in the chapters above should be taken to deny that there are occasions when the use of force is, indeed, the lesser evil, and in such contexts the just war tradition, even in its modern forms, remains a powerful and thoughtful guide to how we might think about such use in ways that are congruent with the moral beliefs we share. But the point, of course, is to be able to assess when such contexts arise. My primary contention in the foregoing was that the combination of teleocratic conceptions of politics and that part of the just war tradition that emphasized force as the punishment of wrongdoing have, at least in recent times, inclined towards a much *greater* number of such contexts than I think either wise or warranted, with the results that I tried to outline in chapters 4 and 5. But that some such use may on occasion be justified (at least after the fact), I have never sought to deny.

In this context, the logic of my argument is that we should emphasize those aspects of the tradition that enable the *constraints* on legitimate force, not those that can be understood at least as warranting a more permissive use of force. It is precisely the growing teleocratic bent of European political thought over the past century or so that facilitated such an understanding, and that was in part why I was (and am) so critical of it.

To the more general point, that I do not give due weight to the necessity of a teleocratic conception of politics given the challenges that face us in contemporary world politics, I would like to suggest a rather different response. The point I have sought to emphasize throughout is not that teleocratic conceptions of politics have no place in our accounts of politics: it is the *dominance* of teleocratic conceptions of politics to which I have objected, not their existence as such. As Oakeshott argued in *On Human Conduct*, the growth of conceptions of teleocratic politics in Europe came about very much as a response to an already extant idea about the appropriate form of political association. So there may indeed be instances or contexts in which such conceptions provide a resource. But that is premised on the associated idea that such conceptions exist alongside other conceptions that can, effectively, balance them. It is that which seems increasingly no longer to obtain and it is that – rather than the fact of teleocratic politics per se – that is the root of the problem.

Which brings me, of course, to the reason why I think a predominantly teleocratic politics is a problem. To get at this, I want first to discuss an intervention that, I think, exposes the character of the problem especially well. This is Michael Ignatieff's recent reflection on what a 'global ethic' might entail.[19] Ignatieff's basic argument is predicated on the claim that talk of 'a global ethic' runs together two rather different things; a global ethic in the singular and a global ethics in the plural. The former – 'a perspective that takes all human beings and their habitat as its subject' – is flourishing, he suggests, in philosophical discussion around the world, has a long and distinguished history, is best seen as a 'view from nowhere', and has, as its central function, the requirement to justify. But this will require confronting the problems inherent, at least in democratic states, between the universal and the particular, for example the conflict between what Ignatieff terms 'democracy and justice' that is, the values inherent in the self-determination of peoples and the values inherent in abstract justice for all individuals. As he puts it, 'in a plural moral universe, the particular faces off against the universal but neither plays as trumps; neither is privileged and both are obliged to justify'.

The latter view, global ethics in the plural, is not a discourse but rather an institutional practice or set of practices enshrined in the four central documents of the post-war order, the UN Charter, the Universal Declaration of Human Rights (UDHR), the Geneva Conventions and the UN Convention Relating to the Status of Refugees. The problem with global ethics in the plural is that these practices offer contradictory priorities and often conflict, the best example being, Ignatieff thinks, the conflict between state sovereignty (enshrined in the UN Charter) and human rights (enshrined in the UDHR). Conceptual bridges can be found – he suggests that the adoption of

---

[19] See Michael Ignatieff, 'Re-Imagining a Global Ethic', *Ethics and International Affairs*, 26, 1, 2012, 7–19. Parts of the next few paragraphs are taken from my response to Ignatieff in the same issue.

Responsibility to Protect is such a bridge as it makes sovereignty conditional on two basic responsibilities – but that does not eliminate the problem.[20]

The real point of 'a global ethic', Ignatieff suggests in his Conclusion, is to force the contradictions inherent in both discourse and practices out into the open and thus to engage in a process of 'recurrent, repeated, behaviour changing justification. The process needs standards – a global ethic provides the view from nowhere, global ethics provides a view from somewhere – and if sides in dispute accept the standard, they argue with each other, not past each other, and if they accept the standard they are more likely to accept the obligation to change when justification fails.'

There is much in this with which I can agree, of course. It is certainly true that the global ethic in the singular has a long and distinguished history (or rather, as I shall discuss in a moment, histories), that it flourishes in contemporary (analytic) philosophy,[21] and that it has raised profound problems of justification for many contemporary practices. It is true also that the founding documents of the post-war order do conflict,[22] and that this then impels us to see if we can find ways of bridging such divides where possible. So if we can agree on so much, where might I disagree – or at least express a doubt about Ignatieff's reimagining?

A first doubt might be over the actual content of the notion of a global ethic. Ignatieff says that the idea of a global ethic has a long history and he is right in the sense that, for example, most of the

---

[20] As we have already seen, and following the initiative of the then UN secretary general Kofi Annan, the Canadian government set up the International Commission on Intervention and State Sovereignty in September 2000. At its third meeting Gareth Evans, Mohamed Sahnoun and Ignatieff himself suggested the phrase 'responsibility to protect' be adopted in place of phrases such as a right (or a duty) of intervention. The commission reported in December 2001 and was adopted by the UN world summit in 2005.

[21] The growth of 'cosmopolitan' ethics and political theory over the past thirty years is testimony to this. Leading figures, as we saw earlier, would include Charles Beitz, Onora O'Neill, Thomas Pogge, Henry Shue and Peter Singer.

[22] This is not just because they are dealing with different problems – Ignatieff's point in his essay – though it is certainly partly that, but also because of the somewhat baroque origin of many of the ideas in the first place. An excellent example in the case of the UN Charter can be found brilliantly discussed in Mark Mazower's excellent *No Enchanted Palace: The Ends of Empire and the Ideological Origins of the United Nations* (Princeton University Press, 2009).

world's great religions hold a 'global ethic' view in one sense at least –
they have a view that they believe to be the true view of the ethical
structure of the human (and in some cases the non-human) world. The
problem, of course, is that the content of these views are in many cases
incommensurable. This does not mean there can be no dialogue, nor
does it mean that such views cannot sometimes change, but it does
suggest that what formally is 'a global ethic' is rather less than this in real
terms. And much the same might be said about the 'cosmopolitan' predilection of many contemporary analytic philosophers. Both 'Kantian'
cosmopolitans (Pogge, O'Neill) and 'consequentialist' cosmopolitans
(Singer) adopt a 'global ethic' but *the contents* of their respective ethics
differ radically.

There is also, perhaps, a wider problem. The moral life, at whatever
level one considers it, displays I think a hybrid character. One form of
it certainly does lie in the exercise of reason to justify (or fail to justify)
the actions we have done or are planning to do. It issues in precisely
what Ignatieff suggests his 'global ethic' does – a requirement for
justification. But another form, as Michael Oakeshott suggests, consists largely in the exercise of habitual affection and conduct.[23] Most
actual moralities are combinations of these two (and possibly other
forms as well). But inasmuch as Ignatieff's essay suggests that 'a global
ethic' would issue in 'repeated, recurrent behaviour changing justification', it looks very much as if his 'global ethic' (of either kind) would
very largely fall into the former camp. And that, surely, would be
problematic. As Oakeshott points out, where the form of the moral
life is *dominated* by this process of constantly reflective self-
consciousness (as opposed to being partly constituted by it) its effects
can be ruinous. This, he thinks, is precisely the problem of the contemporary world: 'morality in this form', he suggests, 'regardless of the
quality of the ideals, breeds nothing but distraction and moral
instability'.[24] In other words, if the task of a global ethics is *constantly*
to insist on the requirements of justification it is going to drain itself of
anything which can support the content of the ethic itself, and we have
heard already that the content of such an ethic is highly disputable in

---

[23] Here I follow Michael Oakeshott's discussion in his essay 'The Tower of Babel'
contained in his *Rationalism in Politics and other Essays*, expanded edn
(Minneapolis: Liberty Fund, 1991(1962)).
[24] Ibid., p. 481.

any event. I hardly think that a cacophonous babel would be the best way of imagining – or reimagining – a global ethic.

So is there an alternative? I think there is, but it is not strictly speaking an alternative but rather an acceptance of the necessary logic of the hybrid character of the moral world. We should first understand that it is precisely the thick commitments of particularity we all possess that flavour the moral life, give it weight and significance and create its real charge for us (whoever the us might be). However, we should also understand that such commitments stand side by side with the requirements of living with others who do not share them – in our own communities and with other communities. This certainly requires, as Ignatieff supposes, 'standards', but the standards will not be substantive but, so to speak, adverbial – they will be the recognition of the values we need to adopt in a world of deep plurality if we are not to do violence to our own particularities or to others' particularities. The final problem with Ignatieff's undeniably powerful essay is perhaps an elision of the procedural with the substantive. His reimagining of a global ethic assumes a level of substantive agreement that I think is not likely at least in the short term but that does not deny that there could be a level of *procedural* agreement that allows for both certain general rules to govern conduct and many thick particularities. He is quite right to suppose that, even at the level of procedural rules, politics will never be far away, but the best image of a global ethic, I think, is one that recognizes not only the depth of our pluralities but the value that might be found in such diversity for its own sake and for the gifts such diversity can offer to all: not enforced and recurrent justification – though this does not mean that justification will never play a role – but rather conversation and dialogue – about similarities and differences, rules and responsibilities, conduct becoming and unbecoming. Of course, people can refuse the invitation to participate in such a conversation; they can try to keep themselves isolated or shout so loud they hope to drown out every other voice. But inasmuch as they do so, they simply move away from the understanding of what a global ethic should involve.

The point of the above discussion is to emphasize that for all the differences of content, the form of a global ethic in Ignatieff's sense must be teleocratic. It must hold itself to the notion of common purposes in form – purposes against which, and in the context of which, justification is appropriate. But this leads us away from the recognition of the plurality and distinctiveness of our contemporary world and assumes at least a universality that is simply not present.

The irony here is that the two contrasting views of international order I outlined above – the realist/pluralist/communitarian and the liberal/internationalist/cosmopolitan – in fact *both* see the world in broadly teleocratic terms, though they interpret the relevant 'purposes' differently. And if Oakeshott's argument that I discussed in Chapter 1 is borne in mind that will hardly surprise. Viewing the international order as effectively a 'state of war' *will* inevitably incline one to see it in terms of 'survival',[25] 'self-help',[26] 'perpetual great power competition',[27] and therefore the relevant common purpose will be that inherent in one's specific community (whatever that is taken to be). And so as the European international order became more consolidated – and the global economy with it – between the sixteenth and the nineteenth centuries the 'international condition' become more and more akin to a 'clash of teleocracies': the 'common purposes' sought by any member would sometimes differ (in the twentieth century especially), but the growing power such common purposes in general had would simply become more and more entrenched, and so the more teleocratic the international order became the more 'uncivil' it became. As Oakeshott also points out, these processes gathered pace in the nineteenth and twentieth centuries, for a variety of reasons.

While one form of teleocracy sees the 'uncivil condition' as the default setting of international relations, however, and derives from that a stark assumption of irredeemable conflict, another offers itself as the *remedy* for this condition. This is the managerialist internationalism that Oakeshott pointed to in post-war international institutions and which one now sees writ large in much of the literatures of international organization, 'international political economy' and 'global governance', for example,[28] and even more so in the

---

[25] Martin Wight's term in 'Why Is There No International Theory?', in H. Butterfield and M. Wight (eds.) *Diplomatic Investigations* (London: George Allen and Unwin, 1966).

[26] Waltz's version in his *Theory of International Politics*.

[27] Mearsheimer's phrase from *Tragedy of Great Power Politics*.

[28] The literature here is immense and I could not even begin to scratch the surface. Some classic treatments would include Inis Claude, *Swords Into Plowshares: The Problems and Progress of International Organization* (New York: Random House, 1988); Robert Keohane and Joseph Nye, *Power and Interdependence: World Politics in Transition* (London: Longman, 2000, 3rd edn); Robert

cosmopolitanism one finds in contemporary analytic philosophy and, in rather different forms, in many non-governmental organizations and international institutions. Here the 'common purposes' are transnational and institutional; they cut across specific political communities and are seeking to encourage new forms of governance with shared purposes and pooled responsibilities and obligations.[29]

What we have in the contemporary international order, then, is not so much the clash of civilizations so feared (or perhaps secretly desired) by some but rather a clash of teleocracies. The conception of the relevant *focus* of the common purpose will differ. The idea that politics, at least in the here and now, is fundamentally *about* such purposes does not.

Why does this matter? It matters, to go back to something I wrote earlier, because of what is lost in the process. The chief casualty of the growing dominance of teleocratic politics is, I agree with Oakeshott, perhaps the greatest achievement of modern European political thought: the idea of civil (and thus non-purposive) association. Like him, I think that that achievement is so important because of what it sought to recognize in us as human beings. In other words, its real importance was extrinsic: it was a form of government intended for people of a certain type.

Modern European political thought emerges not from classical or Roman models, however central these were in second-order terms, but rather from medieval ideas and practices. In particular, it emerges from what one might term the decay of the medieval synthesis. Civil association, for Oakeshott, was the kind of political association appropriate for the kinds of human beings that emerge in that context, as he put it: 'self-determined autonomous human beings seeking the satisfaction of their wants in self-chosen transactions with others of their kind'.[30] He added that the *persona* who is the counterpart of civil association is the *persona* 'who Montaigne and Rabelais celebrated. However, the

---

Keohane, *After Hegemony: Cooperation and Discord in the World Economy* (Princeton University Press, 1992); Anne Marie Slaughter, *A New World Order* (Princeton University Press, 2004); Michael Walzer, 'Governing the Globe', *Dissent*, Fall 2000.

[29] Again, amidst an enormous literature, see the previously cited works by David Held, and by the cosmopolitan just war theorists discussed in Chapter 3, but see also, for a good sampling of relevant material, David Held and Garrett Wallace Brown (eds.) *The Cosmopolitanism Reader* (Cambridge: Polity Press, 2011).

[30] Oakeshott, *On Human Conduct*, p. 315.

persona that Montaigne and Rabelais celebrated was not, as Oake-shott is at pains to point out, 'a savage egoist, nor a cold "capitalist" nor the contemptible *bourgeois* of legend'.[31] Rather he or she is an individual, a 'self determined autonomous human agent' who displays:

a disposition to cultivate the 'freedom' inherent in agency, to enjoy individuality and … to readily concede virtue to this exercise of personal autonomy acquired in self understanding.[32]

In a wonderful passage, elsewhere in *On Human Conduct*, Oakeshott suggests that such a persona displays a

disposition to be 'self employed' in which a man recognizes himself and all others in terms of self determination: that is in terms of wants rather than slippery satisfactions and of adventures rather than uncertain outcomes … And since men are apt to make gods whose characters reflect what they believe to be their own, the deity corresponding to this self understanding is an Augustinian god of majestic imagination who, when he might have devised an untroublesome universe, had the nerve to create one composed of self employed adventurers of unpredictable fancy, to announce to them some rules of conduct, and thus to acquire convives capable of answering back in civil tones with whom to spend an eternity in conversation.[33]

This 'individual' and the mode of association appropriate for such is, Oakeshott insists, a modern creation, but both are rooted in much older ideas; they are, he says, a 'modification' of the conditions of medieval life and thought.

This 'nomocratic' understanding of politics, conventional (in the sense of not related to some supposed 'natural state') but non-purposive, generates its own understanding of order at any and all levels. Such an understanding will recognize and welcome the plurality and distinctiveness of our different selves and, at least in principle – though this is much less a concern of Oakeshott's than of mine – of our different societies and the distinctive engagements to which they also give rise. As the philosopher Stephen Clark has well put it, 'we all live within networks of familial and friendly relationships … states gain such authority as they have only by embodying … values that transcend the merely economic and contractual, that business, sects and nations all have their part to play in a civilized world order whose lineaments are visible in times of war as well as in times of peace … the

[31] Ibid., p. 322.   [32] Ibid., p. 239.   [33] Ibid., p. 324.

world of our human experience ... is ... structured by familial affection, sexual desire and trade, by the demands of hospitality and word once given, by the spirits of our different nations, by war and innocence and the world's beauty'.[34]

'Civil association' is that mode of political life attuned to the 'self-enacted' individual recognizing and opening out towards that wider plural world in which, as Clark suggests, 'the gods ... keep just their ancient places';[35] teleocracy represents a closing down of it.

Civil understandings of politics require, as both Oakeshott and Clark emphasize, an Augustinian recognition of the limits of our knowledge and a humility towards our capacity to alter the conditions of our existence – an 'anti-Pelagian' recognition if you will[36] – and that accommodates us to the continuing importance of charity and mercy and the possibilities that exist for us to make spaces for these and related virtues in our world. Teleocratic understandings, however, close off such options and emphasize the common purposes that would *of necessity* trump the plurality and many-sided 'uncentredness' of a genuinely 'civil' international order.

My reason for being very suspicious of claims that expand the *provenance* of war, even when the claims are predicated on admirable moral assumptions, is that such claims are always going to be the enemy of civil politics understood in Oakeshott's sense. As we have seen, claims about humanitarian intervention and about preventive war often arise from very understandable, and in many respects very welcome, ethical concerns. But such concerns in themselves should also make us wary. This is because one of the central assumptions of seeing politics as civil (and therefore limited) is that in general terms people cannot be trusted with too much power, and expanding the power of the state – or, indeed, of other agencies as proxies for states – to make war, even for very good reasons, *necessarily* (and not just contingently) will give them too much power. As I say, that does not mean that war can never be justified – sometimes the danger is indeed enough to warrant the risk, and the lineaments of a civil world order are (or should be) visible in times of war as well as times of peace – but it does mean that

---

[34] Stephen Clark, *Civil Peace and Sacred Order* (Oxford: Clarendon Press, 1989), p. 159.

[35] Ibid., p. 159.

[36] For an exploration of this sensibility and its significance for modern political thought and international relations, see my forthcoming *Dealing in Darkness*.

trajectories, policies and institutional schemes devised with the intent of making war more permissible – even in very limited contexts – should always be viewed with real scepticism and suspicion. By definition, such schemes run the very real risk – even when their advocates are unambiguously of good intent[37] – of creating a situation where the cure is worse than the disease.

The problem with teleocratic conceptions of politics is that, if unchecked or unbalanced, they turn what is (and should be) an understanding of, and welcoming of, plurality which is the necessary foundation for any genuine civil liberty – whether in the context of the political order of a particular polity, or in the context of the international order of many (diverse) polities – into a monistic conception that will constantly (even if not always intentionally) threaten it – though, as I say, the substance of that monism will be very different for different teleocrats. Not only will civil politics be greatly impaired – ultimately indeed rendered impossible – by such conceptions; the possibility of a fit between the persona we might have and the kinds of politics that can enable it and allow it to flourish will be broken.

Of course, a full defence of this would have to go much further: showing why the persona Oakeshott, Rabelais and Montaigne celebrate should indeed be celebrated and relating it much more fully to both civil association in terms of political association and the lineaments of a civil international order; and that is no part of the present book. But the argument above makes it clear, I hope, why – for me at least – the dominance of teleocratic politics is so problematic. For I do think that, at our best, such a persona is what we might aspire to (perhaps even what we *should* aspire to) and that to abandon it or even gravely to weaken it represents not merely a threat to a sustainable and meaningful political order (at all levels) but a threat also to a manner of living that is far more consonant than any other with what we need at the present time. But that is a story for another day.

A choice or a destiny?

Which brings me, finally, to my closing remarks. What this book has sought to do is to draw attention to a particular trajectory mainly affecting Western states and the institutions they have largely created

---

[37] As most of the advocates of humanitarian intervention and preventive war discussed in Chapter 4, for example, clearly are.

in world politics – in connection principally, in the current context, with the use of force, though (as this Epilogue has I hope made plain) with much wider general ramifications. I must emphasize that I have not said, and do not think, that trajectory is destiny. Indeed, as I remarked at the outset, part of the point of the book is to flag up the fact that it *is not* a destiny but rather a choice, or a series of choices. We could choose to see our political world very differently. We could be much more sceptical about teleocratic styles of politics and seek to breathe new life into nomocratic conceptions that contain (as I would argue) much of what is most valuable in our political traditions, and see how they might be made applicable to the globalizing world of the twenty-first century. As Oakeshott remarked, it is simply a fallacy to believe one could not do that and there is a good deal of work, in many different academic fields, and from outside the academy altogether, that might help us to show how political orders that are essentially nomocratic orders can achieve many of the things we seem to be assuming that only teleocracy can achieve. Given what I take to be the loss that abandoning the field to teleocracy entails, we should surely develop such ideas much more fully than perhaps we have so far. I am not suggesting, of course, that there would not be costs in adopting a more nomocratic view of politics: there clearly would. At a minimum, we would have to surrender the view of the political enterprise as one of 'world mastery' – even if a benign world mastery – and that is something that we seem curiously reluctant to do. But I would argue that the benefits would outweigh the costs, not least in a reduction in the permissiveness we have extended in recent times to the use of force.

At the same time, I am quite aware that the likelihood is that the teleocratic styles of politics I have discussed will retain and in all probability enhance their growing dominance. In many cases, such a teleocratic politics will be of a relatively conventional power-political sort and will probably result rather more quickly and directly in the deepening of the 'uncivil condition' – the world the realist teleocrats see will become even more uncivil precisely because they see it as they do. This is perhaps the world that beckons if the theme of 'rising powers' becomes the signature process of the twenty-first century. But even if one assumes that the more 'solidarist', internationalist (even cosmopolitan) forms of teleocracy flourish instead, and one understands them as genuine attempts to civilize the uncivil condition that is world politics – and it would be churlish to deny the deep seriousness and good intentions of many of those who advocate this path as well as the very real character of the challenges they think force them down this route – then the logic of unrestrained teleocracy will still be deeply problematic. For ultimately – even in this well-intentioned and relatively benign form – the logic of teleocracy will essentially be a functional logic, and the logic of functionalism is always ultimately one of power.

Of course, as Noel O'Sullivan points out in his subtle and illuminating study of the evolution of post-war European political thought,[38] power can be used benignly but even if and when it is, something is still lost, and what will chiefly be lost, I agree with him – and we are both echoing Oakeshott, of course – will be the possibility of civil association and all that goes with it. As O'Sullivan remarks, one might recall, in this context, the situation of Rome after the Battle of Actium:

when Augustus effected a revolutionary shift from republic to empire with such subtlety that few noticed the dramatic change that had occurred ... for two centuries thereafter Romans enjoyed an imperial golden age. They enjoyed it, however, by sacrificing *libertas* to non-accountable *imperium*.[39]

That shift was, analogously, to a model of teleocratic association which might be seen – following Oakeshott's fourfold characterization of teleocratic politics that I discussed in Chapter 1 – as a combination of materialist productivism and enlightened government. And it is by no means obvious that, however benign such a model might be in intent, it will always be perceived as being benign in practice – as the experience of the European Union (EU), the International Monetary Fund and the Greek government and people has suggested all too clearly in the crisis that engulfed them in 2010 and after. There is plenty of evidence too that a similar kind of teleocratic politics holds sway in many contemporary areas of *global* governance as well. The whole point of there being 'common purposes' is that such purposes predispose actors to advance towards them. In such cases, stopping or reversing direction is likely to be seen as, at best, bad form but more probably verging on a betrayal (how, after all, could this not be if the purposes are 'common'?). Independent of the merits of the case either

---

[38] See Noel O'Sullivan, *European Political Thought since 1945* (London: Palgrave, 2004). See especially the argument of Chapter 7.

[39] Ibid., p. 189.

way, the claim that European integration has to be an 'irreversible process', that there is only one legitimate direction, it seems to me displays a similar logic. Moreover, the actions of the EU on several occasions when polities or groups have suggested otherwise – peoples effectively being told to vote again until they 'get it right', for example – surely bear the clear imprint of this logic.[40]

Whichever of these two forms of teleocracy become dominant in the years to come, however, I think that the trajectory that I have sought to delineate in this book is likely to remain a powerful and for the most part malign influence on our societies, our politics and our understanding of international order for the foreseeable future. The just war tradition was from its inception, as I argued in Chapter 3, very aware of the iniquities and unintended consequences that come from any uses of force, and so was very hesitant in its original formulations about how, and under what circumstances, it should legitimate them. The nomocratic conception of politics, as I remarked in Chapter 1, is alien to belligerence and partly as a result of being so has been genuinely open both to individuality and civility. In following the path we have chosen to follow, we have come close to silencing the latter and deeply compromising the former – not a great achievement to pass on to posterity. Nevertheless, as I have tried to emphasize throughout, it *is* a choice. Perhaps there is still time to think again.

---

[40] As I say, I am not offering any view, one way or the other, of whether the 'European project' is a good one or not in principle. I merely observe that the characteristic mode of behaviour of the EU has in practice been irremediably teleocratic and thus, from my perspective, deeply problematic.

Select bibliography

Adcock, F.E., *Roman Political Ideas and Practice* (Michigan: Ann Arbor, 1964).

Agamben, Giorgio, *State of Exception* (University of Chicago Press, 2005).

Allison, Graham, *Nuclear Terrorism: The Ultimate Preventable Catastrophe* (New York: Times Books, 2004).

Angel, Norman, *The Great Illusion* (London: Heinemann, 1933(1911)).

Anscombe, G.E.M., *Philosophical Papers*, 3 vols. (Cambridge University Press, 1981), vol. III.

Arbour, Louise, 'The Responsibility to Protect as a Duty of Care in International Law and Practice', *Review of International Studies*, 34, 3, 2008.

Arend, Anthony Clark, and Robert J. Beck, *International Law and the Use of Force* (London: Routledge, 1993).

Arendt, Hannah, *On Violence* (New York: Harcourt Brace Jovanovich, 1970).

The Origins of Totalitarianism (New York: Harcourt Brace Jovanovich, 1951).

Aron, Raymond, *Penser la Guerre, Clausewitz* (Paris: editions Gallimard, 1976).

Bain, William, *Between Anarchy and Society: Trusteeship and the Obligations of Power* (Oxford University Press, 2003).

Bainton, Ronald, *Christian Attitudes Towards War and Peace* (Nashville, Tenn.: Abingdon Press, 1960).

Erasmus of Christendom (New York: Scribner, 1969).

Bamford, Bradley W.C., 'The United Kingdom's "War Against Terrorism"', *Terrorism and Political Violence*, 16(4), 2004, 737–56.

Barnett, Michael, *Empire of Humanity: A History of Humanitarianism* (Ithaca, NY: Cornell University Press, 2011).

Barnett, Michael, and Thomas G. Weiss (eds.) *Humanitarianism in Question: Politics, Power, Ethics* (Ithaca, NY: Cornell University Press, 2008).

Beitz, Charles, *The Idea of Human Rights* (Oxford University Press, 2009).

Bellamy, Alex, *Just Wars: From Cicero to Iraq* (Cambridge: Polity Press, 2006).

Responsibility to Protect: The Global Effort to End Mass Atrocities (Cambridge: Polity Press, 2009).

'R2P and the Problem of Military Intervention', *International Affairs*, 84, 4, July 2008.

Benhabib, Seyla, *Another Cosmopolitanism* (edited by R. Post) (New York: Oxford University Press, 2008).

Berridge, Geoff, *Return to the United Nations: UN Diplomacy in Regional Conflicts* (London: Palgrave Macmillan, 1990).

Best, Geoffrey, *Humanity in Warfare: The Modern History of the International Law of Armed Conflicts* (London: Allen and Unwin, 1978).

Law and War since 1945 (Oxford: Clarendon Press, 1994).

Bialer, Andreas, *The States System of Europe* (Oxford University Press, 1992).

Bobbitt, Philip, *Terror and Consent: The Wars for the Twenty First Century* (London: Allen Lane, 2008).

The Shield of Achilles: War, Peace and the Course of History (London: Allen Lane, 2002).

Booth, Ken, and Tim Dunne (eds.) *Worlds in Collision* (New York: Palgrave, 2002).

Boucher, David, *Political Theories of International Relations* (Oxford University Press, 2000).

Boyle, Joseph, 'Just and Unjust Wars: Casuistry and the Boundaries of the Moral World', *Ethics and International Affairs*, vol. 11, 1997, 83–98.

Bracher, Karl Dietrich, *The Age of Ideologies* (London: Methuen, 1984).

Bradbury, Jim (ed.) *The Routledge Companion to Medieval Warfare* (London: Routledge, 2004).

Brock, P., and N. Young, *Pacifism in the Twentieth Century* (Syracuse, NY: Syracuse University Press, 1999).

Brown, Chris, Terry Nardin and Nicholas Rengger (eds.) *International Relations in Political Thought: Texts From the Ancient Greeks to the First World War* (Cambridge University Press, 2002).

Brown, Peter, *The Rise of Western Christendom*, 2nd edn (Oxford: Blackwell, 2003).

Buchanan, Allen, *Human Rights Legitimacy and the Use of Force* (Oxford University Press, 2010).

Buchanan, Allen, and Robert Keohane, 'The Preventive Use of Force: A Cosmopolitan Institutional Proposal', *Ethics and International Affairs*, 18, 1, 2004, 1–22.

Bull, Hedley, *The Anarchical Society* (London: Macmillan, 1977).

'The Grotian Conception of International Society', in Herbert Butterfield and Martin Wight (eds.) *Diplomatic Investigations* (London: Allen and Unwin, 1966).

(ed.) *Intervention in World Politics* (Oxford University Press, 1984).

Bull, Hedley, Adam Roberts and Ben Kingsbury (eds.) *Hugo Grotius and International Relations* (Oxford University Press, 1986).

Burchill, Graham, and Colin Gorder (eds.) *The Foucault Effect* (University of Chicago Press, 1991).

Butler, Judith, *Frames of War: When Is Life Grievable* (London: Verso, 2008).

Caedel, Martin, *Pacifism in Britain, 1914–1945* (Oxford University Press, 1980).

  Semi-Detached Idealists: The British Peace Movement and International Relations 1854–1945 (Oxford University Press, 2000).

  The Origins of War Prevention: The British Peace Movement and International relations, 1730–1854 (Oxford: Clarendon Press, 1996).

  Thinking about Peace and War (Oxford University Press, 1987).

Campbell, Joseph C., *The Hero with a Thousand Faces* (Princeton University Press, 1968(1949)).

Caney, Simon, *Justice Beyond Borders: Towards a Global Political Theory* (Oxford University Press, 2005).

Caplan, Richard, *A New Trusteeship? The International Administration of War Torn Territories*, Adelphi Paper no. 341, London: IISS.

Cassesse, Antonio, *International Law*, 2nd edn (Oxford University Press, 2004).

Chatterjee, Deen, and Don Scheid (eds.) *Ethics and Foreign Intervention* (Cambridge University Press, 2003).

Clark, Ian, *The Post Cold War Order: The Spoils of Peace* (Oxford University Press, 2001).

Clark, Stephen R.L., *Civil Peace and Sacred Order* (Oxford: Clarendon Press, 1989).

Claude, Inis, *Swords Into Plowshares: The Problems and Progress of International Organization* (New York: Random House, 1988).

Coady, C.A.J., *Morality and Political Violence* (Oxford University Press, 2007).

  'Terrorism, Morality and Supreme Emergency', *Ethics*, 114, 2004, 772–89.

Coker, Christopher, *Humane Warfare* (London: Routledge, 2001).

Cooper, David E., *World Philosophies: An Historical Introduction* (Oxford: Blackwell, 1996).

Coppieters, Bruno, and Nick Fotion (eds.) *Moral Constraints on War: Principles and Cases* (Lanham: Lexington Books, 2002).

Corey, Elizabeth, *Michael Oakeshott on Religion, Aesthetics and Politics* (Columbia, Mo.: University of Missouri Press, 2006).

Cowling, Maurice, *Religion and Public Doctrine in England*, 3 vols., vol. I (Cambridge University Press, 1984).

Religion and Public Doctrine in England, 3 vols., vol. III: *Accommodations* (Cambridge University Press, 2004).

Craig, Campbell, *Glimmer of a New Leviathan: Total War in the Realism of Niebuhr, Morgenthau and Waltz* (New York: Columbia University Press, 2003).

'The Resurgent Idea of World Government', in *Ethics and International Affairs*, 22, 2, 2008.

Damrosch, Lori Fisler and David J. Scheffer (eds.) *Law and Force in the New International Order* (Boulder: Westview, 1991).

Davis, Grady Scott, *Warcraft and the Fragility of Virtue* (Moscow, ID: Idaho University Press, 1992).

Dershowitz, Alan, *Why Terrorism Works: Understanding the Threat, Responding to the Challenge* (New Haven: Yale University Press, 2003).

Deudney, Daniel, *Bounding Power: Republican Security Theory from the Polis to the Global Village* (Princeton University Press, 2007).

Devetak, Richard, and Christopher Hughes (eds.) *The Globalization of Political Violence: Globalization's Shadow* (London: Routledge, 2008).

Dillon, Michael, and Julian Reid, *The Liberal Way of War: Killing to Make Life Live* (London: Routledge, 2009).

Donegan, Alan, *The Theory of Morality* (University of Chicago Press, 1977).

Donelan, Michael, *Honour in Foreign Policy: A History and Discussion* (London: Palgrave Macmillan, 2007).

Doyle, Michael, 'Kant, Liberal Legacies and Foreign Affairs', *Philosophy and Public Affairs*, 12, 1983 (Summer and Fall): 205–35, 323–53.

'Liberalism and World Politics', *American Political Science Review*, 80, 4, 1986.

Striking First: Preemption and Prevention in International Conflict (edited by Stephen Macedo) (Princeton University Press, 2008).

Duffield, Mark, *Global Governance and the New Wars: The Merging of Development and Security* (London: Zed Books, 2001).

Dyson, Robert W. *Natural Law and Political Realism in the History of Political Thought*, 2 vols., vol. 1: *From the Sophists to Machiavelli* (New York: Peter Lang, 2005).

Ehrenreich, Barbara, *Blood Rites: Origins and History of the Passions of War* (London: Vintage Books, 1997).

Elliott, J.H., *Richelieu and Olivarez* (Cambridge University Press, 1984).

Elshtain, Jean Bethke, *Augustine and the Limits of Politics* (University of Notre Dame Press, 1995).

Just War against Terror (New York: Basic Books, 2003).

Women and War (Brighton: Harvester, 1987).

Emmott, Bill, *Rivals: How the Struggle between China, India and Japan Will Shape Our Next Decade* (London: Penguin, 2009).

Erskine, Toni, *Embedded Cosmopolitanism: Duties to Strangers and Enemies in a World of Dislocated Communities* (Oxford University Press, 2008).

Euben, J. Peter, *The Tragedy of Political Theory: The Path Not Taken* (Princeton University Press, 1996).

Evangelista, Matthew, *Law, Ethics and the War on Terror* (Cambridge: Polity, 2008).

Evans, Gareth, *The Responsibility to Protect: Ending Mass Atrocity Crimes Once and For All* (Washington: Brookings, 2008).

Fabre, Cecile, 'Cosmopolitanism, Just War and Legitimate Authority', *International Affairs*, 84, 5, 2008.

Ferguson, Niall, *The Pity of War* (Harmondsworth: Allen Lane, 1998).

Foot, Philippa, 'The Problem of Abortion and the Doctrine of Double Effect', *Oxford Review*, 5, 1967, 5–15.

Forbes, Ian, and Mark Hoffman (eds.) *Political Theory, International Relations and the Ethics of Intervention* (Basingstoke: Macmillan, 1993).

Foucault, Michel, *The Government of Self and Others: Lectures at the Collège de France 1982–83*, edited by Arnold I. Davidson, trans. Graham Burchill (New York: Palgrave Macmillan, 2010).

Franco, Paul, *The Political Philosophy of Michael Oakeshott* (University of Chicago Press, 1989).

Freedman, Lawrence, *Deterrence* (Cambridge: Polity Press, 2004).

Fritz, Kurt Von, *The Theory of the Mixed Constitution in Antiquity* (New York: Columbia University Press, 1954).

Fukuyama, Francis, *State-Building: Governance and World Order in the 21st Century* (Ithaca, NY: Cornell University Press, 2004).

Fussell, Paul, *The Great War and Modern Memory* (Oxford University Press, 1977).

Gaddis, John Lewis, *Surprise, Security and the American Experience* (New Haven: Yale University Press, 2004).

The Cold War (London: Allen Lane, 2005).

The Long Peace: Inquiries into the History of the Cold War (Oxford University Press, 1987).

Gallie, W.B., *Philosophers of Peace and War* (Cambridge University Press, 1978).

Gamble, Andrew, *The Spectre at the Feast: Capitalist Politics and the Politics of Recession* (London: Palgrave, 2009).

Gaugler, William, *A History of Fencing: Foundations of Modern European Swordplay* (Bangor, ME: Laureate Press, 1997).

Gay, Peter, *The Enlightenment: An Interpretation*, 2 vols. (New York: Wildwood House, 1970).

Geifman, Anna, *Thou Shalt Kill: Revolutionary Terrorism in Russia, 1894– 1917* (Princeton University Press, 1993).

Gilbert, Paul, *New Terror, New Wars* (Edinburgh University Press, 2003).

Gong, Geritt W., *The Standard of Civilization in International Society* (Oxford: Clarendon Press, 1984).

Goodin, Robert E., *Political Theory and Public Policy* (University of Chicago Press, 1982).

Gray, Colin, *Another Bloody Century: Future Warfare* (London: Weidenfeld & Nicolson, 2005).

Modern Strategy (Oxford: Clarendon Press, 1999).

Strategy for Chaos: Revolutions in Military Affairs and the Evidence of History (London: Frank Cass, 2004).

Gray, J. Glenn, *The Warriors* (New York: Harcourt Brace, 1959).

Greenleaf, W.H., *Oakeshott's Philosophical Politics* (New York: Barnes & Noble, 1966).

Grisez, Germain, Joseph Boyle and John Finnis, *Nuclear Deterrence, Morality and Realism* (Oxford University Press, 1987).

Hauerwas, Stanley, *Despatches from the Front: Theological Engagements with the Secular* (Durham, NC: Duke University Press, 1994).

Hayden, Patrick, 'Security Beyond the State: Cosmopolitanism, Peace and the Role of Just War Theory', in Mark Evans (ed.) *Just War Theory: A Reappraisal* (Edinburgh University Press, 2005).

Heinze, Eric, *Waging Humanitarian War: The Ethics, Law and Politics of Humanitarian Intervention* (New York: State University of New York Press, 2009).

Held, David, *Democracy and the Global Order* (Cambridge: Polity Press, 1995).

Higgins, Rosalyn, *Problems and Process: International Law and How We Use It* (Oxford University Press, 1993).

Hoffman, Bruce, *Inside Terrorism*, 2nd edn (New York: Columbia University Press, 2006).

Hoffmann, Stanley, *The Ethics and Politics of Humanitarian Intervention* (University of Notre Dame Press, 1996).

The State of War: Essays in the Theory and Practice of International Relations (New York: Prager, 1965).

Hoffmann, Stanley, and David Fidler (eds.) *Rousseau on International Relations* (Oxford: Clarendon Press, 1991).

Holmes, Richard, *On War and Morality* (Princeton University Press, 1989).

Holzegrefe, Jeff, and Robert Keohane (eds.) *Humanitarian Intervention: Ethical, Legal and Political Dilemmas* (Cambridge University Press, 2003).

Honig, Bonnie, *Emergency Politics: Paradox, Law, Democracy* (Princeton University Press, 2009).

Housley, Norman, *Contesting the Crusades* (Oxford: Blackwell, 2006).

Howard, Michael, *The Invention of Peace* (London: Profile Books, 2001).

Hume, David, *The Treatise of Human Nature*, ed. L.A. Selby-Bigge (Oxford University Press, 1888).

Huntington, Samuel, *The Clash of Civilizations and the Remaking of World Order* (New York: Simon & Schuster, 1996).

Hurrell, Andrew, *On Global Order: Power, Values and the Constitution of International Society* (Oxford University Press, 2007).

Ignatieff, Michael, 'Re-Imagining a Global Ethic', *Ethics and International Affairs*, 26, 1, 2012, 7–19.

The Lesser Evil: Political Ethics in An Age of Terror (Princeton University Press, 2004).

The Warrior's Honour (London: Jonathan Cape, 1998).

Ikenberry, G. John, *After Victory* (Princeton University Press, 2000).

Isaac, Jeffrey, *Democracy in Dark Times* (Ithaca, NY: Cornell University Press, 1998), Chapter 4.

Jabri, Vivienne, *War and the Transformation of Global Politics* (London: Palgrave, 2007).

Jackson, Robert, *The Global Covenant: Human Conduct in a World of States* (Oxford University Press, 2000).

Jeffery, Renee, *Hugo Grotius in International Thought* (London: Palgrave Macmillan, 2006).

Johnson, James Turner, *Can Modern War Be Just?* (New Haven: Yale University Press, 1984).

Ideology, Reason and the Limitation of War (Princeton University Press, 1975).

Morality and Contemporary Warfare (New Haven: Yale University Press, 1999).

The Just War Tradition and the Restraint of War (Princeton University Press, 1981).

Jonsen, Albert R., and Stephen Toulmin, *The Abuse of Casuistry: A History of Moral Reasoning* (Berkeley: University of California Press, 1986).

Kaldor, Mary, *New and Old Wars: Organized Violence in a Global Era* (Cambridge: Polity Press, 2007).

Kaplan, Robert D., *The Coming Anarchy: Shattering the Dreams of the Post Cold War World* (New York: Atlantic Books, 2000).

Warrior Politics: Why Leadership Demands A Pagan Ethos (New York: Vintage, 2003).

Kateb, George, *Patriotism and Other Mistakes* (New Haven: Yale University Press, 2006).

Keane, John, *Reflections on Violence* (London: Verso, 1996).

Keegan, John, *A History of Warfare* (London: Vintage, 1994).

Keen, Maurice, 'Chivalry and the Aristocracy', in *The New Cambridge Medieval History*, 8 vols., vol. VI ed. Michael Jones (Cambridge University Press, 2000).

(ed.) *Medieval Warfare: A History* (Oxford University Press, 1999).

Keene, Edward, *Beyond the Anarchical Society: Grotius, Colonialism and Order in World Politics* (Cambridge University Press, 2002).

Keohane, Robert, and Joseph Nye, *Power and Interdependence: World Politics in Transition* (London: Longman, 2000, 3rd edn).

Keppel, Gilles, *The Roots of Radical Islam* (Paris: Saqi Books, 2005).

Kiernan, V.G., *The Duel in European History: Honour and the Reign of Aristocracy* (Oxford University Press, 1988).

Kingsbury, Benedict, and Benjamin Straumann (eds.) *The Roman Foundations of the Law of Nations: Alberico Gentili and the Justice of Empire* (Oxford University Press, 2010).

Koskenniemi, Martti, *The Gentle Civilizer of Nations: The Rise and Fall of International Law, 1880–1960* (Cambridge University Press, 2003).

Krasner, Stephen, *Sovereignty: Organized Hypocrisy* (Princeton University Press, 1999).

'Addressing State Failure' (with Carlos Pascual), in *Foreign Affairs*, 84, 4, 2005.

Kublakova, Vendulka, and Andrew Cruikshank, *Marxism and International Relations* (Oxford University Press, 1989).

Lacey, Nicola, *The Life of H.L.A. Hart: The Nightmare and the Noble Dream* (Oxford University Press, 2006).

Lang Jr, Anthony J. (ed.) *Just Intervention* (Washington, DC: Georgetown University Press, 2003).

Lang Jr, Anthony J., Nicholas Rengger and William Walker, 'The Role(s) of Rules: Some Conceptual Clarifications', *International Relations*, 20, 3, 2006, 274–94.

Lasch, Christopher, *The True and Only Heaven: Progress and Its Critics* (New York: Norton, 1991).

Layne, Christopher, 'Kant or Cant: The Myth of the Democratic Peace', *International Security*, 19, 2, 1994: 5–49.

Lebow, Richard Ned, *A Cultural Theory of International Relations* (Cambridge University Press, 2008).

Lee, Steven, 'A Moral Critique of the Cosmopolitan Institutional Proposal', *Ethics and International Affairs*, 19, 2, 2005, 99–107.

Leslie, John, *The End of the World: The Science and Ethics of Human Extinction* (London: Routledge, 1996).

Levinson, Sanford (ed.) *Torture: A Collection* (Oxford University Press, 2005).

Lewis, Bernard, *What Went Wrong? Western Impact and Middle Eastern Response* (Oxford University Press, 2002).

Linklater, Andrew, *The Transformation of Political Community* (Cambridge: Polity Press, 1997).

Logue, Christopher, *All Day Permanent Red: War Music Continued* (London: Faber & Faber, 2003).

  Cold Calls – War Music Continued (London: Faber & Faber, 2005).

  Kings (London: Faber & Faber, 1991).

  The Husbands (London: Faber & Faber, 1995).

  War Music (London: Faber & Faber, 1988).

Loth, Wilfried, *The Division of the World 1941–1955* (London: Routledge, 1988).

Luban, David, 'Just War and Human Rights', *Philosophy and Public Affairs*, 9, 2, 1980, 161–81.

  'Preventive War and Human Rights', in Henry Shue and David Rodin (eds.) *Preemption: Military Action and Moral Justification* (Oxford University Press, 2007).

  'Preventive War', *Philosophy and Public Affairs*, 32, 2004, 207–48.

Luttwack, Edward, *Strategy* (Cambridge, Mass.: Harvard University Press, 1985).

  The Grand Strategy of the Roman Empire (Baltimore: Johns Hopkins University Press, 1979).

Machiavelli, *The Prince*, trans. and Introduction by Harvey Mansfield (University of Chicago Press, 1985).

McMahan, Jeff, *Killing in War* (Oxford University Press, 2009).

Malcolm, Noel, 'Hobbes' Theory of International Relations', in his *Aspects of Hobbes* (Oxford: Clarendon Press, 2004).

May, Larry, *Aggression and Crimes Against Peace* (Cambridge University Press, 2008).

Mazower, Mark, *No Enchanted Palace: The Ends of Empire and the Ideological Origins of the United Nations* (Princeton University Press, 2009).

Mearsheimer, John, *The Tragedy of Great Power Politics* (New York: Norton, 2000).

Meinecke, Friedrich, *Machiavellism: The Doctrine of Reason of State and Its Place in Modern History*, trans. D. Scott (Boulder: Westview, 1984).

Mellet, Michael, 'The Theory and Practice of Warfare in Machiavelli's Republic', in Gisela Bok, Quentin Skinner and Maurizio Viroli (eds.) *Machiavelli and Republicanism* (Cambridge University Press, 1990).

Midgely, B.F., *The Natural Law Tradition and the Theory of International Relations* (London: Elek Press, 1975).

Milbank, John, *The Future of Love* (London: SCM Press, 2007).

Theology and Social Theory (Oxford: Basil Blackwell, 1990).

Mueller, John, *The Remnants of War* (Ithaca, NY: Cornell University Press, 2004).

Retreat from Doomsday: The Obsolescence of Major War (New York: Basic Books, 1989).

Münkler, Herfried, *Die neuen Kriege* (Reinbek: Rowohlt, 2004).

Nardin, Terry, *Law, Morality and the Relations of States* (Princeton University Press, 1983).

The Philosophy of Michael Oakeshott (University Park: Penn State University Press, 2004).

(ed.) *The Ethics of War and Peace: Religious and Secular Perspectives* (Princeton University Press, 1996).

Nardin, Terry, and Melissa Williams (eds.) *Humanitarian Intervention* (NOMOS XLVII) (New York University Press, 2005).

Narveson, Jan, 'Pacifism: A Philosophical Analysis', *Ethics*, 75, 4, 1965.

Nye, Joseph, *Soft Power: The Means to Success in World Politics* (New York: Public Affairs Press, 2004).

O'Donovan, Oliver, *The Just War Revisited* (Oxford University Press, 2003).

O'Driscoll, Cian, *Renegotiation of the Just War Tradition and the Right to War in the Twenty First Century* (London: Palgrave Macmillan, 2008).

O'Neill, Onora, *Bounds of Justice* (Cambridge University Press, 2000).

'The Dark Side of Human Rights', *International Affairs*, 80, 1, 2004

O'Sullivan, Luke, *Oakeshott on History* (Exeter: Imprint Academic, 2003).

O'Sullivan, Noel, *European Political Thought since 1945* (London: Palgrave, 2004).

Oakeshott, Michael, *On Human Conduct* (Oxford: Clarendon Press, 1975).

Rationalism in Politics (London: Methuen, 1962).

Rationalism in Politics and Other Essays, expanded edn (Minneapolis: Liberty Fund 1991(1962)).

Ober, Josiah, 'Classical Greek Times', in Michael Howard, George Andreopoulos and Mark R. Schulman (eds.) *The Laws of War: Constraints on Warfare in the Western World* (New Haven: Yale University Press, 1994).

Onuf, Nicholas, *The Republican Legacy in International Thought* (Cambridge University Press, 1997).

Orend, Brian, 'Is There a Supreme Emergency Exemption?' in Mark Evans (ed.) *Just War Theory: A Reappraisal* (Edinburgh University Press, 2005).

Michael Walzer on War and Justice (Montreal: McGill-Queen's University Press, 2001).

Orwin, Clifford, *The Humanity of Thucydides* (Princeton University Press, 1994).

Pagden, Anthony, *Lords of All the World: Ideologies of Empire in Spain, Britain and France c. 1500–1800* (New Haven: Yale University Press, 1995).

Pagden, Anthony, and Jeremy Lawrance (eds.) *Francisco de Vitoria: Political Writings* (Cambridge University Press, 1991).

Pangle, Thomas, *Montesquieu's Philosophy of Liberalism* (University of Chicago Press, 1973).

Pangle, Thomas, and Peter Ahrensdorf, *Justice among Nations: On the Moral Basis of Power and Peace* (Lawrence: University Press of Kansas, 1999).

Parekh, Bikhu, *Gandhi's Political Philosophy: A Critical Examination* (Basingstoke: Macmillan, 1989).

Paret, Peter, *Clausewitz and the State: The Man, His Theories and His Times* (Oxford University Press, 1976).

  Understanding War: Essays on Clausewitz and the History of Military Power (Princeton University Press, 1992).

  (ed.) *Makers of Modern Strategy* (Oxford: Clarendon Press, 1986).

Parker, Geoffrey, *The Military Revolution: Military Innovation and the Rise of the West 1500–1800* (Cambridge University Press, 1996).

Pettit, Philip, 'A Republican Law of Peoples', *European Journal of Political Theory*, 9, 1, January 2010.

  Republicanism: A Theory of Freedom and Government (Oxford University Press, 1997).

Pick, Daniel, *War Machine: The Rationalization of Slaughter in the Modern Age* (New Haven: Yale University Press, 1993).

Piscatori, James, 'Religion and Realpolitik: Islamic Responses to the Gulf War', in James Piscatori (ed.) *Islamic Fundamentalisms and the Gulf Crisis* (Chicago: American Academy of Arts and Sciences, 1991).

Plamenatz, John, *Man and Society*, 2 vols. (Harlow: Longman, 1961).

Plato, *Laws*, ed. and trans. Thomas Pangle (University of Chicago Press, 1980).

Pocock, J.G.A., *The Machiavellian Moment: Florentine Political Thought and the Atlantic Republican Tradition* (Princeton University Press, 2003 (1975)).

Pogge, Thomas, *World Poverty and Human Rights* (Cambridge: Polity Press, 2003).

Posner, Richard, *Catastrophe: Risk and Response* (Oxford University Press, 2004).

Rachman, Gideon, *Zero Sum World: Politics, Power and Prosperity after the Crash* (London: Atlantic Books, 2010).

Ramsey, Paul, *The Just War: Force and Political Responsibility* (New York: Scribner, 1968).

War and the Christian Conscience: How Shall Modern War Be Conducted Justly? (Durham, NC: Duke University Press, 1961).

Rashid, Ahmed, *Taliban: Islam, Oil and the New Great Game in Central Asia* (London: I.B. Tauris, 2001).

Rawls, John, *A Theory of Justice* (Harvard: Belknap Press, 1971).

The Law of Peoples (Cambridge, Mass.: Harvard University Press, 1999).

Rengger, Nicholas, *Dealing in Darkness: The Anti-Pelagian Imagination in Political Theory and International Relations* (London: Routledge, in press).

'Just a War Against Terror? Jean Bethke Elshtain's Burden and American Power', *International Affairs*, 80, 1, 2004, 107–16.

Political Theory, Modernity and Postmodernity: Beyond Enlightenment and Critique (Oxford: Blackwell, 1995).

'Realism Tamed or Liberalism Betrayed: Dystopic Liberalism and International Order', in R. Friedmann, K. Oskanian and R. Pachacho (eds.) *After Liberalism* (London: Palgrave, in press).

'The World Turned Upside Down: Human Rights and International Relations After Twenty Five Years', *International Affairs*, 87, 5, September 2011, 1,159–78.

Reus-Smit, Christian, *The Moral Purpose of the State* (Cambridge University Press, 1999).

Richardson, Lewis Fry, *Arms and Insecurity* (Pittsburgh: Stevens, 1960).

Richardson, Louise, *What Terrorists Want: Understanding the Terrorist Threat* (London: John Murray, 2006).

Richmond, Oliver, and Jason Franks, *Liberal Peace Transitions: Between Peace Building and State Building* (Edinburgh University Press, 2009).

Roberts, Adam, and Richard Guelff, *Documents on the Laws of War*, 3rd edn (Oxford University Press, 2000).

Roberts, Adam, and Benedict Kingsbury (eds.) *United Nations, Divided World* (Oxford: Clarendon Press, 1988).

Robin, Corey, *Fear: The History of a Political Idea* (Oxford University Press, 2004).

Rodin, David, *War and Self Defence* (Oxford University Press, 2002).

Russett, Bruce, *Grasping the Democratic Peace* (Princeton University Press, 1993).

Schelling, Thomas C., *The Strategy of Conflict* (Cambridge, Mass.: Harvard University Press, 1960).

Schmitt, Carl, *Der Begriff des Politischen: Text von 1932 mit einem Vorwort und drei Corollarien* (Berlin: Duncker und Humblot, 2002).

Die Diktatur (Berlin: Duncker und Humblot, 1921).

Schroeder, Paul, *The Transformation of European Politics 1763–1848* (Oxford: Clarendon Press, 1994).

Sherman, Nancy, *Stoic Warriors: The Ancient Philosophy behind the Military Mind* (Oxford University Press, 2005).

Shklar, Judith, *Montesquieu* (Oxford University Press, 1987).

Shue, Henry, and David Rodin (eds.) *Just and Unjust Warriors* (Oxford University Press, 2006).

(eds.) *Preemption: Military Action and Moral Justification* (Oxford University Press, 2007).

Simms, Brendan, and D.J.B. Trim (eds.) *Humanitarian Intervention: A History* (Cambridge University Press, 2011).

Skinner, Quentin, *Liberty Before Liberalism* (Cambridge University Press, 1997).

The Foundations of Modern Political Thought, 2 vols. (Cambridge University Press, 1978).

Visions of Politics, 3 vols. (Cambridge University Press, 2003).

Skinner, Quentin, and Martin Van Gelderen (eds.) *Republicanism: A Shared European Heritage*, 2 vols. (Cambridge University Press, 2005).

Slaughter, Anne Marie, *A New World Order* (Princeton University Press, 2004).

Smith, Michael Joseph, 'Ethics and Intervention', *Ethics and International Affairs*, 1989, 1–26.

'Growing Up with *Just and Unjust Wars*: An Appreciation', *Ethics and International Affairs*, 11, 1997, 3–18.

Sunstein, Cass, *Laws of Fear: Beyond the Precautionary Principle* (Cambridge University Press, 2005).

Taylor, Charles, *A Secular Age* (Cambridge, Mass.: Harvard University Press, 2007).

Modern Social Imaginaries (Durham, NC: Duke University Press, 2004).

Thompson, Judith Jarvis, 'The Trolley Problem', *Yale Law Journal*, 94, 1985, 1,395–415.

Thucydides, *History of the Peloponnesian War*, trans. Thomas Hobbes, ed. David Grene (University of Chicago Press, 1989).

Tilly, Charles, *Coercion, Capital and Modern European States: 990–1990* (Oxford: Blackwell, 1993).

Toulmin, Stephen, *Cosmopolis: The Hidden Agenda of Modernity* (University of Chicago Press, 1992).

Return to Reason (Cambridge, Mass.: Harvard University Press, 2001).

Tuck, Richard, *The Rights of War and Peace: Political Thought and the International Order from Grotius to Kant* (Oxford University Press, 1999).

Vanderpol, Alfred, *La Doctrine scholastique du droit de guerre* (Paris: Pedone, 1919).

Vincent, R.J., *Non-Intervention and International Order* (Princeton University Press, 1974).

Voegelin, Eric, *Collected Writings*, ed. Manfred Henningsen (Columbia, Mo.: University of Missouri Press, 1999).

The New Science of Politics, 34 vols. (University of Chicago Press, 1951).

Walker, William, *A Perpetual Menace: Nuclear Weapons and International Order* (London: Routledge, 2011).

Waltz, Kenneth, *Man, the State and War* (New York: Columbia University Press, 1959).

'The Continuity of International Politics', in K. Booth and T. Dunne (eds.) *Worlds in Collision* (London: Palgrave, 2002).

Theory of International Politics (Reading: Addison-Wesley, 1979).

Walzer, Michael, *Arguing about War* (New Haven: Yale University Press, 2004).

'Governing the Globe', *Dissent*, Fall 2000.

Just and Unjust Wars: A Moral Argument with Historical Illustrations, 3rd edn (New York: Basic Books, 2000(1977)).

'The Moral Standing of States: A Response to Four Critics', in Charles Beitz et al. (eds.) *International Ethics* (Princeton University Press, 1985).

Politics and Passion: Towards a More Egalitarian Liberalism (New Haven: Yale University Press, 2004).

Spheres of Justice (Oxford: Basil Blackwell, 1983).

'World War II: Why This War Was Different', *Philosophy and Public Affairs*, 1, 1, 1971.

Weiss, Thomas, *What's Wrong with the United Nations and How to Fix It*, 2nd edn (Cambridge: Polity Press, 2012).

Welsh, Jennifer, 'Implementing the "Responsibility to Protect": Where Expectations Meet Reality', *Ethics and International Affairs*, 24, 4, 2010.

(ed.) *Humanitarian Intervention and International Relations* (Oxford University Press, 2004).

Wendt, Alexander, 'Why a World State Is Inevitable', *European Journal of International Relations*, 9, 4, 2003.

Wheeler, Nicholas J., *Saving Strangers: Humanitarian Intervention in International Society* (Oxford University Press, 2000).

White, Stephen K., *Political Theory and Postmodernism* (Cambridge University Press, 1991).

Wight, Martin, *Systems of States* (Leicester University Press, 1977).

'Why Is There No International Theory', in H. Butterfield and M. Wight (eds.) *Diplomatic Investigations* (London: George Allen and Unwin, 1966).

Wilde, Ralph, *International Territorial Administration: How Trusteeship and the Civilizing Mission Never Went Away* (Oxford University Press, 2008).

Wilkinson, Paul, *Terrorism versus Democracy* (New York: Frank Cass, 2001).

Wilson, Peter H. (ed.) *A Companion to Eighteenth Century Europe* (Oxford: Blackwell, 2008).

Wright, Quincy, *A Study of War* (University of Chicago Press, 1942).

Yack, Bernard, *The Problems of a Political Animal* (Berkeley: University of California Press, 1993).

Yoder, John Howard, *The Politics of Jesus* (Grand Rapids, Mich.: W.B. Eerdmans, 1972).

Zakaria, Fareed, *The Future of Freedom* (New York: Norton, 2003).

  The Post-American World and the Rise of the Rest (London: Penguin, 2009).

Zartman, William (ed.) *Collapsed States: The Disintegration and Reestablishment of Political Authority* (Boulder: Lynne Rienner, 1995).

Zimmern, Alfred, *The Greek Commonwealth* (Oxford: Clarendon Press, 1911).

Index